Coming Home to Tibet

Coming Home to Tibet

A Memoir of Love, Loss, and Belonging

TSERING WANGMO DHOMPA

Shambhala
BOULDER
2016

Shambhala Publications, Inc.
4720 Walnut Street
Boulder, Colorado 80301
www.shambhala.com

9 8 7 6 5 4 3 2 1

First Shambhala Edition
Printed in the United States of America

⊗ This edition is printed on acid-free paper that meets the
American National Standards Institute z39.48 Standard.
♻ This book is printed on 30% postconsumer recycled paper.
For more information please visit www.shambhala.com.

Distributed in the United States by Penguin Random House LLC
and in Canada by Random House of Canada Ltd

Designed by Dean Bornstein

LIBRARY OF CONGRESS CATALOGING-IN-PUBLICATION DATA
Dhompa, Tsering Wangmo.
Coming home to Tibet: a memoir of love, loss, and belonging /
Tsering Wangmo Dhompa.—First Shambhala edition.
pages   cm
"First published in Hamish Hamilton by Penguin Books India, 2013"
—Title page verso.
ISBN 978-1-61180-329-7 (paperback: acid-free paper) 1. Dhompa, Tsering Wangmo.
2. Dhompa, Tsering Wangmo—Travel—China—Tibet Autonomous Region.
3. Tibet Autonomous Region (China)—Description and travel. 4. Dhompa, Tsering
Wangmo—Family. 5. Mothers and daughters. 6. Mothers—Death. 7. Home—
Psychological aspects. 8. Place attachment. 9. Tibet Autonomous Region (China)—
Biography. 10. Tibet Autonomous Region (China)—Social life and customs. I. Title.
DS786.D56 2016   951'.505092—dc23   [B]   2015027116

To Tsering Choden Dhompa
Beloved Mother

Contents

Prologue

My mother was still settling into the role of being wife to a chieftain of a nomadic clan in 1959. She accepted the new name, Tashi Dolkar, given to her by her in-laws. She parted her hair on the unfamiliar side. She stopped wearing trousers under her dress. She was eighteen.

It did not alarm her at first when she heard the Chinese army had encircled all strategic Tibetan towns and cities. Nomads in her village professed to witnessing two suns, or two moons, or a barren sky. Trees collapsed. Rivers grew tumid. Then came news that entire villages of central Tibet were fleeing for Nepal or India.

My mother packed valuables. She followed her husband out of her home on a cold night. They set out for an unknown country. A hint of summer held grass upright.

She disciplined her memory to give up counting her losses. She gave her suffering one name: exile.

All of her exiled life she waited to return home. She spoke of exile as something that would be expunged over time. When *this* is over, we can go home.

She waited from year to year. She carried a hope that if we waited long enough, *this* would end.

This is not a simple story.

Every summer my mother culled images of flowers from her childhood. There were the ones with white lollipop heads that grew with cheeky profusion impeding her stride; there were the lissom blue beauties, translucent and shapely as a glass bottle, who fooled her into thinking they were half-reptilian; and the waxy and purple bull-dog-faced flowers she could never uproot because they hugged the ground so tenaciously.

"Did they look like this?" I would ask her, holding up buttercups or primroses that grew in the yards of neighbors who had larger families and correspondingly, more plants.

The flowers in Tibet were more beautiful, according to my mother.

"What about those?" I would point to stocky bushes of wild daisies that grew alongside paths in Dharamshala where we lived until I was twelve years old.

The flowers in Tibet were always taller, more fragrant and vivid. Her descriptions, imprecise but unchanging from year to year, had led me to an inevitable acceptance that her past was unequaled by our present lives. She would tell me of the knee-deep fields of purple, red, and white—plants never named or pointed out to us during our years in India and Nepal—that over time served to create an idea of her fatherland, *phayul*, as a riotous garden. I pictured her wilderness paradise of flowers by comparing them not to the marigolds, daisies, and bluebells I crushed with my fingers, but to the shapes of household artifacts around me: lollipop, broom, bottle. Disparate objects that surrendered to and influenced the idea, space, and hope of a more abundant and happy place.

When there are just two of you, you appropriate images from each other and inhabit one tongue until the stories that compose your two worlds become interchangeable. It was so for my mother and me.

We would return to Tibet someday, mother said when she came home from a long day in the office and was too tired to cook dinner for us, or when she labored under the weight of grocery bags in the summer heat. I lived with the notion that, as refugees, our life in exile was temporary. It was easy to accept that idea in our two-room house in Dharamshala where everything we owned fit into the four aluminium steel suitcases under our two twin cots.

Phayul: the word was a constant reminder that everything wonderful that eluded us in exile waited for us in Tibet. Existing without proof of photographs or contact, this Tibet was our real home.

A new year's morning is indistinguishable from other mornings if you are traveling through small villages and towns on the Grand Trunk Road leading to the city of Chandigarh. Early morning fog hovers above wheat fields. One or two light bulbs cast a brumous glow into the spaces between modest brick houses visible as silhouettes. My mother and her three friends had hired a jeep and a driver to take them from Delhi to Dharamshala. The sun rose lazily on the first day of January 1994.

A man emptying his bowels in a field witnessed the collision on the highway. A truck is a powerful beast, he would comment later to a police officer. He saw a jeep spin like a dizzy house sparrow. The man's peaceful morning ritual had been shattered by the intrusion of death.

A police officer who was among the first to reach the scene of the accident told me that my mother had looked "intact" to him. "I did not think she would die," he said to me on my visit to the Karnal police station two months after the accident.

The doctor who had tended to her had known otherwise. He was reluctant to speak to me or to elaborate on the postmortem documents.

I asked if she had suffered.

"What does it matter? She is dead," he replied. "How can I remember? People die every day."

I asked again if she had suffered. He handed me five documents with "Unknown" scribbled untidily across the top of each page. He could not tell me which of the pages contained my mother's information. I had glanced at the descriptions of the unnamed dead knowing I would find clues to the person I loved most.

Unknown: Female. Age: Unknown. Maroon jacket. Brown dress. No bra or underwear.

My mother did not return home during her lifetime.

CHAPTER ONE

The Abode of Snow

My aunt Tashi wipes away her tears with the sleeves of her shirt as I walk toward the exit of the new Xining airport. The white of her shirt lends an austerity to the misshapen black of her *chuba* held together by a red cotton belt. Her right hand is out of the long sleeve of the traditional dress, as is customary in her hometown of Kyegu. The airport is silent save for the clanging of carts and the susurration of a man sweeping the floor. Shoes squeak. There are no announcements at this hour.

I touch my forehead to hers in greeting and then embrace her. We have not seen each other for a few years.

"Is your body tired?"

"There was no trouble."

"Is your body tired?"

"Not anymore."

After years of English, I slip into the Nangchen language and feel the happiness that comes from speaking in the mother tongue. We go through the list of people we love, checking if they are still alive and well. Once we bridge the years of our absence, our words gush out with unabashed greed.

Not here Lhasa's melancholic beauty. Xining is business and bustle. Row after row of buildings sit in a monotonous monochrome. But closer to the city's center, in the new high-rises, color and geometry suggest a slight shift in aesthetics, and more pertinently, the city's exultant participation in China's new prosperity.

Walking in the polished and marbled halls of a new mall, I hear fragments of Tibetan languages and catch glimpses of heavy black chubas that command a second look from those who are not Tibetan. A salesman shows me a range of outfits when I wander into the wedding photo studio. He suggests I consider a billowy white gown. He says that, with my height, the gown could transform me to look "like a beauty." A full wedding album includes an array of backdrops and costumes—Western white gowns, traditional Chinese and Tibetan garb—images of glamour that contrast oddly with the actual wedding-day photos.

Xining was not always favored by Tibetans. There are elders in my family who remember their years in the city long before it became so attractive to their children. Their memory of the city is of a prison that enclosed them within the walls of the labor reform camps, the *laogaidui,* of the People's Republic of China. It is in these prisons that many tens of thousands of Tibetans are said to have perished.

Qinghai Province was known as the Chinese Siberia to which many former Kuomingtang army officers, police officers, and rightists were sent in exile in the early 1950s. During the 1960s, the *laogaidui* entered into industrial and agricultural production and began to serve two functions: detention centers as well as commercial enterprises. Xining was a *laogai* city with five or six major camps inside its city limits, I am told, and with as many as twenty-eight camps spread across its neighboring provinces.

The elders in my family—my aunt Parchen, my mother's cousin Ashang Lama, and five other cousins—were charged with either being a rightist or a counterrevolutionary simply because they were born into or affiliated with a prominent religious, social, or political class. A dozen other relatives languished for decades or died in such prisons performing grueling manual work and undergoing thought reforms meant to purge them of incorrect beliefs and attitudes. Those who survived their imprisonment, like Ashang Lama, cannot forget the years spent in the camps but are not at ease recalling them.

In this world of concrete, Tibetans find a way to live. Every morning and evening the women gather in the courtyard of my cousin's apartment complex to dance to Tibetan music. This is their exercise and indulgence. This would not happen in the small towns the women hail from: dancing in spandex pants and blouses bursting with prints of tiny flowers, or giggling in a square in view of all passersby. When they are home in Dritou, Chumaleb, or Zatou, these women go for circumambulations around the monastery stupa in a uniform of white blouse and brown or black chuba. Here in the city, however, they are anonymous and they dance in merriment. They do not have to follow the decorum expected of a mother or a grandmother, nor are they ridiculed by their peers for this dancing and this gay abandonment that they bring to joints niggled by rheumatism and other aches. Their husbands, brothers, and fathers do not join them. The men are embarrassed to dance, but they don't stop the women from doing so.

"Look how my old lady is transformed in the city. And watch the Chinese women trying to learn the slow and repetitive steps of our dance," a family friend chortles, pointing toward his wife, who has become the leader of the evening dance.

Aunt Tashi does not join the dancers. She takes delight in watching her friends dance.

"Why don't you dance? It will be good exercise," I coax her. She laughs.

She tells me it would not suit her to dance, not as a widow, and not as a woman of sixty-seven. Then, as though to show she is suggestible, she adds mischievously that she'll join in if I do. But we are who we are. We are both content to watch.

The following evening Tashi takes me to a new park in the city's center where a crowd of people dance every evening. She holds my hand and leads me to the front of the circle of bystanders. The song resembles Tibetan traditional folk music in its use of the Tibetan guitar and flute, but the melody is Chinese. The leader of the evening's dance routine, a slight Chinese woman, leads a group of forty people—Chinese of all ages and a few Tibetans—in slow, repetitive steps that gradually pick up pace to a complex footwork beyond my ability. I am surprised to hear Chinese onlookers around me refer to this as a "Tibetan dance." They say it so familiarly, as though they have been amidst this form for a long time, as though they know who the Tibetans are. I cannot distinguish all the younger Tibetan dancers, in their jeans and T-shirts, from the Chinese; the elders I can correctly identify from the way they move their bodies. Tashi says she can spot Tibetans wherever they are, even if they stand in a sea of Chinese people.

How can she tell Tibetans apart from the Chinese?

She says she recognizes her own people.

We linger a few days in Xining so that I can acclimatize and prepare for Kyegu, which sits at 14,400 feet above sea level San Francisco, from where I have flown. On a sunnier day, Tashi, two cousins, and I make our customary pilgrimage to Kumbum Jampa-ling Monastery—one of the six largest monasteries of the Gelugpa sect in Tibet—founded in 1583 by the Third Dalai Lama. In 1958 there were thirty-six hundred monks; today the monastery is allowed a modest limit of six hundred monks and they are monitored closely. Kumbum—that is, a hundred statues—refers to the monastery's one hundred thousand statues of Lama Tsongkhapa, the founder of the Gelugpa sect of Tibetan Buddhism. Today these statues are viewed in greater numbers by tourists than believers.

A busy bazaar leads to the monastery's main entrance. Statues of deities, prayer bowls, and religious artifacts from India and

Nepal are placed outside the stores so visitors cannot avoid browsing. Each shop plays a different song, all devotional. Our entry to the monastery coincides with the arrival of a busload of Chinese tourists. I listen to the guides, all Chinese, explain in rehearsed voices the history of the monastery. They also give explanations about the Tibetan people, their Buddhism, and their culture. When a guide points toward my group, I sense he has made the calculation that I am the beneficiary of China's modernity while Tashi is of an older Tibet. Members of his group smile at me in recognition—the jeans, the hiking boots, the T-shirt—and they smile at my aunt with awe and indulgence. For them, as the government had hoped and believed, Tibet must serve as a symbol of China's largesse, an example of its capacity for progress, tolerance, and diversity.

A naked Tibetan boy crawls on the ground, in the corner by the entrance. He grins and bares two front teeth.

A guide walks toward us while we compose ourselves into a group. He turns away when Tashi signals we do not need him. A few minutes later, a woman approaches us and asks if we want a guide. She is almost skipping in her attempt to gain the maximum stride allowed by the restrictive hemlines of her skirt. Her shoes tap noisily on concrete. I can tell by her walk that the leather is exhausted. She looks efficient and young but her face betrays weariness. This is not a place she thinks of as home; it is a place of work, perhaps even hardship.

A cousin tells her we do not need her to tell us our own history.

The young guide looks confused for a moment and steps aside without revealing how the words have affected her. Her hair is short. It hugs the base of a neck which is very slender and which she bears stiffly as she walks away from us. A few minutes later, I see her lead a group through the monastery gate as a monk ushers them in with folded hands.

CHAPTER TWO

The Wild East

He is loneliest when he is on the road.

"It is the land," Rinchen, the driver of our jeep explains. It is not just the distance between destinations that brings on desolation. "It is too beautiful," he says. Close to six feet tall and carrying a frame the girth of a door, Rinchen is bigger than most Tibetan men I know. Coming from his taciturn lips, the words are beautifully haunting. He understands distance as an interminable terrain where everything he sees is either too far ahead or suddenly speeding past him. He says it is possible to feel adrift and alone after hours of looking at an unattainable horizon. He cannot imagine living anywhere but in Tibet, he says with the obdurate self-possession of a lover. It is the same love that makes him stick to the thicker vowels of a language spoken in his village of twenty families in Trindu county even though he left home for Kyegu many decades earlier.

It is the beauty of the land that makes loneliness palpable. So was it, I believe, with travelers in the past who came to the interior lands of Tibet bearing the burden of an ineludible feeling of being one and alone of their kind. Still, they came, cautioning each other and being forewarned themselves against the perilous journey. It was for the eastern regions of Kham and Amdo that people, even Tibetans, reserved their most persuasive warnings.

In 1945 when Heinrich Harrer was making his way toward Lhasa, he was warned against the *khampas*, people of East Tibet.

He recalls the undertone of mystery and terror in the voices of non-khampas when they referred to a khampa: "At last we realized that the word was synonymous with 'robber,'" he writes in his book *Seven Years in Tibet*.

Such fears were necessitated because brigands did indeed spring from behind boulders on lonely stretches of land, terrifying pilgrims and travelers, as the French explorers Andre Guibaut and Louis Liotard found out on 10 September 1940. Liotard died in an ambush while crossing a pass on their way to Golog.

An earlier French explorer, Dutreuil de Rhins, also met his end from a brigand's bullet—in June 1894, not too far from Kyegu, home to most of my relatives in Tibet. Dutreuil's death was announced in the *New York Times* on 7 August 1894, under the simple headline "Explorer Killed in Thibet." His body was found in the river Dzachu that becomes the Mekong.

A journey to the high herding communities in Kham continues to come with warnings: no roads, no electricity, no plumbing, no hospitals, no vegetables, no shield from the brute manners of khampas, no privacy, and absolutely no comfort of familiar languages and customs. Today there are no longer fears of bandits bearing down on travelers with old rifles, but there persists, still, the insult of knives carried and used unsparingly by khampas.

For me, it is the dead who bring me here. It is they who give me a place in Tibet.

The new road leading out of Xining is luxurious. It is built, I think, with some other destination in mind and not for the little towns with boxy houses that no longer seem consistent with the China proclaimed on billboards. The new luxury apartments and office complexes are empty for now. Dust intrudes everywhere and wraps everything in a gray lethargy.

Rinchen drives silently without asking for a translation of the signs guiding us in English and Chinese. As we move farther and farther from the city, tall buildings give way to lower and humbler structures constructed from mud and brick. Trees step out in salubrious green alongside the road. The land forms undulating fields resembling step farms in the hill stations of northern India and Nepal. These farms narrow as the road inclines and then they too disappear and the land is not the same. Or that is how I see it, because I know we are on Tibetan territory judging from the prayer flags visible on rooftops. The flags are bleached to a dreary silver. In this wind they will need to be replaced soon, perhaps before the end of the year.

So easily do Tibetans give themselves away, I tell Tashi, pointing to the prayer flags. The green farmlands that thrilled my eyes have disappeared. Cars do not follow us anymore. Stripped of all company, we crawl up the mountains. Every now and then the tent of a nomadic family appears within sight and yaks lift their eyes to us, as though questioning our purpose on their grounds. A few yaks graze just feet away from the road. I want to tell them we are not the ones who have brought electric poles, jeeps, and concrete a hand's length from their grazing land.

After an hour of traveling southwest, past the last brick building of Xining, we meet the NyiDa NyiKha, the "Sun and Moon Pass." Once on the pass, Tashi says we truly are on Tibetan soil. Her body relaxes. Even though Kham and Amdo are scattered in the Chinese provinces of Sichuan, Gansu, Yunnan, and Qinghai, Tashi refers to Tibet by its Tibetan names of Bhod, or Chol-ka-sum. Five decades ago it had taken her close to twenty days to reach Xining on horseback from Kyegu. When jeeps began to cover the same distance in twelve hours, she thought it was by some divine machination.

"Now I can take a plane from Xining and be in Kyegu in the time it takes me to make bread," she says in wonder.

Farmlands have transformed into grasslands and yaks wander

in open fields. We go on and on into the hypnotizing green. As we approach the Tha La Pass which marks the border of Amdo and Kham, I keep paper prayers, the *lungtas*, ready in my hands. Mountain passes are homes for deities and local protectors and each time we cross a pass, we make offerings to the protectors of the land we are traveling through. We ask for safe passage, we ask their permission to enter and to leave their abode, and we ask for all beings to be protected. This custom is still ours to remember and we have our papers ready each time we cross a mountain pass. This is our toll in acknowledgment of reaching a difficult and strategic place in our journey.

Tashi remains in the jeep while Rinchen and I get out shouting, *La so, la so, lha gyalo.* May the gods be victorious. We toss pink, blue, white, and yellow squares of papers printed with prayers in the direction of the wind. We remembered to purchase the *lungtas* from Tibetan traders selling Buddhist wares in Xining. If we were truly prepared, we would have burned incense and carried fabric prayer flags to hang on the wooden poles that are already heavily bedecked. And if I were more wedded to the land and its ways, I would have walked to the top of the hill and prostrated, as my mother might have done, and requested the deities of the region to receive me after these years of absence, to watch over me, and to deliver me to safety.

At 4,824 meters, we hear the insistent wind whistle across land that has not seen grass for six months. It is June and the earth is slowly warming. Snow gives up inch by inch its adoration of the soil and green shoots rise in clenched temerity. The ground is still cold and I think it must be a painful process, this period of thawing, even for stones and mud. Soon, beyond the pass on lower grounds, the grass will grow tall and inhibit easy walking, and then it will be impossible to think of the grasslands as being any other color but green. And yak and sheep will be unable to separate their dreams from their wakeful wanderings, thinking of summer as a delectable feast.

There is an uncommonly harsh beauty to the Tibetan landscape. Its nakedness makes it seem incapable of deception, but under its calm deportment it conceals winds so brutal that yaks are known to die while their jaws are in masticating bliss. On hot summer days the sun licks up the rain within minutes. No puddles are formed; no moisture lingers in the air. It is only the droplets on tiny leaves of the baby turnip plant that betray rain.

The names of towns along the highway—Tsigor Thang, Dhomda, Matou—are spoken once and then forgotten. Low buildings of white or startling pink tiles and of forgettable architecture hug the edges of the highway; they appear to be still in progress or already in ruins. Again, an odd courtship or statement by people who have lived their entire lives in blackened tents or mud houses. Rows of buildings indistinguishable from each other are separated by billboards in Chinese and Tibetan signaling the many reasons that call for a pause in the journey: food, beverages to meet every desire, gasoline, yogurt.

The road is framed by rows of billiard tables over which young men and old men stand poised with sticks raised in a warrior's stance. They are a blur of black hats and black jackets. Their brows are knitted into frowns, their bodies straining to scatter a handful of colorful balls into four corners. Rinchen slows down the jeep and we watch the players.

"What is this fascination for the game?" I ask Tashi.

"People are going crazy," she responds.

Each town we pass along our journey entertains tables on the sidewalks. A game is always in progress. There are no women beside them; perhaps the women are committed to nothing else but work. I wonder if the Chinese see these as strange places for habitation, even impossible, with the relentless monotony of blue skies and unbroken stretches of land. Only those who were born in such places would remain out of love or helplessness, or those who come to such places willingly must have taken flight from worse, unbearable ordeals to have to live where no company or comfort will protect them from the remorseless numbing cold. Yet they too are here, the Chinese. They run restaurants, they set up billiard rooms, they own motels where we stop to get gas. They have stores where even cattle might beg not to be kept. In these shops they sell in abundance the commodities Tibetans have never produced and now consume blithely: instant noodles, gasoline, innumerable brands of soft drinks, cigarettes, and beer.

Tufts of grass grow in fields of pale yellow that will signify the short summer of this land. "Even though the grass looks poor here, it is very nutritious," Tashi informs me.

Little spots of green come and go and aside from tall electric poles nothing else, perceptible to me, distresses the land. The stretch of wire indicates human endeavor at the outposts of this region—or subjugation, for it is the Chinese who have brought electricity here. Only one or two people enter our vision. Tibetans are somewhere on this land living as nomads. Water emerges as small lakes, blindingly blue to the eyes.

Once the high passes are left behind, the contours of the mountains become gentler and rounder. We are going west, toward regions known for famous yogis and intransigent warriors. Wildflowers begin to dot the fields. They sprout at the most indeterminate places, as though their existence ought to have a story, and most often, they do. Factors other than wind and sun bring them here.

"The flowers are made for the goat, the flowers are made for the sheep, and the flowers are made for the mountains," Tashi tells me. She says nomads believe the first to gain color on the land is grass and the last to lose color is a flower of blue-purple. This flower alone keeps her hue while everything else turns ochre. She has the body of a bell. She is petite and succulent. She is beloved and called the "turquoise of the grassland," *pangyen yulo*.

All around us is the summer permitted in June: the green puerility of grass peeps from the ground, an impunity of color bursts from the tight heads of midget flowers, cerulean water travels by our side. For the past few hours an unending spread of grass has fallen sweetly on my eyes. I had not noticed the passage of time. Then, the moment I acknowledge time and space, the green becomes a burden and a longing takes over me to turn away to see something else. Perhaps this desire comes with the comprehension that there is nothing I can do to get closer or away from the land. It takes my entire body to see this land, and still, there is more.

This land is not built like Kathmandu, New Delhi, or San Francisco, where I have lived. Cities I have come to know through street names, borders, and maps that allow for a particular security and permanence. There are no signs here other than sporadic reminders on the highway that the closest town is far away. Try as I may, I cannot avoid thinking of the fragility of human existence. The more I look into the mountains the more I recognize my naïveté in assuming I comprehend anything at all, least of all the essence of what I do and what I know: work, family, love.

"There is no land more beautiful than our land," I tell Tashi and the driver.

"The winters are long," Tashi begins. "The wind is terrible, the altitude is hard on the heart, the cold wrecks our bones, and the dust is a devil." She is not afraid to speak of the small inconveniences this land brings. She has not been taught to praise what she loves.

It is similar to the way my mother would announce my failings to her friends when they praised me. "She is stubborn. She does not like Tibetan tea," or "she does not write Tibetan." To protect those listening from feeling less themselves, we do not praise the ones we love.

Tashi tells me how winter blankets the land for more than half the year, driving people to forget the shape and function of the river, the fungus, the grass, and the springs they rely on. And then summer arrives, she says, as though it was always there and people recollect what they love just as water returns without premeditation to its old rivulet paths. Tashi is poetic when she speaks of the land.

Small clusters of houses serving as a village come and pass by in a flash, a prelude to what will from here onward be the land of eastern Tibetans, as much as it is possible under Chinese rule. The houses are built of mud and the newer houses have white tiles for decoration. Colorful prayer flags flutter from the roofs of homes or from the walls encircling courtyards. Tashi points out specifics to me: patties of yak dung drying on walls, men reclining on grass, and a stupa in the distance. She asks Rinchen to halt for a moment when the monastery of Dhamkha faces us from its place atop a hill.

Keeping her eyes steadfast on the monastery, she says her prayers. The lama is well respected and has students all over the world, she informs me. The popularity of Tibetan Buddhism in the West as well as among the Chinese in Taiwan, Singapore, and Hong Kong has enabled some Buddhist lamas—both those in exile and those in Tibet—to raise funds to restore their shrine halls, to build prayer halls, and to maintain monks in the monasteries. The Chinese government does not seem to interfere much with the rebuilding in this region if the lamas remain apolitical and maintain a low profile. They are perhaps relieved at not being called upon to reinstate the monasteries—approximately six thousand—they partially or completely destroyed during the invasion and the Cultural Revolution. Quite often the Chinese government presents the prosperity of the monasteries and the lamas to their advantage: to refute accusations of religious intolerance and of subjugation of Tibetans.

Tashi tells me excitedly each monk in this monastery has electricity in his room, and that water is pumped from the river to reach the taps in the bathrooms. The luxury of it appeals to her, she who has traveled to Nepal and India three times and knows the pleasure of daily showers. "The monks can take showers and wash their faces all year round," she tells me.

In Kyegu she relies on the well in her compound for water, and because she does not have a bathroom with hot water she must go to the public bathhouses run by the Chinese once every three months for a hot shower. It is not a pleasant experience and her distaste is compounded by her prejudice. She does not like the reminders she gets from the strands of hair on the floor, the dried mucus or blood on the walls, that anybody can take a bath there.

"I feel as though I return home with the dirt of strangers," she says.

As we drive yet closer to the town, now twelve, thirteen hours into our journey, the road is adorned on either side with poplar trees. They were planted a few years ago by school children and government employees. Tashi tells me some of my relatives were among those fortunate to have been given the day off from work to plant them. Doctors, accountants, police officers, secretaries, cooks, and sweepers: all had worked side by side and enjoyed the reprieve from their offices.

"In the beginning there were no trees in this high plateau area," she tells me. There is a story for everything that exists and Tashi knows this from having witnessed many births and deaths. Seventy years ago, she begins, a lama from Trindu county in Qinghai Province brought the first saplings of the poplar from Xining. He wrapped each sapling carefully in plastic and transported them on the back of yaks over several weeks. He had in mind to build a perfect village where streets intersected each other neatly in a grid akin to contemporary cities. He wanted everyone in his village to be able to get around easily. He envisioned each street lined with trees and every house with a yard.

Naysayers whispered the lama was wasting his time. If this land was meant to shelter trees, wouldn't they grow on their own, as the grass did, and the juniper?

The trees thrive still in his perfect village. During summer they are bright green and thrill birds who flit from street to street. In autumn, leaves the color of gold and copper decorate the gray stone streets and the perfectly stacked stone houses—the village becomes an image of a bride on her wedding night.

"Every tree we see in town and in the surrounding towns is the lama's gift," Tashi explains.

A river enters our view to our west and the hills to our east sprout untidy clumps of juniper and grass. In October these hills will be shades of saffron and turmeric.

Then fields of wild clematis, aster, delphiniums, and edelweiss lead us into Kyegu.

CHAPTER THREE

Town of Nine Lives

Kyegu is a perfect locale for a western movie: the swirling dust, the woebegone stray dogs, and the air of bravado of men on the streets. The men here are omnipresent and they are made bigger and taller by their fur-lined sheepskin jackets, cowboy hats, and the stentorian manner in which they speak their dialects. Whether resting against streetlights, half-astride on motorbikes, or sitting on the steps of shops in the marketplace, they tower over the Chinese and look like bandits or lords. Everything about them indicates it will take but a tiny cough to incite them into a brawl. Many of them were born in nomadic villages in the six regional counties that make up the Yushu prefecture.

There are those who take trouble with their hair, hair that is blacker than ordinary black, and immobile against their spine. Not even a breeze displaces the shiny strands from their position. There are others who braid red silk threads into their hair and wrap the strands around their heads like snakes wrap around tree trunks. There are men with high cheekbones and lean bodies whose pictures I can imagine in travel magazines, and about whom visiting women, usually tourists, refer to, more than once after they return to the safety of their own homes: the long-haired men from whom they are so lucky to have escaped.

Mingling among the idlers are the equally imposing warlords of commerce who reveal jewels and sometimes musk from the inside pocket of their jackets. They take up positions in the middle of the street across from a busy square and insist people pause to inspect the strands of turquoise, agate beads (*zi* in Tibetan), and coral beads they wear around their necks. I am not certain who buys from them. There are only a few Western tourists and I cannot imagine the young Chinese backpackers being interested in the exorbitantly priced stones, symbolic and of value to Tibetans. The men carry the precious stones with an air of submissive impropriety. They look like adolescent boys waiting to be noticed at the entrance to a woman's sanctum. They cannot be ignored, and even though local Tibetans walking past them are not looking to buy jewels, they slow down, let their eyes linger over the strutting bejeweled men before continuing onward.

Once the shock from seeing the men is acknowledged, other details of the town arise: the becalming view of the Kyegu monastery sitting atop the hill, yellow and indigo window frames that look like painted eyes, lace gloves protecting the hands of women from being burnished to a blue sheen, mothers who move briskly in black unlike the languorous gait of the opposite sex, the inventive hats worn by monks and nuns, dust on eyeglasses, dust on the ends of trousers, and dust on dry, cracked lips.

The Yushu prefecture is known for its riches. Three of Asia's mightiest rivers originate from its mountains—Mekong (Dza Chu), Yellow River (Ma Chu), and Yangtze (Dri Chu)—and minerals, gold, and iron ores await to be plundered. This is the heartland of Tibet for me, where more than half of the population continues to live as high-plateau herders, as their forefathers did for generations. It is a region defined equally by the isolated clans and chiefdoms who made their name assailing each other as by famous Buddhist teachers and yogis.

Ask a khampa and he will speak gladly of the torrential vehemence that stirs his blood. Ask the people in Lhasa, for they too have heard stories and will ratify the quick temper and brashness of the khampas. Mistaking me for a central Tibetan, a shopkeeper in Lhasa had advised me on a previous visit to proceed with caution when dealing with khampa traders. Perhaps my use of the central Tibetan language spoken in exile aided in masking my origin. She had said khampas were volatile.

Young men on the streets look surly enough to instill the fear that even an innocent brush against their sleeve will produce a reaction or a revolution. Instead, I am courted by their courtesy. In shops, on sidewalks, it is young men who stop to translate for me or help me decipher what the Chinese say to me. They are always helpful. *Sister,* they say softly, casting a slow smile. *Sister. Lady. Big sister.*

Kyegu, the capital of the Yushu prefecture, is undecided on its identity and the hesitancy has much to do with the rustic roots of most of its inhabitants who meet the dictates of the city with irreverence. The schools, Western-style hotels, and new shopping complexes indicate Kyegu's attempt to modernize, but still, the city cannot disguise a disheveled look, nor can its bureaucrats accomplish the simple task of scattering Tibetans who loaf and socialize at street intersections. Traffic lights installed a year ago at two focal locations in town are repeatedly ignored by pedestrians and drivers alike, and the occasional traffic officer standing in the middle of the street would be better off reading or drinking tea, so inconsequential is their presence.

Fifty years ago, the chieftains of this region fought regularly with one another over land, matrimonial alliances, and cattle. Chiefs forged alliances with other chiefs to surprise their rivals with murder. They also enlisted the help of their lamas to pray to their protectors so that their foes, along with their descendants, were cursed to short lives, sickness, or, even more wicked, to have no sons. Such curses besiege families to this day. It is widely known in my mother's village of Dhompa that when my seventeen-year-old granduncle outwitted the much older and established Asha chief in court in the 1930s, the older chieftain claimed his revenge by murdering my granduncle: some say his reins were coated with poison, some say his drink was. The Asha chief was called before the Nangchen king's court and as penalty for killing my granduncle he had to offer a portion of his land and some of his people to my grandfather. This further enraged the Asha chief, who is said to have asked his lama to put a curse on the Dhompa family so that longevity was never to be enjoyed in the line. The chief and my grandfather never did make peace and so no attempts were made to reverse the curse. My grandfather, uncle, mother, and aunt all died close to or at the age of fifty and people make references to the curse as the reason for their brief lives.

Fifty years ago, it was common to hear of nomads losing fifty horses or a hundred yaks to bandits or to neighboring clans. To steal from a family member or from one's clan was shameful and punishable, but to steal animals or land, or even kill aggressors, from rival clans was lauded. Physical strength was admired and men fought hard to preserve their dignity as good horsemen and brave fighters, and as loyal sons, brothers, or friends. Living by such beliefs and customs, nomadic chiefs and their people established a somewhat ignoble reputation as they preserved their land, culture, animals, and status from outsiders and from each other.

There were times when fifteen chieftains from all over the state of Nangchen gathered at the king's residence in Nangchen Gar or in Kyegu to settle disputes. A handful of the chieftains would be cajoled into renouncing their enmity and made to enter a pact of friendship they generally honored until their deaths. Some offered land and animals to the wronged or pledged their children in marriage as evidence of contrition.

The khampas' proclivity for troublemaking has not abated. There is always some issue that keeps Kyegu abuzz—a murder over a trivial argument, a stolen car recovered, a fight at the square, an automobile accident, a visiting healer or shaman—and because the town's infrastructure and planning is as haphazard as its growth, all news travels a convoluted path and augments, until a story, by the day's end, is three times its size.

"Is it true there are many young patients brought to the hospital with knife wounds?" I ask a young doctor who is married to a family member. "Would it be correct to state that there is a man brought to the hospital once a week, or perhaps once a month, due to a scuffle?"

He admits it would not be entirely incorrect to say that five people are brought to the hospital every day because of a fight or because of a car accident. "I do not know why our people are so quick to use their knives," he confides. "If we kill each other, who will the Chinese have left to kill?"

Knives are a traditional ornament and worn at the waist by khampa men and women alike, and while nomads continue to wear their knives, the men in town are no longer legally permitted to do so. Still, men devise ways to conceal a knife inside their clothes. I do not want to be the one to say I come from people who will use their knives more readily on a fellow khampa than they will use their hands to strike down a pesky fly. Yet there are many unnecessary deaths in town to prove it, including a nephew who died during a night of drunken revelry with his friends. The pride, the physical prowess, and the impetuousness of the khampas that we fear and boast of in exile are exhibited to dire consequences on their soil. There are many examples and the most talked about murder during my visit involved a family of six, which included a young child. The story goes back a few years.

Seven years ago, one of four brothers from the region of Dege was murdered in a business squabble. The three remaining brothers, keeping to a tradition of revenge, vowed to avenge their dead brother. They moved to the town of Shinze, a few miles outside Kyegu, and took up work as stone carvers. Every day for seven years they toiled at a laborious vocation inscribing Buddhist prayers on small stones and rocks which they sold to pilgrims. In seven years they were able to find the identity and location of the man who had murdered their brother. One day they put aside their prayer stones and drove to the town of Chumaleb, four hours away from Shinze. They entered the house of the man and killed everyone in his family, including the young child. Six people died as punishment for the murder of their brother.

"The child had to be killed," a cousin reasons. "If they had let the child live, the child would grow up and kill the three brothers to avenge the death of his own family and it would continue into the next generation or until everyone in both families is dead."

<hr />

When dust storms pass through town in the late afternoons, shopkeepers pull down their metal shutters and hangers-on pull up their shirtsleeves to cover their mouths and nostrils. The dust is thick and ties tongues into silence. It forces eyes to remain half closed. The sun too invokes its wrath on the easily browned Tibetan faces and applies a toasted hardiness or a look of frontier belligerence to their features. Women don white cotton masks over their mouths and noses. Their eyes hide behind sunglasses with lenses as huge as two tennis balls. It is as though they are all hiding from someone. And yet, this is nothing compared to the windstorms of winter. From December through February the air bruises the population. It blinds you, it cuts your skin; its force is hellish. You can pass by your own child or lover and not recognize them, my cousins complain.

A morning of modest rain washes the town of all signs of efficiency and order: drains overflow onto streets; flies disengage themselves from their hiding corners to buzz and buzz; piss and feces rise to the top of little pools of water in backstreets. Each step has to be thoughtfully planned: what we step on is what we carry home. I see a few trash bins on the streets, but to many people the river passing through the town is a more convenient garbage disposal. The brown river carries an unending revelation of desire—cans, plastic bottles, old car tires, the waste from the city's new sewage system, and remnants of the night's libations—all these float alongside the occasional sanitary napkin, gaping bloodily. Not much attention is given to personal and public hygiene; people are more observant than they were five or ten years ago, but much more is needed to alter habits and to learn the true and unretiring nature of synthetic packages that have them enraptured for now.

Kids loiter near gutters; they stray into the water and wet their feet when they can, kicking out of the path of their bare feet the broken bottles, syringes, and plastic wrappers. Many thousands are being spent to create a promenade along the river, but it does not stay clean for long, I am told. I ask an eleven-year-old girl playing near me if she notices anything unusual. She says she has never seen fish in these waters. She has never seen the river look blue. She drops a candy wrapper from her hand. A man cycles past us and spits. His spit flies in a perfect arch, floats over the young girl's head as she leans forward, then plunges into the river. I see its entry before it is carried deeper into the city's stomach.

A few years ago new houses in Kyegu boasted blue-tinted windows and outside walls of white tile. When I told family members tiles were best in bathrooms they would argue it made no sense to hide them inside the house when they were so clean and grand to behold. Much to my relief, this year traditional houses are more prestigious. The authorities enforce their version of a Tibetan architecture upon buildings on the main streets, in order to present an authentic Tibet to government officials visiting from mainland China and to tourists—an increasing number of them Chinese. So once again, older buildings are torn down and replaced with those carrying Tibetan motifs etched along the roof awnings and window frames. The new houses have indoor bathrooms and plumbing, but the old residences, which account for more than half of the town's buildings, continue with the out-houses and rely on wells for water.

Even so, Kyegu is kind to gardens in summer. Poppies, geraniums, cosmos, and nasturtiums bloom without modesty. These are flowers I recognize and can mention. The poplar grows well here too and it is a tree that people and street dogs search for during dry, hot afternoons.

Summer is a season of hope for everyone but more so for nomads who come to trade their most lucrative crop for cash. In recent years, caterpillar fungus, or *yar-tsa gun-bu,* translated as "grass in summer, worm in winter," also known as *bu,* or worm, has accomplished what the Chinese government has not since 1959: to bring cash to nomads, rural Tibetans, and marginalized urban populations and integrate them into China's economic machine. These populations have come to depend on the fungus so entirely that they organize their year around the short harvesting season that begins in May and lasts often through July.

If the animals look longingly to the grasslands for grass and flowers, their keepers, the nomads, look even more hopefully for the fungus that determines their income for the year. The fungus hides among grass and nomads spend two months of the year with their eyes glued to the ground from dawn to dusk. It is hard work and only those with keen eyesight and steady hands make good pickers. Teenagers often make the best pickers as they are quick and they can withstand the long hours spent on knees or stomachs. A good caterpillar fungus is one which has its whole body intact. It can be as long as a finger and as wide as a chopstick, and it looks like a miniature sea urchin, an insect carved out of wood. The browner it is, the more it is valued. Each piece of fungus is counted in yuan.

The streets in town are empty and business is slow during the fungus-picking months. Even schools in Kyegu and nearby Nangchen close for a month and a half to enable children to assist their parents. Nobody in town travels to visit family in villages because they know only the elders, monks, and toddlers remain home, the ones either prohibited from or unwilling to partake in this bounty expedition.

Once the collecting season ends, the market squares in Kyegu fill with nomads bargaining for a good price for their fungus. Nomad sellers and Chinese buyers circle each other warily: the dark cowboy hats worn by Tibetans make the *taqiyas* worn by Muslim traders appear delicate and tidy. People sell their best fungus for as much as sixteen yuan a piece and the mediocre for twelve yuan or less. In a good year, a family that collects four or five pounds of the fungus earns a few times the salary of a high-powered government official in Kyegu. During this time storekeepers in town keep their shops open for longer hours, knowing their best business months are upon them. In a lucrative fungus year, nomads have enough to buy a car, a motorbike, and sometimes a house in addition to treating their ailments and stocking up on staples for the year.

As the fungus moves farther and farther from the hands of the nomads, its price escalates, from the lowest five yuan to the highest fifty yuan. Nomads say the best quality fungus can be sold in

China for more than its weight in gold. Nomads—many of whom
have only recently become acquainted with the workings of market economy—laugh at the whimsy of fortunes. See, anything is
possible in a lifetime, they say.

And then, what would summer be without skin and hats of all
styles. The necks, the arms, the white of flesh hidden for seven
months are revealed, and the women in town are suddenly women
with shapes and women for whom songs seem applicable and
obligatory. I tease a cousin that summer must be the time when
mothers like her feel anxious for their daughters and observe the
men in the neighborhood as potential marauders. Even the main
street with its identical shops take the long days seriously, I say.
All day, large speakers, placed at the entrance to stores, tirelessly
flaunt love songs sung by Tibetan singers who are pictured with
carelessly worn long hair and leather jackets.

> *When, from a distance, I glanced at her*
> *Beautiful Rinzin Wangmo looked back at me . . .*

There are many singers in Kham. In the town of Kyegu itself
there are more musicians and singers than there are in the entire
community in exile. I hear the old favorites—like Yadon and
Kunga—as soon as I step out of the house and new singers who
are also invoked by their first names, such as Riga and Sherten.
It is not difficult to figure out the hit songs, for they precede my
steps on the streets, day after day, so that I come to learn a few
lines and hum along without any effort.

> *White clouds please move away*
> *So Rinzin Wangmo and I can go together . . .*

Popular love songs carry strains of Buddhist philosophy even
as the songs attempt to convince the beloved of the sincerity of
amorous feelings. Young singers sing of their attachment to the

land, their devotion toward their parents, and despite the threat of being thrown into jail they employ metaphors and traditional images to praise and invoke the Dalai Lama. Their music videos carry images of snow-peaked ranges, lush grasslands where yaks and sheep graze in the background, and the nomads who are not always welcome on the streets of towns are shown to exude grace, innocence, and jungle agility as they gambol in the mountains. Even here, on Tibetan soil, Tibetans rely on the beauty of the land to express themselves. The singers appear in their own songs wearing chubas and they turn prayer wheels in monasteries, prostrate before lamas, and move their feet to traditional dances. Such are the images we hold of this land and people, images that bedazzle the television screens in busy shopping centers in Chinese cities where Tibetan singers are increasingly recognized.

When I cannot see my lama, my mind is saddened. Oh my lama...

The elders are enraptured by devotional songs and videos of the monasteries of Golog and Yachen, in Kham. They say the best singers come from Amdo and Golog and point to the intimations made to the Dalai Lama, Panchen Lama, or the Karmapa in the songs.

Tashi notes the changes in town and remarks Kyegu has grown over the years, spreading far east, south, and west, even to the very hips of the mountains. On warm days she sits on a short stool outside the gate to her house and observes people. She says it is the elders who feel cold in the summer. It is they who wander to the monasteries to pray, who wake up early to buy fresh milk and yogurt from nomads in the town's main square, and it is they who persist in eating *tsampa* for breakfast despite the proliferation of Chinese bakers selling breads in various shapes. She asks the same questions, sits in the same spot, and repeats the stories I know by heart. I rewrite notes I took down three, five, ten years ago. Quite often I have to resist the urge to go back to my room when irritation or fatigue overcomes me listening to the unnecessary and long diversions in the storytelling, but it is precisely at these moments I remind myself—a story does not have to make sense. Someday, I tell myself, the relevance and the wisdom of these moments will be revealed to me.

Tashi, like most elders in town, has led a turbulent life. She does not speak bitterly of the years under the Chinese rule but refers to it as though recalling a story she has heard elsewhere. When her friends visit her, they usually speak of the people they knew, people who have died since, or places they lived in during the Cultural Revolution. Every now and then an elder will mention a significant detail of his or her life, but it is inserted between the commonplace observations of a day in progress or while we are speaking about another place so that its seriousness passes by unchecked. Many elders ask me about India and say they have heard there is much suffering and poverty in India. They ask if it is true that many people don't have enough to eat.

In the course of such a conversation, an elder might add that many people in Kyegu have died of starvation. He might remember Kyegu as having 170,000 people before 1959, and then there being only 90,000 people left in 1961. If I were to press for details and ask how the particular numbers came to be in his possession, he will offer no explanation. He will say he knew many people died because he survived.

When I ask the chief of Kyegu how many people he had on his land before 1959, he says there might have been a total of 650 families in Kyegu: 400 who paid taxes and about 250 poor families who did not. Official documents state there were 2,092 families, or 9,591 people, under the Kyegu chief in the regions covering Kyegu, Parthang, and Shinze in 1959. Most original inhabitants of the town have since moved to Xining and the present population consists largely of nomads from the six counties.

The elders in Tibet remind me of the elders in exile in the way they drop statistics in their conversations without providing any source, in the deliberate way they linger over their words, and in their habit of repeating punch lines two or three times, as though the story will improve with repetition.

They preface their lives by speaking of time as before the Chinese and after the Chinese. This rupture is contained in their use of the term *ngabchu ngabgay*, which means "1958," or simply *ngabgay*, "'58." They also refer to the change in Tibetan history with the term *dhulok*, which means "when time collapsed" or "when time overturned." *Dhulok* signifies a change from good to bad. The elders say they can exhale now; they did not think they would survive the Cultural Revolution.

They carry their past in them as though safekeeping it for someone else. Very often they look at me and say, "poor thing." They say I have lost a mother and am alone in the world. They feel compassion for me, for a loss that comes to all; they disregard their own extraordinary suffering.

All day they finger their prayer beads and at the suggestion of a misfortune they send money to the monks in Kyegu monastery perched on the hills overlooking the town. They also give money to local representatives of several famous monasteries who fax the list of prayers every evening to their monasteries, some more than a day's journey away. I suspect most elders spend their allowance on prayers and butter lamps. Many of them cannot walk to the top of the hill to the Kyegu monastery, so they seek the streets in town from where they can view it while saying their prayers.

The monastery is a becalming solace to them. It helps to ground them in this life and reminds them of the next life. I suspect it has something to do with knowing there are people whose lives are dedicated to prayer. And that they can, on other people's behalf, pray for them, negotiate their fate, defer or even remove obstacles. They are the mediators, the spiritual lawyers, the upholders of the culture and language.

The elders continue to wear layers of clothes as though their bodies are indifferent to summer. Summer after summer has come and gone and still they don't desist. They are used to the weight of lambskin and woolen trousers knitted by relatives and they cannot shrug the layers off. They are warm, they are uneasy, but they cannot do without the weight. Tashi wears two pairs of cotton trousers under her chuba. She feels naked if she removes them. When she is unbearably hot, she pulls the lower end of her chuba up to her knees and flaps it back and forth. This action cools her. The chuba as worn by the women in this region is not very practical nor does it make any effort to provide a feminine shape. It is worn like a wide bathrobe, with sufficient material to be folded and secured at the waist. It is a dress that hides the body well and is wonderful for cold days. Tashi wears a layer of a lighter material as a lining under her chuba and together they weigh as much as she does. This is her summer dress. For winter she exchanges the cotton pants for woolen ones and the heavy wool chuba for one lined with sheepskin.

It is a hot summer day. Tashi tells me the Chinese government is making rain this summer. She has heard from people that an airplane flies in the sky and sprays a chemical in the air that helps form clouds and makes rain. She thinks the Chinese should ask the lamas to pray for rain as the people have done so for many centuries.

"The Chinese do not beseech the sky deities for rain, they assault the sky," she explains. She is mystified and partly in awe of what the Chinese can do but she is always wary of their methods. "Their rain cannot be good for the land, for humans, and for the animals," she states firmly.

Tashi does not accompany me in the evenings to a small temple and stupa where I take my circumambulations. She does not walk much despite my entreaties to her to join the elders who walk around the stupa early in the morning and then again in the late afternoon. Three years ago I walked through fields of wheat and barley to get to the stupa; now the fields have been replaced with new houses and shops. There are always twenty to thirty women, four to ten men, and a handful of teenagers walking around the temple. Most elders complete their morning prayers at dawn, and after getting some rest they return for their evening rounds. They look happy enough as they sit on wooden seats along the edge of the *kora* path sharing tales between prayers. A few of them need the aid of walking sticks and they require a break after each round of the stupa.

I overhear snippets of their conversations when I walk past them and in this way feel justified for not reading any newspapers (there are none produced in this town): eight young students died when their car flew off the road approaching Zatou and one of them is in the hospital with a broken leg (so many young men die in cars, they say and mutter prayers); Chinese soldiers were patrolling in armored vehicles early in the morning (only the old are awake at that hour, they mumble); two trucks are selling juicy pears at fifteen yuan for five kilos outside the main hospital; of the three who killed seven members of a family in Chumaleb, one brother managed to evade the police and has disappeared into the labyrinth of arteries that will take him elsewhere (perhaps he will escape to Nepal or India and begin a new life, wishes an elder). Information on heart medicine, cold medicine, pain reducing tactics for gout and arthritis are exchanged.

Kora, as we refer to circumambulations, is part of the Buddhist religious life. Tibetans walk around all sacred structures, man-made as the stupa, or born of nature such as sacred mountains and lakes. The elders believe the body is cleansed of its impurities if placed in the vicinity of sacred grounds and so the stupa, in this case, becomes the symbol of purity. This act of worship involving body, speech, and heart is said to have the power to ful-fill wishes and add merit toward the next life, so the elders recite their prayers out loud and imagine the many deities as they walk with their finicky and troublesome bodies.

What do the elders hope for? If they are praying for better health, riches, and happiness in their next life, they do not make these wishes known to me nor do their prayers reveal their inner-most fears or desires. As far as I can tell, they recite prayers for the happiness of all beings in the world.

I do not walk around the stupa to help establish a better next-life. I would prefer to experience happiness in this life. I walk because I enjoy the company of elders who make their journey solely on faith. It is enough for me to hear their voices rise in a haunting litany to the deities who they believe surround us. There are always one or two women who sing their prayers out loud. Perhaps they were known to have a singing voice in some period of their lives and there is a quality in the tone they dare to take that hints of those times. A tune sung out loud alters the after-noon air, permitting a sweetness and a friskiness that takes the present hour outside of time. I am not certain how much of the day the elders give to prayers but it is very possible that they com-mit to their deities as many hours as I do to a full-time job in San Francisco. Who knows if they are rewarded for this effort and if it makes any difference once they are dead, but they believe in the merit of taking their bodies around sacred relics and in rolling their fingers repeatedly over their prayer beads until the wood of the beads is whittled to the size of rice grains. The able-bodied walk, the wounded walk, and even those whose bodies are bent at the waist like walking sticks attempt to make a kora.

They devise little tricks to keep track of their prayers and their circumambulations, for what would be the purpose of not keeping count? Most elders employ their prayer beads and there is a system to the beads that makes it possible to count until the millionth prayer. Once a million prayers are said, they take the shell from their prayer wheels (the ambidextrous among them use prayer bead in one hand and prayer wheel in the other) and wear it around their necks. An elder I befriend reveals the pebbles she holds in her hands.

"To fling at dogs?" I ask.

"To count my koras," she explains. It is a foolproof system. She places twenty pebbles in a pile and with each round she completes, she picks one pebble from the pile and begins another. When all the pebbles are transferred from one pile to the other, she knows she has finished her twenty rounds.

She also stops along her kora to read a prayer tucked into the walls behind the prayer wheels encircling the stupa or to pull out photos of lamas from the cracks in the walls. These photos are placed on her head as blessing and then hidden again in their places. I see a picture of the Dalai Lama only to find it disappear after a few days, then it reappears again in the hands of an elder who impales it on the wall with a wooden popsicle stick. A photo of the previous Panchen Lama comes and goes on the same wall. Through such small gestures, Tibetans assert their desire and their need for their spiritual leaders.

Who are these people who can put aside their own suffering? Their torn socks and flimsy cloth shoes make me wish they would devote themselves to their own comfort. At dusk I see many elders disappear through a gate to a dreary concrete dwelling that is a state-run elderly home near the stupa.

I do not speculate as to what brings the young to the stupa. Lovers walk side by side, their hands brushing slyly and shyly; it would not do here, among the praying elders and the monks, to hold hands and display carnal desire. Young girls hold prayer beads in their hands. Perhaps they played around the stupa, as a dozen kids do today while their parents do their prayers. Kids run clockwise and counterclockwise, and despite their state of inattention, they must, over time, pick up a few lines of prayers and a few habits like carrying prayer beads and putting insects out of the path of shoes.

One evening I watch two young boys chase each other around the elders and past two drunk men sitting on the steps leading to the hall of the shrine. On my second round I notice the two men beckoning the little boys to come to them. The men, who speak only Chinese, are unsteady even as they sit. They pat the heads of the boys and ask questions in Chinese.

I tell the boys, in Tibetan, to go home. They are surprised by my tone and I repeat myself gently and say they should go home because the men are drunk.

The two men speak to me in Chinese.

"Go home. Wherever you are from," I tell them in Tibetan. "Leave the boys alone."

They imitate me and laugh. They do not speak my language. The little boys do not speak Chinese yet. I am angry but do not know what to do. I ask an elder to tell the men to leave the boys alone.

Why, he asks.

I don't know how to put my unfounded fear and prejudice into words for the elder.

"Because they are drunk," I say.

The elder admits he does not speak Chinese and walks on.

I do not know how to be angry in Tibetan. The men watch me. "Leave the boys alone. Go home," I say in English. "Assholes," I mutter under my breath when I have nothing else to say. They laugh at me. In Tibet, these two migrant workers from China have more legitimacy to be here than I do. They do not understand me and perhaps do not understand why I am angry. They are far from their families and their people; perhaps they have children where they come from. In Tibet I develop hostility toward the ordinary Chinese. I see them as the oppressor. I am ashamed of feeling this way, yet there is little I can do to quell the emotion. In Tibet I feel dispossessed of my land more directly than I do when I am outside it.

In my confused anger, I enter the hall of the shrine I am walking around. A statue of the Buddha commands the center of the room. Butter lamps sputter, and then hold still as the eyes of the Buddha gaze ahead in a semi-seeing dreaminess. The Buddha's face glitters in the quavering light. My heart aches and I want to weep, for nothing in particular and for everything that has happened to us: the elders who walk with faith in deities they do not see, my grandmother, my aunt, my mother. I cannot forget the past when I am in Tibet. It stays in me like a tightfisted bud.

The caretaker tells me to take the butter lamps he has just prepared if I am interested in lighting them. "You can pay after you light them," he instructs.

A woman comes to my side and whispers to ask who the caretaker is as though his presence in the hall is a matter of great relevance to her. She speaks to me as though she knows me. In a town of Tibetans, she will know someone who will know someone who will know the caretaker as well as me, and our places will be revealed. The two Chinese men she does not inquire about: they come from places she has never been to; they come from families she has no knowledge of. The Chinese are the people from whom she buys her cooking oil, her flour, and her vegetables. They are people she is forced to live with; the Tibetans she can avoid if she so chooses.

Shadows from pillars, statues, and butter lamps offered to one's preferred deity form a mandala on the cold mud floor. Dust falls in jaundiced patches. We are silenced by legions of sculpted bodies.

A man's voice breaks in from outside, *I am separated from you in this life . . .*

The women turn away from the caretaker and look to corners in the room. That we should acknowledge love in this room of deities feels sacrilegious yet the words linger. The caretaker removes the bulbous black heads of decimated wicks from the butter lamps. The walls are black from smoke and portions of the wall murals are obscured, demonstrating a lesson in impermanence and the only certitude in life: that all things perish. He wipes the silver lamps, pushes in new wicks, and pours melted butter over them. This is his daily ritual. This is a rite he shares with most Tibetans—even those of my age and younger—who continue to maintain an altar in our homes. A frown travels halfway down his left cheek like a snail trail.

A bell rings faintly and I hear someone reciting her night prayers. I light lamps for those I can name—Doma, Chenresig, Guru Rinpoche—and for those I cannot recognize but accept as part of my Buddhist faith. Tashi offers, as I know other elders do, to the monasteries and lamas what she will not spend on her own pleasures. I have faith enough only to partake in small offerings. I see lamas as human and, therefore, fallible. My faith makes fearful gestures. It has shallow roots.

It is dark outside. The lights of the city come on, one by one, and form a map that illuminates more pointedly how the town is changing. Night nibbles the heads of poppies in the courtyard of new homes purchased by nomads who have done well selling caterpillar fungus and Tibetan mastiffs. A child's wailings get louder by the minute, protesting over his mother's persuasions, from one of the houses. Another night is taken in habit as the day shuts like a book in midsentence. *If only, if only,* the wretched must say to themselves over and over, I think.

Almost every day I too have thought, *If only my mother were alive.*

CHAPTER FOUR

Born in Exile

Dharamshala, a town in northern India nestled against the Dauladhar mountains and sitting atop the valley of Kangra is where the Tibetan refugee community has set up a government-in-exile under the leadership of His Holiness the Dalai Lama. In Hindi, the word *dharamshala* generally refers to a "shelter" or "sanctuary," usually for pilgrims. With its temperate summers and the majestic backdrop of mountains, Dharamshala has been an auspicious sanctuary for Tibetans. My mother moved to the town when she was voted to represent the people of East Tibet in the highest legislative body of the Tibetan government-in-exile, known as the Assembly of Tibetan People's Deputies. We lived in a two-room apartment provided to representatives. The surroundings afforded forests of pine and deodars under whose covering I spent most of my afternoons playing hide-and-seek with other children.

Throughout the day I would peep through the window into my mother's office. I took questions to her: Can I wash my hair? Can I change my shirt? Can I play in the woods? Sometimes she would put her hand to the wired mesh that covered the window and trace my palms with her fingers. The interruptions never seemed to distress her unless she was in a meeting—then she would reproach me with a stern look. On the days my mother attended late-night meetings, I sought the company of neighbors. I realized her role was different from the mothers in our apartment building who were home all day and who began their preparations for dinner when the clock struck four. I sensed their admiration for my mother for working alongside their husbands and fathers and I also saw their compassion toward her.

My mother would rest a while when she got home and then she would prepare dinner for the two of us. She was my constant companion as I was hers. How was it we had no family other than each other, I would ask her.

Mother did not know where her family was. She did not know if they were alive.

How was that possible?

They were left behind in Tibet.

Why?

The Chinese had taken over our country and she had escaped in 1959 by traveling on horse and by foot all the way from her home in eastern Tibet to the borders of Nepal.

Why did China invade Tibet?

Fate.

Why did her family remain behind?

It was their fate that imprisoned them there.

Three people had escaped from her region: my mother, a monk who moved to Canada and who wrote letters to her, and an older man who visited us every week when we relocated to Kathmandu.

Mother was frugal with her references to her father and mother, and when she did speak of them she would rush through the stories as though to linger would cause her grief. If I asked questions about them, she would feign a headache and suggest I wait for a day when her memory wasn't sullied by the day's humdrum. When I persisted in seeking details of their appearances she would say they each had one nose, two eyes, and one mouth. I didn't know their names because it is not auspicious to speak the names of those who have died. My mother referred to her parents as, "my father who is no more" and "my late mother." She did not name them for fear of disturbing their peace. When I was in my early teens, she pointed out a man in a faded photograph in a book on the history of Nangchen. The man was her father, my grandfather.

Only once did she speak of her father's death and she went over the story very quickly. She allowed no questions. She presented dark rooms and narrow corridors. Her face was tight and her voice clarioned as she rushed toward the end of the story as though she were simply summarizing it for herself. Her memory allowed for no personal revelations.

Mother said her father's death had been her first introduction to suffering. He had died from a blocked throat. I tried to see her as a young child of eight or nine years eavesdropping on the servants and older relatives and their whispers about the end of the Dhompa chief, how he was losing his strength and how he couldn't eat.

How had he died?

Tea leaves had settled sideways in his throat.

Tea leaves killed my grandfather! For a long time I was disappointed that a chieftain whose name was known all over the kingdom of Nangchen died such a lackluster death. There was nobody to contradict my mother's story and it was only on my first trip to Tibet, after her death in 1994, that I stumbled upon information about other events held responsible for his end.

The winter I was twelve, my mother received news that changed our lives: her family in Tibet was alive! Not enough of them. Not her mother, not her paternal aunt—a crusty nun who occasionally fed her a spoonful of yogurt made of milk from her favorite female yak, which my mother believed was the best she ever ate—nor her maternal aunt with a son so devious not even family members crossed him. But enough people, to give my mother the comfort of family once again, were alive.

The reemergence of family prompted a series of changes in my mother's life, the first being a relocation to Kathmandu a week after hearing the news because she longed to be physically closer to Tibet. She said she felt a veil lifting from her heart. At the age of twelve I was asked to memorize the names of people I was to love: two aunts, one uncle, twelve first cousins, and my mother's four cousins. I never thought to question Mother, I never thought it impossible to love without seeing or knowing these people. I loved them because I loved her.

Prior to this list of absent relatives of her family left behind in Tibet, the only image I had was the lone portrait of a young Tibetan man in our house. He was also the only male presence in our home. In my unenquiring state, I thought of him as her father, and sometimes as my father or my great-grandfather. His name, I later learned, was Phuntsok Wangdak Dhompa, and he was my mother's brother, older than she by three years. She had asked an artist to paint him from a photo he had taken in Lhasa in 1956.

I never queried my mother about my father—to me she was both mother and father; the painting of my uncle accompanying us wherever we moved fulfilled the function of a man in the house. My own father I neglected even as I grew up. My mother had separated from him before my birth. I forgot he was alive. I never loved him, I never disliked him, and I did not attempt to know him. Every now and then grown-ups asked if I knew who my father was: Was he a certain lama? Was he her ex-husband? Was he an Indian lover? To these people I said my mother was my father and if they wanted to know more they could ask her.

I did feel, however, the absence of grandparents, aunts, uncles, and cousins. My friends in the compound had parents and at least one other sibling. I noticed grandparents, aunts, and uncles living with them or visiting them. I was giddy when we had guests: I danced, sang, and entertained the grown-ups and was delighted when they ruffled my hair and called me a "funny girl." Every now and then my mother would warn her friends, "Don't turn the radio on."

Her friends would kiss me and give me candy. And I would spin in joy from one guest to the other.

"I told you not to turn the radio on."

It had not taken me long to understand who the "radio" was. I would beg her friends not to leave when the evening turned late. I acquired an ability to appropriate anyone who was remotely connected to Mother and me: a man called Sorry who lived on the top of a hill with his mother and older brother and brought us cow milk in a small aluminum pail; a young Tibetan girl who came to help my mother with laundry and shopping on weekends; and a storekeeper, Uncle Raj, whom my mother had befriended. She had objected to and stormed out of his shop hearing the outrageous prices of cotton fabrics on her first visit. But on subsequent visits he cajoled her into becoming a frequent customer. Most Sundays we would pay him a visit and enjoy the tea and samosas he offered us.

My mother showed her gratitude for her life in exile by pointing to India's modernity: the expansive railway network; the Bollywood movies she came to love for their tumultuous stories which ultimately conceded to the cardinal guidelines she held in her own life—love, family, and duty; the Birla and the Tata industries whose products of tea, fabric, and trucks were ubiquitous; the asphalt roads laboring into refugee settlements named Paonta Sahib, Dalhousie, Mussoorie, Simla, Bylakuppe—names she distorted to her own sounds: Ponta Sab, Dallahossy, Masori. Still, it was Tibet's antiquity that anchored her in exile. It was *phayul* she longed for when her skin was scorched by the summer heat of India's plains. When she drank milk she compared it to the milk of her childhood, for such sweetness and creaminess was not easily forgotten, and when she felt nauseous riding the buses that weaved their way around curvaceous mountain roads, she spoke of the horses she had loved to ride.

And there were evenings when sitting with others like her—her friends and coworkers known to me as Uncle, Grandma, or Aunty—who had left their homes and made their own journey to India, I came to learn the purpose and the effort of the words and images they adopted to help them identify happiness. They recalled the silhouette of the land in the hushed night late in June or September when a mountain took the form of a hunched rat, in the leather slippers left cold beside the bed, in the smell of a certain grass which they compared to the aroma of fresh homemade Tibetan flatbread, the surprising dampness of dew, the suppressed sniffles of sisters and mothers as their homes disappeared from view with each step. They explained the beauty of the calamitous mountains and rivers of Tibet in economical sentences, relying on approximate replacements in exile so their land would turn real for us, the children who came after the upheaval.

"In my village you could drink from the river and it was sweet. Not like this river. Wretched you," an elder would remark while explaining how she used to help her mother collect water from a mountain spring. "You too could have entered this dreamland if China hadn't swallowed our country as a lizard gulps a fly." As far as the elders remembered, Tibet was wonderful precisely because it was isolated. It was a powerful metaphor: this place of fulfillment, this place of fullness.

As a child I experienced loss for what I felt was withheld from me: the delicious milk, the mountains of flowers I could not roll in, the cousins I could not play with, a beautiful house on a plateau. As the years grew with me, I became aware of absences that impacted me directly and indirectly: the loss of place, of stories, of family, and of citizenship.

Mother considered her birthplace, Dhompa, named after the family, the most beautiful place on earth. Flowers that knocked against her knees, sky impaling sky, a place where she had mounted her horse and ridden all day and all night.

I can say now, now that I have been there: Dhompa is like no other place. Granted, within Tibet it is a place perhaps better known for its ordinariness. It has verdant summer plains, the river Kyichu, and several spectacular but haphazard hills like those positioned all over Tibet's vastness. None of our people were among the leaders of the armed resistance movement that was formed in East Tibet in 1956, nor do we have renowned poets and singers like the regions of Amdo, but those who are from Dhompa look out at the land and feel a love that wounds us. We say we are good and loyal people because our land is so beautiful. Our land is our ornament.

Dhompa's immediate neighbor is Bongba, the region to which my mother went as bride to their chieftain when she was seventeen. It was the last extravagant wedding the people of the region witnessed before the Chinese came. She had left with a train of fifty men on horses, fifty men on foot, and an army of yaks, sheep, goats, and horses. The air had reverberated with songs of praise sung by my mother's wedding party, reminding the groom's contingent how precious and beautiful she was. There was never a more sullen bride leaving her home, my mother would say of herself. Nobody had noticed the swell under her eyes and the tears that obstructed her vision for most of the day.

In the present day, as they were in the past, the people of Dhompa are recognized as *drokpas*, nomads, for they live as pastoralists herding yaks, goats, and sheep. They are known for the size of their herd and for their ability to care for their animals and the land. They relocate their home and animals four or five times a year. Well above twelve thousand feet, these are lands of extreme climates, of splendid summer months where every growing thing on earth turns green and lush, and of excruciating long winters when man and beast are inert and huddled indoors.

My mother's people accept me as the niece of the Dhompas, the family that has been their chief for over two hundred years. They see in me versions of the person they could have been if they had escaped from Tibet: of India (*gyagar rowa*), and from an outside country (*chi-gyal*), and every now and then I am mistaken for a Chinese because I wear trousers and my skin is smoother and lighter than their burnished and leathery complexion. They know I am not one of them. They say my walk gives me away. They say my clothes fit differently and that the language does not flow effortlessly from my lips.

Children cannot decide if I am a man or a woman: my hair, worn shoulder length, is not hidden in a neat bun as their mothers' and sisters' hair. I let my hair loose, as men do here, and walk in trousers that do not hug my frame. It is apposite I be undefined here, even sexually. For the duration of my visit, be it one month or five, I remain in a state of having just arrived. My mother's people say I am good to love this place and this allows me a temporary role amongst them. It allows them to believe it was the protector of our land who escorted my mother out of Tibet and that it is he who brings me back.

CHAPTER FIVE

Histories of Self

Peering closer at the calendar in my room in Tashi's house in Kyegu, I realize that I am in 1995. I find another calendar in the kitchen hidden behind a cleaning towel. The year has been ripped out of its corner but from the yellowed edges of the paper I see the faint outline of a word: October. An October of distant years.

I seek out my aunt and ask her for the date. She says it is the first day of the fifth lunar month of the Tibetan calendar and that we are in the Year of the Fire Dog, 2133. I ask her for the Chinese date. She does not know.

The multiplicity of time and, therefore, its displacement is appropriate. This town, this time of the year, feels unbound of linear time. In Tibetan cosmology, time is without a beginning and an end. In the beginning there existed a void. This unnameable emptiness allowed for a gentle wind that twisted for countless eons to ultimately form the texture and weight of a mass. This mass, let us call it a thunderbolt, created clouds and brought rain so ponderous it fell to the ground for many ages. The rain grew into a body of placid water.

Then followed a long period of stillness. Then again, a mild wind stirred the water to deliver a delicate layer of foam to its surface, just as butter is created from cream. The foam formed layers of matter that gradually pushed upward into the shape of mountains. Then came the wind again, restless to make clouds, and thus were born the salty oceans of the earth.

In the beginning, this world was home to happy gods. Their celestial bodies emanated light to create what we know as daylight. There existed no pain or sickness in this perfect place. One day however, while wandering around, one of the gods stumbled on a creamy substance growing on the land. He tasted it and found it to his liking. He took it to the other gods and they too found it pleasing. From then on the gods ate nothing else but this delicious, rich food. The food made them slothful and sluggish. Their effulgence dimmed and no longer lit the entire world. Fortunately, they had committed sufficient good deeds in their past to create the sun, the stars, and the moon. Therefore, when we look up at the celestial bodies in the sky we are looking into our own history and at a world that was once peaceful, beautiful, and free from suffering and greed.

We are the people of Khawachen, the "abode of snow." We are as enraptured by it as are those who dream of it from afar. We are a people so grateful to be in a place where Buddhism flourished, adrift from the rest of the world. It is not difficult then to understand how bereft my mother was: to not be in this land and to be far away from the myriad seen and unseen inhabitants of the mountains, lakes, and crooked streams. Elders in exile still pray to the deities of their old land. It is not easy to speak of people and land in simple terms beginning with a beginning and ending with an end.

When I am with family and friends from Nangchen I see them through my mother's eyes. They were part of her life and they were characters in the stories I heard from her. Through storytelling, she revealed others and herself; through each story a narrative of a place and people were formed. Even before I met my mother's younger sister I knew her laugh carried the same deep-throated chortle as my mother's and I knew my mother's older sister walked with the elegance of a feather drifting in air. I had been forewarned of my uncle's tendency to gloom and of a nephew's sixth thumb. My aunts were delighted I knew so much about them and their childhood. It touched them deeply to realize just how much my mother's life in exile had been haunted by memories of the family. They compared the stories my mother told me to how they remembered them and through numerous retellings we uncovered more of the family history. In this way, something as simple as the details of my grandfather's death turned into high drama.

I had first learned of my grandfather's death when I was eight. Old enough to surmise that my entire family consisted of my mother and me, I began to beleaguer her with questions about her parents. That's when she told me her father died choking on tea leaves.

My cousin Karma, my aunt Tashi's only son among seven children and who would have been the Dhompa chief, were we still in the old Tibet, has never heard of the tea leaf accident. He thinks it impossible that tea could have proved fatal to a man so fastidious. He offers another explanation. Our grandfather, he tells me, had accompanied the king of Nangchen and four other chieftains to Xining to offer a thousand horses as tax to the Machu government. Rinchen Tsering Drawutsang, the chief of Kyegu, who is the only man alive today from that mission, confirmed that the journey did take place in the winter of 1949 or the spring of 1950. On their way to Xining they ran into young Chinese soldiers who explained they were running away because the Communist party had taken over. Rinchen Tsering said the chiefs decided to continue their journey and offer the horses to the new ruler, reasoning that one Chinese party was the same as another.

My grandfather took ill on the return journey. My cousin Karma says it was food poisoning. Our grandfather had stopped to rest in Matou, a wind-terrorized place in present-day Golog, before continuing his journey. He would have had with him a retinue of attendants.

Matou is a village on a plain so vast that it seems a topographical error. Sitting at 4,300 meters it has no cover from the wind. A row of restaurants and hotels invite routine and commerce; the people on the streets are either nomads from the region or Chinese who run businesses or travelers who stop for a meal or to rest for a night. There are no summers here, I am told. It was June when we passed through and my bones ached from the stinging chill in the wind that seemed to blow at 50 kilometers per hour. I was convinced I would be plucked from the ground and taken far away if I allowed my body to relax so I had planted my feet apart, and pressed deeply into my hips. I had stood as I imagined an ox would.

My grandfather had rested in Matou to regain his strength and when he was stronger he had continued toward Dhompa. Journeys took many days, even weeks, on horseback. When he reached Dhompa he showed signs of recovery, but after a few days his health took a turn for the worse and he died. The exact sickness was never identified. Something to do with his intestines, is all Karma can say.

Another cousin is convinced our grandfather was assassinated. She said I would have to remember my mother was only a child when her father had died and people would have tried to hide the truth from her.

"Your late mother had the wrong version," she said. "The Chinese poisoned him."

"Who?"

"The Chinese."

Was she referring to the Communist government?

She pondered the question as though it had caught her by

surprise. She shrugged her shoulders and repeated she meant the Chinese.

I persisted with my questions: Why would they want to kill some small chieftain from eastern Tibet who wasn't even involved in any insurgency and who wasn't influential except in his little area?

My cousin replied that when he had left Xining he had bled for a long time.

"But why would *they* want to kill him?"

"I do not know."

I wondered if I ought to persist with more questions. I had been taught to accept the words of elders without confronting them. I reminded myself she was not much older than I.

"How do you know this?"

My cousin had heard the story from a relative and hadn't thought to challenge it. She said it did not matter because the dead are dead. Most elders who witnessed my grandfather's life and his death are themselves dead, and the few (such as Tashi and my mother's cousin Ashang) who are alive resist taking his name, for he is no more. They all agree my grandfather died of a sickness: stomach, throat, and liver—nobody can say for certain. It does not matter, they say. They reason that the Chinese would have killed him anyway had he survived his sickness. He was fortunate to have died when he did; there were lamas and monks present to pray for him, they say. They list the names of those who died in the years following 1950, people who had no prayers conducted for them.

It is as though people have accepted the whimsicality of memory and in doing so they know one story cannot be the only truth. My knowledge is only partially true: the malleability of history revealed in the versions of my grandfather's death indicates just that. How could we, born under different circumstances—though of the same bloodline—come together to have a singular understanding of history, even the history of a family?

The elders in the family refer to the lives of those who are no more in one or two laconic sentences. I am left to draw my own conclusions, both of the history of the family and of the region.

I am a niece of the Dhompas. I have taken my mother's father's name. I have never given the name any special consideration in exile, but while I am in Tibet people refer to me as the niece of the Dhompatsang, the family of the Dhompas, or as the "daughter of the one who passed on in Nepal." I am of a lineage rooted in a specific location and culture. More than eleven generations of Dhompas have been chieftains. The name is more than just a title; people have died because of their association with it, the family reminds me. Those of my generation speak with assurance that the future will be better, that their children will not suffer because of their father's name, as they did.

My grandmother is remembered as a beautiful woman. No, she was the most beautiful woman in Nangchen posit two women now living in Kyegu, who were themselves very comely in their youth. There are no photographs or paintings of her. Her name was Dechen Choden. There are no names for the women before her who married into the Dhompa family and had sons and daughters. The sons are mentioned and remembered for their sons. The daughters were married off to other chieftains or became nuns. Their names don't appear in any of the stories, written or oral. My grandmother is mentioned because there are still many alive who knew her and because she came to Dhompa as a bride under unusual circumstances: she arrived with a daughter and a son. The son was my grandfather's but the daughter was fathered by the Chungho chief who had been courting her before my grandfather intervened.

Thutop Gombo Dhompa, my grandfather, was the chieftain of Dhompa, one of the twenty-five nomadic clans in the kingdom of Nangchen that fell under the territory of Kham, or East Tibet, also known to its people as Chu Shi Gang Druk ("four rivers and six mountains"). Kham, a region of six kingdoms, is designed with geographical cunning of such formidable rivers and mountains, and possessed of such belligerent kingdoms and chieftains, that for much of its history it managed to eschew a fixed political or administrative center.

My grandfather was the eleventh in the lineage of the Dhompas that began with a man known as Tsador Jal Dhompa, some two hundred years ago. Not much is known of Tsador Jal, but according to an older lama he came from Dhomda, a cold and bleak region in what is now the Golog prefecture. Forsaking his home, Tsador Jal brought his family and a group of people to Dhomna, a small settlement outside the main town of Nangchen. It is said he helped the Nangchen king triumph over his foes and as a reward the king gave him land and people and named him chieftain.

There were twenty-five chieftains—four of them known as *behus* and the rest as *becangs*—who held their allegiance to the king of Nangchen. *Behu*, a translation from the Chinese *baihu*, "commander of one hundred (military) households," and *becang* from *baizhang*, "commander of one hundred men," were titles most likely bestowed by the Qing court in 1725. The status and rank of chieftains was established according to their accomplishments and their relationship with the governing Nangchen king. At the time of the Chinese invasion in 1950 the four ruling behus, directly subordinate to the king, were Asha Behu, Chungho Behu,

Dhompa Behu, and Gyatsap Behu. These four chiefs spent most of their time at the king's residence overseeing the day-to-day administrations of the twenty-five clans and their people. When my grandfather was not with the king he was in Dhompa, ruling on his own terms and without much interference from the king of Nangchen, the government in Lhasa, or the Chinese.

It is said Thutop Gombo fell in love instantly upon seeing my grandmother during a festival at the Nangchen king's palace. Dechen Choden was tall and delicate. Her hair was as black as the pupils of the yaks and as thick as the juniper branches that grew in Dhompa. Murmurs around the court suggested she was being pursued by many chiefs but was not easily swayed. She was well read and unyielding. She was phlegmatic and wise and her wisdom yielded to a sweetness that served only to enhance her physical grace, according to Tashi, who as the daughter-in-law is a reliable source for such details.

My grandfather, on the other hand, relied heavily on his reputation as a competent chieftain and as an astute man. He was rather unremarkable to look at. In the only picture I have of him, he stands behind the king wearing an impassive and brutish expression. His features are harsh and irregular. His hair is shorn savagely as though cut hurriedly by a blunt knife. He had not taken the effort to press his hair down with butter or water for the photograph.

The Chungho chief was my grandfather's rival. He had a bit of an advantage over my grandfather because he had fathered my grandmother's first child, a daughter named Parchen. Chungho was also handsome and he had a way with words, but my grandfather, being the craftier man and the king's most trusted chief, won Dechen Choden as his wife. It was a decision that put him at odds with the family and the ministers who had hoped he would marry a chieftain's daughter. Dechen Choden, they surmised amongst themselves, brought no beneficial alliance to Dhompa. And how would they explain the shame of the child begat by the Chungho chief? It is said that my grandfather threatened to give up his responsibilities if his people did not accept my grandmother as his wife. He stayed with her for two years according to one narrator, Tenzin, who was my mother's playmate.

Love stories that took place in nomadic Tibet are impossible to authenticate. The time spent with Dechen Choden resulted in a son and my grandfather was entreated by his people to bring her home. He had established the continuance of the Dhompa lineage. He also brought Parchen with them. There are no accounts of my grandmother's first impression of my grandfather.

After my grandfather's death in 1950, it was Dechen Choden who presided over Dhompa. In this hinterland world where power was maintained by prowess in conspiracies, and the force and reputation of sons, my grandmother managed to keep her place secure. But she did not have very long, because the Chinese came soon after and the family and the people of Dhompa were plunged into a different course.

When the Chinese army entered Dhompa in 1959, the family was scattered: my mother was with her husband (she had married the previous year), my older aunt was in Zurmang with her four husbands (chiefs and regional leaders of the Tibetan resistance movement, they were killed while defending their land against the Chinese army), and my uncle was under house arrest. When the Chinese surrounded my grandfather's house, there was nobody to stop them from entering and destroying it. There are men, who were boys then, who remember shells being dropped on the property and around it. Some say the army came down the mountains like a herd of yaks and slaughtered the Tibetans in their path. The large repository of guns my grandfather was famous for—it is said he owned more guns and machine guns than the king of

Nangchen—were of no use in protecting the family because nobody was home to employ them.

My grandmother, alone with my youngest aunt, left for a nearby monastery to consult with the lamas. Together they plotted their escape route and set off late in the night, but they were apprehended by the Chinese army not too far from the monastery. The Chinese decided to take the prisoners to Zatou, where many other lamas and chieftains from Nangchen were being held. My grandmother was told she was going to have to walk over the high mountains. She, as well as the lamas with her, had heard of the hundred monks and lamas who had perished in Zatou; yet they walked. It is said by the elders of Dhompa that my grandmother, who was a proud and courageous woman, showed her indignation toward the Chinese by walking in the cold in her thin petticoat—more likely an inner layer of the chuba. It is said she refused victuals. That the soldiers made her take off her clothes in front of the lamas and her people to humiliate her. I do not know if all of these stories are true. But walk she did, over mountains, and for days.

The lamas of Dhompa and my grandmother might have suffered less if they had been killed in Dhompa. Instead, they were tied to each other like yaks at night, and they were led, two by two, on a long march without sustenance and warm clothing.

Chinese soldiers walked beside my grandmother prodding her with their guns and taunting her. When the group finally reached the precincts of the town of Zatou and they could see the gray walls of the houses across the river Zachu that becomes the Mekong, my grandmother kissed her young daughter, untied herself, and leapt into the river with a loud plea to her spiritual lama. Her last words were, "Karmapa, take heed of me!" *Karmapa khyen-no!*

A spray of bullets followed her and nobody ever saw her again. The hour of her death is lost in the jumble of events that preceded it and those that followed. My grandmother had seen to it that she would not be taken too far beyond the borders of her land.

Whenever she visits Zatou, Tashi stops at the bend of the road where my grandmother is said to have jumped into the river. She seems certain of the exact spot as though she had been there with my grandmother. The river is a long drop from the road. The water glistens below us on the day we pass through Zatou. Gray cement buildings form a tight puzzle. The hour of the past is without shape. We throw some blessed rice grains into the water and pray for my grandmother, wherever she is in her new life.

In writing about my grandmother's death I wonder why it feels necessary to think about how the light might have reflected on her face when she looked into the water, or to know her last words to those around her, or to see the tilt of her body as she met water. I wonder if there were trees near the river or whether the water was blue that day or yellow as it gets after the rains. Did she kill herself because she did not want to die at the hands of the Chinese? Was she afraid of the humiliations and punishments ahead of her?

These are questions I pose to myself but will never dare ask anyone else because I know they serve no purpose to anyone but me. The fact is, here was a woman who knew my mother before I did and who loved her first. In that, I am bound to her. In that I have a grandmother I cannot know and whose face I will never see.

CHAPTER SIX

How to Find a King

Once a week my female cousins follow a sprightly sixty-year-old who is a cousin's mother-in-law on her weekly circumambulation. Sonam, like most elders in my family, takes comfort in walking around sacred sites. Her favorite walk takes us around Kyegu's sacred hill, which is said to contain a billion prayers to Padmasambhava— or Guru Rinpoche—who was responsible for introducing Buddhism to Tibet in the eighth century. One circumambulation of the hill is believed to bring each person the benefit of a billion prayers. It is generally the elders who walk this trail with their troublesome limbs early in the morning before the sun gets too warm or in the late evening before the sun disappears.

Gout restricts Sonam's movements more and more each year. She has undulating flesh, abundant and light, and a singing voice that echoes the tenderness of a teenage girl's elbow. We amble slowly up the hill, stopping often to talk or to watch the streets of Kyegu shrink. At the top of the hill we meet stones with prayers carved into them and stacked on top of each other to create little stupas. Prayer flags stand tall around the cairns in a succession of blue, yellow, green, red, and white, their colors conforming to the elements of water, earth, wood, fire, and cloud.

Sonam does not lie on the grass as I do when she reaches the top of the hill. Standing tall, she flings her head back and sends her voice into the air.

How to Find a King

Her voice reverberates around us. She believes her prayers will take the birds and the animals into higher realms when they die. Her words will bless everyone whose ears are open even if they don't understand the words.

We see a few Tibetan partridges and a warbler.

A bird floats above us. It twists slowly in the air, its body not quite its own but borne of the wind in the crisp evening air. It is as though the bird has surrendered totally to the air to keep itself in place. A beauty with a yellow crest and blue-purple plumage.

A cousin asks about deities other than the ones we believe in.

I had considered myself a Christian when I was nine, I tell them. I had converted after hearing my teachers speak emphatically of the eternal fires of hell awaiting those of us who did not believe in Jesus. I had struggled through many nights debating on remaining a Buddhist and going to hell with my mother or on being unsinged but alone in heaven. For three years I went back and forth between hell and heaven. I prayed to Jesus and thought of heaven when I was in school and I reverted to being a Buddhist when I went home to my mother during holidays.

I would hide in corners of the house to read the Bible fearing that if my mother caught me at it she would berate me as the teachers did in school. Instead, my mother asked me to tell her stories from the Bible and when her friends visited, she'd ask me to tell them too. It was conceivable to her and to her friends that Jesus could walk on water and turn water into wine. She said Jesus was a compassionate man to die for everyone.

A cousin interrupts to ask if Jesus was the son of a king.

He was the son of a carpenter, I tell her.

The most beautiful of birds flying above us ought to be the king of birds but he is not, she says, starting to tell me a story.

The bird nation wanted to find a king amongst them. They wanted someone with a voice of gold and a voice of the sky. Someone they would want to listen to in the air and on the ground. The crested bird was a popular choice because he was beautiful and was already in possession of a crown but his voice had not been tested. Before the selection was made, the bird went to his favorite spots to decide on a voice. He listened to the rustle of barley stalks in fields, to the stride of yaks in meadows; he lay with his ear to the ground for underground springs and listened to overhead thunder. He waited for rain. He wanted to hear rain hit mud roofs, rain hit rivers, and rain hit stones. He heard the gurgle of water over rocks and found himself leaning into the sound; he liked how water never rested on its feet. He decided a gurgle was complete in itself. He listened again with care: to the rush of liquid drops crashing collectively, to water's impetuous and fickle movements. Yes, he reasoned, it was self-contained. He went to the community and allowed water out of his mouth. They were appalled. He could not be king! His was not an omnibus voice. The crested crown was a sign but a king had to have a voice that commanded. Thus it was the plainer of birds with a sweet voice who won the throne.

I look to the sky and sing for the handsome bird who could have been king.

CHAPTER SEVEN

Home on a Throne

All night she was riding a horse, my aunt Tashi informs me when I enter her room to wish her a good morning. It is a rare day when she declares her body to be free from small inconveniences.

She is tired from riding in her dream. The horse was as beautiful as the one she loved best when she was a teenager. She recalls the biting slap of wind on her face and the feeling of slicing through air. Old age has taken horse riding away from her, she says. Her joints, her body weight, and her unreliable eyesight push her toward a sedentary life. She was young once, she adds. Agile and strong. It is cumbersome to bear a body that has been through so much, she tells me. She is only sixty-seven.

"Your late mother and I spent whole days on horseback," she continues. They would take provisions of tsampa, tea, and butter from the cook and ride until they were tired. "Those were the happiest days of my life, but I was not aware then of my own happiness."

"The heart is a small organ. There is only so much we can bear," I tell her.

She says the heart is incapable of forgetting sadness. She turns to happier memories and to the days when she was admired for physical graces we do not see in her anymore.

She tells me of the trip she took to Lhasa with my mother and grandparents in 1957. Oh, how the world beyond Dhompa was rendered real to her! How she and my mother thrilled to walk through the rows of shops along the sacred Jokhang Temple! The stores boasted goods they could not recognize. She remembers vividly their visit to the Potala when they joined the queen and king of Nangchen to receive a blessing from the Dalai Lama. She and my mother imitated the foreign lilt and formality of Lhasa's language and met their own images in a photograph for the first time. She thinks the visit to Lhasa opened my mother's mind to life outside Dhompa and made her realize that my grandfather's name ceased to be recognized instantly once out of the environs of tightly knit Khampa chiefs and their people.

Tashi speaks of my mother with great love. My mother was the third of four children but she was the child who ruled everyone's lives being her father's favorite, and because her intransigence was accompanied by a sharpness of wit and intelligence. The retainers in my grandfather's house feared my mother, for she was full of antics and vengeance if they ignored her or failed to do as she wished. There are countless tales about her misdeeds as a young girl: she drew faces on the bald head of one of her caretakers and scolded him if he moved when she was drawing; she made a hole in a retainer's chamber pot; she stole rides on the horses of visiting guests; she insisted on a weekly bath in a big tub but avoided the jewelry her mother urged her to wear; she donned trousers under her chuba; and she studied Tibetan texts as meticulously as the monks. It was obvious she was not made for a sedate, cloistered life as a nomadic chieftain's wife, everyone said.

Tashi recalls the beautiful summer afternoons they frittered away, lying on their stomachs in the fields or gazing at an old lady's buttocks—an odd pastime, particularly for the daughters of chieftains. How entranced they were, she states. It was all my mother's idea, of course, to offer meat and butter to a vagabond in exchange for close and deliberate study of her bare bottom.

Tashi remembers how my mother would send her maids home

with food she stole from the pantry. Then there were the days when my mother ordered her younger sister and a cousin to steal food from the tall wooden cupboards in the pantry filled to the brim with tsampa, meat, butter, and dried cheese. She would command them to meet her in the fields and when the provisions were brought, she would lead them down a track overgrown with dandelions, forget-me-nots, and the miraculous blue flower, *namchak* ("sky shit"), and farther still to the narrow paths and hidden coves near the river's edge. The two younger girls would follow her until she stopped at a grassy knoll near the rivulet where rocks rested lazily and where my mother's friends waited.

It was only half a mile from the house but to the young girls these were adventure-filled expeditions. Mother would promulgate the rules and her young sisters would be appointed to attend to her friends, who—squealing and already knee-deep in water—cleared the center for her. She was beautiful and dandy. They would watch her dangle a cigarette from the corner of her lips and walk as the men did: heels bruising the ground, shoulders ready for combat or a horse race, a tilt of the head suggesting well-earned arrogance. As far as the girls were concerned, there was nobody like my mother in Dhompa.

She broke all the rules of decorum she was expected to follow as a chieftain's young daughter. She was willful, she was opinionated, and she knew canonical Buddhist texts better than was expected of her as a woman. She would bring either disgrace or honor to the lineage of the Dhompas, one elder prophesied early on.

Not many nomads traveled out of Dhompa. Lhasa, Dartsedo, and Kyegu were only names. One would only hear of distant lands:

traders bought and sold cotton and blended wool from India; silk, tea, and hard candy from China; and guns with names like Tazig, Burra, Rupin, Pame, Moda, Ghazam, and Lhi Bhuchung. Only the wealthier nomads could afford luxuries. And Lhasa, the holiest of all cities, was a pilgrimage everyone hoped to undertake once in their lifetime but very few nomads from Dhompa ever made the four- to six-month-long round trip on yaks and horses. Lhasa was too foreign, too far from the lives of these herders and its news and politics got old by the time it reached them, if it ever did. The stories narrated in Dhompa were those relating to the accomplishments of the lamas and the wiles of their chief and his forefathers.

The route out of Dhompa has not changed. As in the old days people leave the region by road through Zatou or Shornda, the capital of Nangchen. Today there is an unpaved road to both towns although most nomads opt to come through Shornda because that is where many nomads from Dhompa settle if they leave their herding lives.

The Kyegu–Shornda route has always been busy. Just three decades ago, people traveled on horseback for over a week, stopping to rest in villages now made obscure by the highway route completed in 2003. The highway has altered the experience of distance for everyone, but markedly so for businessmen and state officials who make the journey in one day, unthinkable just a few years ago. There is a range of transportation options for the present-day traveler: public buses, private jeeps, taxis, and minibuses.

Competition has not yet tempered the impertinent attitude with which many Tibetan businessmen run their businesses. Some days no private cars are available, no reasons or warnings are given, and so travelers are forced to return home and postpone their journey by a day. Other days vehicle drivers wrangle over passengers as numerous cars are ready to take off at the same time, resulting in a hullabaloo. There is a system, I am told, but I am never certain who is in charge. Besides, there is, not unexpectedly, someone in the crowd who knows someone known to us and my travel decisions are settled on that basis.

Tashi and I plan on making our visit to Dhompa to enjoy the bounties of summer. I am neither brave nor foolish enough to visit it past the month of September when wind and bitter cold paralyze the land. As we head out of the town of Kyegu I inspect the jeeps, trucks, minibuses, and numerous motorbikes on the road with us. Men on motorbikes weave in and out of the traffic. I watch a passenger on a bike ahead of us balance a plastic bucket on his lap. The bucket contains a school of wriggling anchovies.

Will the fish survive the bumpy journey?

He purchased them from a Chinese in Kyegu and is going to set them free in a small pond outside town, he tells me.

Will they be safe in the foreign pond, I ask when we meet up again at an intersection.

He had not thought of that. Now he frets that he bought the fish to free them only to lead them to their death.

I am full of remorse for throwing questions that have only served to bring his judgment into question. I tell him the fish will be okay wherever they are set free. He nods abjectly.

The journey to Nangchen takes us through the rich valley of Parthang, the white rocky mountains of Rashu where ruthless bandits were known to hide (drivers from Yushu and Nangchen drive hastily through the town for fear of being bullied by the long-haired and easily incensed Rashu men), the curvaceous loop of river and hills that lead into Zurmang, and finally the dramatic gorges that signal our advancement into Shornda.

Shornda, more commonly called Nangchen (which is the

name for the whole region of which Shornda is the capital), is a
town like most others in rural Tibet, where a street of single shops
serves as the town's main center. The street ends at the foot of
craggy, stony mountains whose hoary heads are bunched together
like a congregation of ancient seers. The earth blushes red here.
The people, representing various nomadic villages of Nangchen,
wander in black suits, white shirts, and wide-brimmed hats. They
look like they've crawled out of a sandpit. Their hair is coarse and
their skin tinted with sand grains. The place is choked with motorbikes, and in my first hour in town I gesture to a few, who drive
with their eyes trained not on the street but toward pedestrians,
to attend to the road. They laugh without removing their gaze
from my face and without questioning my impudence in berating
their inattention. Red dust coats everything. It is impossible to
keep clothes from turning brown.

My host, a cousin's husband, tells me he can trace almost everyone's lineage in Nangchen because it is so tiny. He tells me, "If
you go to Lhasa and get into trouble, Nangchenwas will come to
your aid. If you go to Xining and get into trouble, forty, fifty people from Nangchen will come to help you." By aid, he means that
groups of men will come help fight off the other party.

Nangchen people are the most devilish of all tribes in the
Yushu prefecture, I am told by proud Shornda citizens. My host
tells me our people are watched closely and dreaded by Chinese
authorities. I gather it is a compliment to be looked on unfavora-
bly by the Chinese. The people of Nangchen are not the kind to
sit quietly and turn into Chinese like the people of Kyegu, my
host continues.

He sits silently enough in his house minding his own business.
He points to huge posters of the Dalai Lama on the walls of his
shrine room and plays a VCD of songs composed and sung by
local men. Phunda is his favorite. He plays a song in which the

singer recalls a dream from the previous night when he saw the face of Tenzin Gyatso, the Dalai Lama.

"*What happiness, what joy,*" the singer sings. My host expresses his anxiety for the singer. Surely he will not escape the scrutiny of the authorities for long. How can he when he sings of seeing the beloved faces of the Dalai Lama and of the Karmapa, both considered "splittists" and frowned upon by the Chinese? Phunda is not the only one to sing of forbidden dreams and lamas. There are many singers all over Kham and Amdo who put their lives in danger singing of their hope for Tibetan lamas in exile returning to their land.

The people of Nangchen are discontent, my host apprises me. Last year, a day or two before 10 March, commemorated as the Tibetan Uprising Day when the people of Lhasa staged a massive uprising in 1959, someone—the authorities never did catch the person—managed to replace the Chinese flag with a Tibetan flag at the entrance to the main government office in Shornda. It took two whole days before the flag was noticed because nobody looked up at the sky, my host says. It is believed the flag was noticed only after the news was leaked on the Internet.

"Imagine," he says, "people in other countries knew about the flag before we did."

He thinks the local officials are good Tibetans who subdue small skirmishes quickly before news reaches higher-ranking government officials in Kyegu and Xining. Last year a handful of monks marched along the town's main street with a Tibetan flag and shouted for freedom. They were quickly disbanded.

I am surprised to hear of these incidents. I tell him that people in exile tell me the people of Nangchen are not known to make any protests.

The people of Nangchen are not like the people of Kyegu, my host repeats.

I ask him what he means by that.

People in Nangchen do not boast like the Kyegu people do, he says smugly.

I tell him people in Kyegu speak well of people of Nangchen. He is unmoved.

I had always thought people from Nangchen were gentle and inhibited.

Not so, I am told by my host.

I tell him the people of Nangchen I know in Nepal are the least colorful of all khampas.

He says something must have happened to us in exile. Nangchen people are troublemakers in Tibet, he tells me with pride. He predicts there will be small protests and uprisings against the Chinese in the future.

All along the main street, men like him stand in groups. My heart lifts to hear various renderings of the Nangchen dialect. I am happy to see silhouettes of men and women in black chuba and big hats. I am even happy when a shopkeeper picks me, from the multitude, to ask where I am from. "You do not look like you are from here," he states dryly.

"I am from Nangchen," I tell him.

Where?

Dhompa.

He allows a smile. He is from Nangchen; he carries the names of the twenty-five clans in him.

CHAPTER EIGHT

Phayul

Tall rocks press into us like a healing suture. We move slowly; it is easy to drive headlong into oncoming cars on this narrow road.

Tashi says on a perfect day it takes six hours to travel the 125 kilometers to Dhompa from Shornda. On not-so-perfect days the road falls apart at the slightest provocation and the journey can take two days. Rain, snow, or hailstorms can turn the road muddy and cause the wheels of vehicles to spin pointlessly without moving forward. On this bullish terrain, our driver says he keeps one eye on the road and the other on deities.

The faces of tall rocks are painted with images of deities or with the ubiquitous prayer OM MANI PADME HUNG or OM BENZA GURU PADME HUNG. Like sacred scroll paintings and frescoes on the walls of monasteries, these images bear no name or biography of the artist. The art is an offering to the deities and to all beings who see them. They are a reminder to travelers of our impermanence.

We are jostled and shaken like puppets on some portions of the road. Impossible green blurs my vision. I catch sight of brilliantly colored birds who remind me of pictures I have seen of partridges and wagtails. I notice nomads camped on distant hills. Their animals are small black dots on the landscape.

We drive for miles and miles without meeting any other vehicle and I am swallowed by inertia. Once we cross into the territory of Dhompa, Tashi calls out the names of the mountains and gestures with her chin or finger to where monasteries hide, invisible from where we are. She points in the direction where people she knows have their summer camps. We halt twice to greet nomads who stand in the middle of the road to stop us. They exhort us to walk to their summer camp for tea. They are distant relatives, I am informed. Their tents are as black as the hair on their yaks.

Tashi has not seen a cartographical map of Nangchen but she carries a map in her mind anchored in stories of ancestors, deities, and lamas. She employs phrases like "this side of the mountain" and "that side of the river" to indicate boundaries and borders between clans and villages. Much of these traditional territorial distributions still exist or are incorporated into the new maps drawn by the Chinese.

Figures appear as in a mirage as we travel deeper into regions known as nomadic. I note men on horses, little girls in bright headscarves minding yaks, and small mud huts that boast orderly patches of turnips in the front yard. Also, much to my alarm, motorbikes pass by us galumphing and blabbering under the direction of monks and young men. Some riders have radios or tape players screwed onto the front of their bikes and the music (devotional songs are popular with monks and Tibetan or Chinese pop are popular with everyone else) competes with the grunts from the machine to create a discordant medley. Photos of lamas hang from the handlebars. Rugs of the type used for centuries on the back of horses cushion their bottoms.

When did monks start to ride motorbikes?

Tashi tells me many nomads own motorbikes. Thanks to them, she can get to places. She cannot walk, she cannot lift herself on a horse anymore, but she is able to hop on a motorbike if the driver can balance her weight behind him. She peers out of the window and I feel an anxious and pleasurable anticipation arise in me. Will I recognize the shape of the hills, the sinuous curve of the river, the flowers? Three years is a brief time here, indeed a very brief time if we consider the history of this land. To my untrained eyes, not much has changed in Dhompa since my first visit in 1994. The dirt road we drive on meanders between a few houses; it passes by the one big store in downtown Dhompa, the only school, and the entrance gate to the monastery called Bagsigon, and comes to a halt in front of a small bridge that has already collapsed in its center. Water sprays the front windows of the jeep as we push through the low river.

The years have brought no new buildings, I say to Tashi.

She informs me about new classrooms that have been built for the school by a nonprofit organization in San Francisco. A shrine and classrooms have been added to the monastery with the help of a lama in India and another lama in Switzerland. The Chinese government has built homes for nomads. The road we are on, she tells me, has been lengthened so that it extends westward all the way to the village of Karjung. Most villages in Dhompa, however, remain far from the road so people continue to use the dirt paths created by horses, humans, and, now increasingly, motorbikes.

The jeep comes to a sudden halt. We have arrived bruised and tired at the bottom of the hill where my mother's family once lived. The jeep can push no further. Tingsikha waits for us at the top of the hill.

Tingsikha is my mother's favorite place on earth. When asked about Tibet, my mother would begin with this location: this was all the Tibet she knew as a child. Tingsikha—which means "sitting on a throne"—gets its name from the plateau's resemblance to a throne. The hill rises out of the valley as though to serve as a butter lamp or a lama's seat. Tingsikha boasts a spectacular view of fields, mountains, and a river named Kyichu—"happy water"—that flows sluggishly hugging gravelly banks. All around us, red hills sprout stumps of juniper and spruce.

In the old days, a permanent tent to the far left of the main house served as a waiting room for visitors who came to see my grandfather to lodge complaints, seek advice, or settle disputes and grievances. It is not certain if my grandfather followed a specific legal system but it is certain that he was aware of and perhaps was influenced by the laws—the Twenty-One Laws as Clear as Crystal—written in the seventeenth century. These documents provided some guidance for general offenses. For example, the five grave offenses were matricide, murder of a holy man, patricide, creating discord between lamas, and causing hurt to good men. For these offenses any of the following were appropriate as punishment: to gouge out the offender's eyes, to cut his throat, to cut off his hands, to toss him from a high cliff, to throw him into deep water.

The elders of Dhompa do not recall such punishments being meted out to general offenders but they do remember hearing about thieves whose kneecaps were removed and adulterers who had a portion of their nose severed from their face. In the old days, a majority of crimes were over land and cattle. Most offenses were rectified by paying to the victim either money or a stipulated number of yaks or horses. Some offenders sought the protection of neighboring chiefs and cleverly avoided punishment. There were no prisons in Dhompa; what would be the purpose of having a permanent structure in a culture where people were peripatetic?

While there is no written document in Dhompa of a legal structure, the elders say the chief and the ministers adhered to a practice of justice that minded local customs, superstitious beliefs, and regional divinities. For example, while it was permissible in most clans to kill wolves, a nuisance and threat to herds, it was a serious transgression in Dhompa because Ghoye, the protector deity of Dhompa, was believed to wander the land in the form of a wolf. And while it was not a crime to kill deer in Dhompa, nomads of Zatou were punished if they maimed or killed one. And if you were caught killing a deer in Rashu, you were certain to lose a thumb. A benign law ruled Dhompa, the elders tell me. My grandfather was a just and kind man, they say. How could he not be? He took care of thirteen monasteries, they state.

The family house is a timid version of its former state. How big it once was I cannot say for certain. My mother would speak of it as though it contained one hundred rooms and Tashi suggests it was three, four, or five times bigger than it is now. I think it was a simple structure of mud and wood, as it is now, with no more than thirty rooms. Tashi tells me the most resplendent room of the house was the large shrine filled with beautiful antiquities and paintings of Buddhist deities and protectors. The jewels, the statues, the resplendent *thangkas*, and the largest private collection of guns in all of Nangchen—all are gone. I hear a few of our own people from Dhompa came into the house and took what they could. I also hear Chinese soldiers took away what they found of value before they bombed the house and reduced everything to dust.

The only remnants of the original house are two pillars in the kitchen, a doorframe, and a large stone now used to pound Tibetan medicine. Its surface is velvet-water. When my mother was a child the mortar served to grind gold to gild the faces of the statues in the shrine.

Tashi has rebuilt on the grounds of the house a beautiful shrine, a kitchen, and two spartan bedrooms. Pillars of wood hold the roof upright and very little light enters through the tiny windows covered with plastic sheets. On days when the wind is strong the plastic flaps to a ruckus. On rainy days drops of water seep through the mud-packed roof to fall on our heads. A tent might offer better protection but for Tashi this is a house of many splendid memories. It is home to me even though I did not grow up in it.

The kitchen—*jhakhang*, which translates as "teahouse"— exists on its former premises and as in the old days, it is allowed no windows. The darker and dirtier the kitchen, the more auspicious it was believed to be for the family. For many decades, the cooks at Tingsikha took great pride in the dingy light-shunning kitchen with its oil-dank cobwebs and sooty beams. In the days when my grandfather was chieftain, the stove glowed all day, feeding visitors with tea and victuals. My mother was not encouraged to go into the kitchen but she would sneak into the dark room and beg the cook to make eggs for her. He would fuss a great deal about how an egg represented life and how his karma was being tarnished by her desires but he would always concede to my mother's wishes. Tashi is evasive when I ask her how eggs reached Dhompa in the first place. (I have never seen a hen there.) Mother would ask the cook to roast meat for her even though roasting was forbidden, for it was believed the smell of it made deities imagine it was their skin that was being scorched. To this day meat is not roasted in Tingsikha. The cooks were also careful not to spill water or food into the burning stove for fear of raising smoke and offensive smells that would upset the deities and cause them to be indisposed. They believed the deities would bring sickness, sorrow, and misfortune to the family if angered or irritated. Such were the beliefs held and followed in the kitchen.

The winter house of the Dhompa family used to be a few feet away from the Bagsigon monastery in Bagsikha, and a fifteen-minute ride on horse from Tingsikha. I am shown a patch of wild foliage where once stood a house of mud and wood. In springtime, the family moved to Shorka, a few miles south of Bagsikha. The herd was left in the hands of caretakers who roamed the mountains.

The people of Dhompa are *drokpas,* a common reference to nomads or high-pasture herders. They are estimated to number two and a half million in Tibet. The animals they own—female yaks (*dris*), male yaks, goats, and sheep—and the traditional systems they follow as subsistence herders is the same for the most part throughout Tibet despite variations in altitude and the luxuriousness of grasslands. Prior to 1959, there were 450 families, or 1,700 people, in Dhompa. Rich households are believed to have had one hundred to three hundred yaks, of which eighty or more were young lactating females, and as many as five hundred to a thousand sheep and goats, while poor families had as few as two to four yaks and a dozen sheep.

Rich nomads could afford to barter their animals for goods. Forty *dris* or five *drels* (the *drel* is an offspring of a donkey and horse, a mule, used to carry goods) would fetch a gun such as the Burra from Russia, which was favored in Dhompa, or the also popular Pame or the Ghazam. A cheaper gun, the Ghibe, could be traded for twenty-five yaks or two *drels*. Precious jewels, brocade, and religious statues were acquired in similar exchanges. As nomadic herders, people moved along with their herds for most of the year and left their possessions in the mud houses on their winter plot. Those without a winter base stored their belongings and their meat in the regional monasteries and took shelter in tents made of yak wool during the cold months.

The poorest nomads did not own cattle. Those who tended to the herd belonging to the chief or the lamas received meat, milk, and butter for their consumption in lieu of a salary and each year they would get a lamb or a yak as reward. The poor—those without land and herd—were exempt from paying taxes, while everyone else offered meat, butter, and yak tail or yak hide to the chief according to the size of their herd. Nomads were also asked to make offerings of "butter to fill two or three yak hearts and eight full scoops of dry cheese" to the king of Nangchen. This offer was merely a gesture but gifts of gold-plated statues, painted scrolls, brocades, and other valuable gifts were probably offered to the king exceeding the value of the symbolic tax.

Nomads lived on land that remained in the family for generations or was leased from the chieftain or the monasteries. They took care to observe a fixed grazing route and learned to exploit the very brief grazing season, typically mid-May to mid-September or early October. They planted turnips and other plants on their winter land so they had some sustenance for both humans and animals during the long infertile winter months. Herders were mindful not to encroach on each other's grazing lands and in particular not to enter the winter encampments where each family stored food supplies. If a horse or an animal wandered into a neighbor's herding land, the offender paid a small token as an offering of contrition.

In the past it was common for three to six families of herders, often related to each other, to share their summer grazing land. This was a precaution against bandits who preyed on single herding families. Herding life presented many dangers and uncertainties; herders had to keep guard against bandits all summer long and then hope that a severe snowstorm or disease did not kill their animals during winter. In order to minimize risks and find alternate ways to support themselves, those herders who could, bartered their products for goods and grain. I suspect the practice of polyandry, where a woman married all brothers in a family, ensured that there was always one brother with the herd and one brother trading. Polyandry helped to keep the herd, the land, and the family together.

Tibetan herders are perhaps as close as you can get to pure pastoralism although they supplemented their food with grain and tea they purchased or bartered with butter and wool. Nowadays nomads have a few cups of instant ramen tucked under their clothes in their tents. Everything else they eat comes from their cattle—butter, milk, yogurt, dried cheese, and dried meat. Their tents are made from yak wool, their clothes are of sheep wool or lambskin, and the bags used to store their tsampa are either made from yak hide or woven from yak wool or sheep wool. Nomads are also able to make a little money selling yak tail and the wool from their herds; these communities, however, were never ranchers and they are still not raising their livestock to be sold in quantity to meat markets. Nomads are attached to their herd and their prosperity is measured by its size. Even though they know herding is a risky business and they lose a few animals to the cold each winter, they are loath to exchange their animals for cash.

Instead of selling or killing their animals in the middle of summer when the demand is often higher, nomads wait until late autumn when the pastures lose their color and their potency and when their herd is at its healthiest. Tashi tells me nomads want the animals to enjoy the summer after the long incarceration of winter. She says they feel the happiness of their animal and they can taste in its milk the warmth of the sun and the sweetness of the flowers.

The hills around Tingsikha are full of wildflowers, purple, yellow, and white. Part of the hillside looks like it is covered in snow. I take morning walks bearing a heart already in love with the land. I smell juniper even though juniper is growing on the other side of the hill. The flowers are abundant and when the wind blows the hills look like dancing magicians in resplendent robes. I stare at the waves of undulating flowers for a long while and enter a moment of clarity when nothing else exists. It is a moment separate from thoughts, cravings, and regrets. I feel awash with bliss and contentment. Then, that too passes.

We are fools to leave such beauty and build cities of glass and stone. I think this but know I will return to such cities. For now though, here, I am a few decades behind my life in San Francisco.

There are six of us in my mother's ancestral home: Tashi, Tenzin, Dorje, Kunga, and Gutso. Tenzin's father was a minister in Dhompa under my grandfather and as a child he visited Tingsikha frequently. He has been a monk for twenty years and is much sought after for his fine craftsmanship in building wood cabins; every year he spends five months in Tinsgsikha. As for Dorje, he was the region's first and once-most-prosperous businessman in addition to being its most notorious drunk; he lost all his money in reckless business ventures and, I suspect, generous drinking parties, and now leads an itinerant life. When he heard I was going to visit Dhompa, he insisted on accompanying my aunt and me to serve as our attendant and chef. Happily, he happens to be the one person in nomad land who can cook both Tibetan and Chinese cuisines.

Kunga is the seventeen-year-old son of a cousin who had decided on a whim to accompany his grandmother Tashi and me to Tingsikha. He had decided it would be fun to spend his summer with us. We were but a day into the journey when he betrayed signs of misgiving. Gutso and his wife, who I rarely see, are paid a paltry sum to live in Tingsikha to maintain and turn the large prayer wheels in the shrine room. We are an odd but compatible group. Aside from Tenzin, who works all day, the rest of us have no duties. Nobody asks me what I intend to do here; they understand that I should be here in my mother's land.

We have two visitors upon us before I have had time to walk the grounds. The ladies come prepared to spend a whole afternoon or perhaps a day or two with us. After a few days Tashi and

I adopt an easy routine around the guests who drop in. Some days we have as many as fifteen. Tashi thrives in the company of the people who can return to the days when she came as a bride and for whom the present is a stage for the past. I find ways to be alone by wandering in the mountains for two hours every morning. In the afternoons, I read beside the guests, listen to their stories, or nap as they talk.

Day after day Dorje asks to walk with me. Who will carry your water bottle and your camera, he asks sincerely. Who will show you the land? What if you fall?

Day after day I tell him I am all right on my own, that I am used to being alone. Then one day, moved by his relentless concern, I give in and from then on he is my walking companion.

While in Kyegu, Tashi had heard a rumor that her old friend Yungyang had died and she had even sent money to a local monastery to conduct prayers for her. Imagine our happiness when we hear Yungyang is alive. We know the news of our presence will reach her and that she will visit us. Three days into our arrival, she comes clinging to her grandson's waist as he manuvers his motorbike up the hill. We fuss about her as if she has been resurrected from the dead. She comes with her prayer wheel and her eating bowl and states she is ready to stay with us for as long as two weeks. She tells me later she is happy to give her grandson and his wife a break from tending to her. She does not like to be a burden on them but she has no other home or family. Her only son lives far away and does not or cannot visit her.

Yungyang was my mother's maid and playmate. She remembers my mother's uncommon love for bathing and for wearing trousers. She says there was no one like my mother—not then, not since. In those days Yungyang, like other women, was not allowed on the premises of the Dhompa household. When she wanted to join my mother and Tashi at play, she would yell to them from the hill across from the house and they'd meet in the fields below. After my mother got married and left home, Yungyang began milking the female yaks and goats in Tingsikha.

Yungyang's face is obscured by soot; it is a challenge for me to see if she has aged in the three years since I last saw her. Her eyes still have their mischievous glint. The deep lines around them and on her forehead are drawn in black. She resembles the charcoal pillars in the kitchen. It is the twenty-first century and Yungyang is encountering a banana for the second time in her life. She has not had a banana since my last visit. Three years ago, she had asked me how she was to eat it. Now she peels back the skin and bites into the soft white pulp of the fruit. Did the Chinese make this, she asks.

Her grandson, a thin man with a face marked by the hardships of his young life, asks if he should wash a banana for me. Yungyang bursts into a girlish giggle and says he is just like her, an old nomadic fool. She takes the fruit and holds it as though she is wielding a knife and prepares to peel it for him. He marvels at its plush and squishy texture. Yungyang opens her mouth to reveal her bare upper gum and says it is the kind of food she should eat.

Yungyang wears a deep brown shirt. It is a handsome color on her and majestically coated with dirt so old it has become a layer to the fabric. Butter, meat, and years of grease lend her dress an excellent versatility: it looks both untenable and durable. The fabric glistens. Yungyang's face is a shimmering black and when I ask her if she will wash her face for me, she thinks I am teasing her. Upon realizing I am serious, she says she has no reason to wash her face. Besides, she adds, she has no features to speak of. Her eyelids are light; they betray her true color. Were she to wash her face, I think she would not recognize herself.

She has not bathed for a long, long time; nor has she washed her face or brushed her short hair. She cannot say for how long but guesses it could be many decades. She pauses and says perhaps she has never washed—ever! She fears she will fall sick if she were to bathe. She wonders what I am sloughing away seeing as I clean my face and brush my teeth each morning and evening.

She asks, "What is there to wash away? There is no dirt on your face." Tenzin waits with her for my answer. They watch me indulgently as I wash. They even remind me on hot days to go to the river to take my weekly bath, although they think it is a ridiculous and unnecessary habit.

On my previous visit when Yungyang came to stay with us in Dhompa she had told me she was in her early sixties. This year she says she is in her mid-seventies. Tenzin and Tashi tell me she is probably sixty-eight or sixty-nine according to the Tibetan calendar. She is upset to discover she is younger than she thought she was. She cannot go back to being sixty-nine.

She wears rows and rows of blessed sacred threads around her neck. She is certain they keep her safe. Like many older Tibetans she wears the shells from her prayer wheel around her neck, serving as an ornament, but also as a mark of achievement in having said a million prayers. She studies the locket around my neck that contains the hair and nails of lamas: precious relics my mother put together when she was alive so I would be safe. In San Francisco, I keep it in my handbag and sometimes under my pillow. A man I once loved had asked me why I believed the odds and ends on my neck would protect me. I had no answer that would make sense to him. I know it is ludicrous to trust bits of hair and nail to keep me from harm's way, yet I have never lived without my sacred protection kit near me.

I ask Yungyang if she feels discomfort in carrying so many sacred talismans around her neck and she laughs disbelievingly at me. She says she does not remove them from her body. She tells me she has not removed her chuba for a long time either.

She sleeps in it and wakes up in it. I ask her if she has ever washed her chuba and she says she has not and that she will wear it until it falls off her body. I am quite sure she does not have a spare chuba. My question propels her into a story she has told me before.

Tsering, a young nomad, was sent to school and she was so intelligent she got a scholarship to attend a medical college in a large Chinese city. Tsering's studies kept her busy and away from her family and it was a few years before she was able to visit them (they were too poor and far away to contemplate a visit to the city). Finally, the happy day came when she was able to travel home. Tsering watched the familiar mountains; she saw yaks grazing in the distance, and realized she had been away too long. She saw tears glittering in her mother's eyes from a distance and noticed how anxiously she rubbed the sides of her dress. Tsering ran toward her mother with a heart filled with happiness and love.

For the first three days Tsering would not leave her mother's side. She woke up early to help her milk the female yaks, she helped her make butter during the day, and she tended to her three younger brothers and two sisters. She helped her father round up the herd in the evening. Tsering was happy; she was home. By and by, Tsering found herself thinking of the city. She lingered in bed on mornings the sun went into hiding; she found the sheepskin bed too hard, the tent smoky, the stream where she washed her face too cold, and her siblings dirty and noisy. She noticed how unkempt her mother was. The sharp odor of butter and meat on her mother's dress and her wild uncombed hair began to bother her. She was revolted by the dirt between her mother's nails.

"I think you should wash your chuba," Tsering said to her mother one afternoon.

Her mother was taken aback. She had never washed her chuba. "I am as clean as I know to be," her mother replied.

"I think we should wash your sheepskin chuba," Tsering repeated.

Tsering and her mother went to the river and they washed the dress. They left it out to dry in the sun. Tsering had brought some trousers for her mother. Her mother refused to wear "Chinese clothes" and was content to wear a petticoat. She was going to wait for the chuba to dry. A few days later it was dry but had shrunk to half its size. This was her mother's only sheepskin dress and now the dress was too small for her.

Yungyang laughs hysterically as she reaches the end of the story, as though she is reminded of something entirely unrelated to what she has just narrated. This story is passed down from nomadic parents to their children. It is a way to teach the young that old traditions are to be respected and if young nomads wander into the city they must continue to remember their heritage.

"Mothers are not to be ashamed of. Dirt is not dirty," she states firmly.

I tell Yungyang that the girl in the story, this Tsering, could not be from Dhompa. I tell her about a man in Chumaleb who had told me the same story a month ago. He said the girl in the story was Chumaleb's first female doctor. He had met her once. She still lived in Xining. He said that for most of her life she was ridiculed and referred to as Amapaktsa: "mother's sheepskin dress." Tibetan nomads did not believe they could wash their sheepskin and so people had laughed at her when they found out she had suggested her mother wash hers. But now in the cities Tibetans get their sheepskin jackets dry-cleaned. Amapaktsa had been right all along. To the man in Chumaleb the nomads are the ignorant ones.

Perhaps this story originated in Chumaleb and then traveled to Kyegu and from there onward to Dhompa, I suggest.

Yungyang shrugs her shoulders and says she has known this

story for a while. She cannot remember when exactly she heard it or from whom.

Maybe there's an Amapaktsa in every nomadic village, I offer.

Yungyang says she has never washed her clothes nor had her mother ever washed hers. She will wear the same dress for years until it falls apart. That's how it will always be for her.

I tell her it will be many years before a dry-cleaner comes to Dhompa.

Mothers are not to be ashamed of, she says. That is her story.

I wonder if she feels betrayed by her only child who has not visited her since he left for a town in Sichuan. She does not speak very much of him. She says he must be poor where he is, and unable to visit her, his poor mother. She does not return to memories of him as a child, whether good or bad. She does not speak of her dead husband either.

Tashi tells me there are daughters and sons all over town who went to school in Chinese cities and are ashamed of their parents. The children are embarrassed because their parents are poor nomads and do not know how to read or write. Tashi complains that educated children think they know everything. "But for all their knowledge they don't know how to say their prayers, milk the animals, make butter or cheese," she states.

How could people be expected to read when there were no schools in nomadic Tibet, she asks. "Only monks, nuns, and children from wealthy families were able to get an education."

Tashi cannot read or write Tibetan. Her father, a chieftain and a lama, had not found it necessary to educate her. He had chosen to put his riches and reputation to use in finding her a good husband instead. When she came to Dhompa as my uncle's bride at twelve, she was not forced to study with my mother because my grandmother felt sorry for her. In 1959, Tashi had over five hundred yaks and as many as one thousand sheep. Today, she owns sixty healthy yaks and over a hundred sheep and goats. These she leaves in the care of a young couple who are paid a small stipend each year and who are allowed to kill one yak and one goat for their use. Each summer, she threads the ears of young goats and baby female yaks with bright-colored wool. From then on these animals are known as *tsethar*, "freed for life." They will never be killed or sold. She has now decided to set all her animals free. She is proud and happy with her decision. She believes that saving the lives of her herd will help her and her children to live better and longer. This practice of ensuring animals will not be slaughtered for consumption or trade is becoming increasingly popular among herders in the villages, among monasteries who buy animals and allow them to roam on monastery grounds, and even among townspeople, who offer money to herders living close to town to set their animals free. More and more people are attempting the impossible: to give up meat, the staple of a Tibetan diet. Those who cannot swear off meat completely abstain from eating it on the six or ten days of the month that have religious significance.

Tashi attributes these practices to persuasive Buddhist teachings from monks who graduate from the philosophical schools of Yachen and Serta. She says good monks are making people rethink the everyday nuances of being a Buddhist. The Chinese, she tells me, view these trends as impractical, as examples of the inability of the Tibetan nomads to exploit their strengths and become the successful, self-sufficient pastoralists that China had hoped for when it disbanded communal herding. These old thoughts, she tells me, are what the Chinese believe will lead to the eventual degradation of the grasslands. Overstocking of herd is one stated concern.

There are Tibetans in town who believe the herding life of the nomads is a setback to the rest of the nation careening toward progress and development. They think the old ways keep the nomads backward, illiterate, and poor. I, too, wrongly harbored a notion that herders led a less-demanding life, that they were less ecologically knowledgeable compared to, say, farmers in the lowlands. But the very fact that nomads have survived for as long as two thousand years and even prospered at times on a harsh and unpredictable land indicates a tremendous sophistication in their traditional knowledge and management of land and herd.

It is not possible, Tenzin tells me, for nomads to herd on the land as they did in the past, due to the changing land and herd policies introduced by the Chinese, but at least people have animals and they are on their own land. For now, he says, people are doing okay.

The Chinese purported to liberate Tibetans from imperialists and old feudal systems, and one of their main strategems to achieve this liberation was to annihilate the old thoughts and ways of the people. The first reform that took place in parts of Kham and Amdo in the mid-1950s—the confiscation of all individual livestock and the formation of collective herding communes—was not enforced in Dhompa until after the fall of 1959.

All efforts to maintain pastoral productivity through collective herding was a failure in Dhompa; the grass was quickly depleted and large numbers of animals died, resulting in the death of many people as well. Still, the Chinese insisted on collective herding all through the Cultural Revolution, even after a majority of the men had been sent to labor camps or prison. During this period several other schemes were enforced to sever traditional kinship and identities: people were forbidden to practice Buddhist rituals, nomads were dislocated from their villages to other areas, women and young children were separated from their men. Men above the age of nineteen, which included Tenzin and Dorje's fathers, uncles, and cousins, were taken away from their families, many never to be seen again.

In the 1980s the policy changed from collectivism to a system of personal responsibility, where families were permitted to own their own herd. The government even distributed cattle to nomads according to the number of family members, so that large families automatically had more animals. One by one, commune systems were dismantled and although the land now belonged to the government, herders could purchase rights to the land for periods of fifty years or so. This enabled many nomads to return to their ancestral homes and to start anew. There are five hundred families of five thousand nomads living in Dhompa today and many of them live on their ancestral land. The nomads have reverted as much as they can to traditional herding practices and they maintain a winter-spring home base and spend summer months from mid-May until mid-October moving across the grasslands with their animals.

The duties are not equitably distributed in most nomadic families—it is the women who wake up at four in the morning to milk the animals and they milk them again in the late afternoon. It is women who are up late at night rounding up the herd or out in the mountains searching for those animals that have not returned. It is women who provide the food and care for the children of the household. The men of the family tend to the more seasonal and business aspects of herding life. In this world children are valuable workers and it is not unusual to see children as young as five out with the animals. It is a hard life, yet herders say they cannot live without their animals, each of whom they know by face and demeanor. They certainly cannot live in the towns where the air is thick with poison and the land rendered so ugly.

It moves me inexplicably to be surrounded by my mother's

people and to hear the Nangchen language everywhere I go. I have lived my life carrying her tongue and was raised within her memories. Here, on the land where she was born to a chieftain and married to another nomadic chief, where she contracted smallpox, and where she earned several inconsequential heartaches, I piece together the pictures she drew for me.

A distortion of long-held images of flowers and animals find their place in English: yak, horse, marmot, buckwheat, cinquefoil, paintbrush, monkshood. The blue flower with elegant lines is delphinium and the smelly white flower with its nodding head is bistort. The protector of the land, Ghoye, is a wolf in spirit and a mountain in its physical form.

I have lived my life defined as a refugee in Nepal and India, a resident alien and immigrant in the United States. At last, I am a Tibetan in Tibet, a Khampa in Kham—albeit as a tourist in my occupied and tethered country.

CHAPTER NINE

Insider

We have brought a tray of plums, apples, and peaches with us. Tenzin wants to know if the peach is a fruit or a vegetable. He is quite certain it is a form of turnip. Should he boil it, he asks me. Yungyang pulls out a knife to skin her fruit; she says she knows how to eat it. She has decided to eat it and not save it for her grandson. Everything else I share with her goes into a plastic bag she keeps in the corner of the kitchen: six sticks of chewing gum, squares of chocolate stuck to the wrapper, and hard candy. She places a peach on a strip of sheepskin while she wipes her hand on her dress. Her fruit is covered with dust and hair.

The Chinese are so clever to make such tasty fruit, she says to me. She sinks her three good teeth into the fruit. Her pupils dilate as her tongue registers the sensation of peach.

Yungyang cannot hear well and even when she does, she is never sure she has understood my Tibetan, or what she deems as the Lhasa language or the Tibetan language. I speak the Nangchen language but one that borrows some terminologies from the central Tibetan tongue. For Yungyang, central Tibet and Lhasa are different countries altogether and define a politics and language not privy to her. She has never stepped out of Dhompa. She has not met anyone from Lhasa and in her imagination the sacred city is as far away as Canada or Australia. She will never be so fortunate as to see the Potala before she dies, she says. She will never understand the language of the Tibetan people, she laments.

I ask her if she remembers the number of yaks and sheep my grandfather had. She says he had "so many" animals. She cannot be persuaded into giving a number but for my sake, she makes an attempt. She tilts her head to one side like a retiring tulip, the right side of her lips pursed tightly. She takes two minutes, even using her fingers at one point as though in preparation to count.

"So many," she says resolutely. She probably knew each animal and had names for them.

I ask her if she has memories of my mother as a young girl.

She says my mother had beautiful hair and was a very good horsewoman. And she washed her hair more often than anyone else did in Dhompa.

Yungyang has always been poor and under my grandfather she was given no chance to alter or improve her life. She would have continued to serve the family without any remuneration until the end of her days. She has not benefited under the Chinese rule either. Her name, Yungyang, "a bounty of turnips," hints at her class. The *yung* grows with little effort here and is the poor man's food. Nomads dry the *yung* until it becomes hard and like the brown of molten chocolate, they eat this as a snack while they are out in the mountains herding their animals. My mother called it nomad candy. The leaves of the *yung* plant provide nourishment for the animals in winter. Yungyang thinks her birth might have coincided with a bountiful yield of turnips allowing her family to eat well and have extra to dry into small balls for the following year.

I am surprised nomads discard the onomatopoeic phrases, proverbs, riddles, and metaphors they use to embellish their stories and settle for obvious caricatures when naming their children: Singhi, "lion"; Singho, "lion's head"; Matuk, "boy soldier"; Changho, "wolf's head." Children born during the Cultural Revolution could not be blessed or named by lamas as the lamas were all in prison. A name had to indicate as little as possible in a time when everyone's imagination was subdued to conform to a common culture espoused and enforced by Mao's Communism. I meet forty-year-old men called Mo Tsering and Mo Tashi, the Mo a salutation to Mao. Perhaps their fathers ascribed to and were cadets of the Red Guards and thought the names would serve their children well.

Traditional names are back: Tsering, Pema, Tashi, Karma. Unimaginative sobriquets continue to abound though, and Tenzin explains that nomads often give temporary names to their children and never get around to asking a lama or an elder for a proper name, so the nickname remains. Here and there adults have names reserved for dogs: Oyo and Atuk, "little puppy." Oka, "white puppy." Men and women are named so because they were born after a child who did not survive. The parents give a dog's name to mislead the one who brings death so their child will stay alive. A dog's life is an onerous life in these mountains and even death does not covet it.

Tashi says nomads keep to the routines and customs they learned from their parents and they know the basic truths: that life is full of suffering, that suffering can be understood and lived through, that their actions and intentions will determine their future lives just as the past has allowed for this present life. They do not assume this life of suffering is particular to Tibetans; they think the rest of the world, as humans, must suffer too and that their spiritual practice, if not Buddhism, must speak of it.

We have semi-dried meat, yogurt, milk, tsampa, salt, white flour, and the vegetables we brought with us. The vegetables are stored in the shrine, which as the coolest room serves as our refrigerator. The meat, dry on the outside but raw inside, has to be carefully observed for the tiny worms that fester in its flesh. Tenzin has spinach growing in the garden. Although Dorje is the designated chef, I cook when I can. At night I stick to noodles but try variations: *thenthuk*, pulled noodles; *bhakthuk*, miniature conch-shaped noodles; and sometimes when I am pressed for time I take the easier path and use the knife to cut the dough in thin strips. Tenzin and Yungyang have not eaten *bhakthuk* for a long time and they marvel that I can make food of the old days. They remark how I am so Tibetan despite my having lived outside Tibet.

Tenzin says I am who I am because I am educated. Educated people are different, he tells Yungyang. Educated people appreciate culture and their own history.

Tashi says I am who I am because I had a good mother.

Yes, of course, Tenzin says.

Why does Tenzin think I am more Tibetan than some Tibetans in the town of Nangchen?

He says I speak the dialect and know the names of the lamas and monasteries. I love the land.

Is that all the knowledge required to live on this land? What is our history?

Even he, more literate and learned than lay nomads, does not offer much information beyond the achievement of the lama he reverentially calls "the mute," who would give accurate predictions through gestures his monks learned to decipher, the Dhompa chief who was known as the Nangchen king's "ear," and yogis of the land who could bring rain, stall snow, and resuscitate people just a breath away from death. Citizens of Lhasa can point to the Potala, the Jokhang, the monastic institutions of Sera, Drepung, and Ganden that abound with scholars, artisans, and thinkers, but here in Dhompa the elders do not articulate specific achievements of the present. They simply point to the land.

Tenzin says he was taught to protect Buddhist doctrines as a Tibetan. He identifies the lifestyle nurtured by Buddhist culture as Tibetan. It is not too different from my mother's view. Even though her homesickness for her birthplace never abated she never forgot the fortune of being exiled in the holy lands of India and Nepal where Buddhism was born. I was encouraged to learn about Buddhism so I could maintain my identity as a Tibetan.

"What do you mean when you say you are Tibetan?"

"What is there to explain? It's obvious we are all Tibetan— the Lhasa people, the Khampas, the Amdos. We are all *nang-pas* ['insiders,' people who share the Buddhist faith] because of our belief in Buddhism."

I tell him there are people who point out that the regions of Kham and Amdo in East Tibet were not part of Tibet when the Chinese invaded Tibet and that therefore we are not part of political Tibet although we think we are Tibetan.

Geographical and political territories have never been his concerns. He, like Yungyang, rarely steps out of Dhompa, and has yet to see a map of Tibet. I tell them decisions on the political sovereignty of Tibet seem to happen outside the struggles of our day-to-day existence in exile, in the same way perhaps that it happened for them long ago when China invaded Tibet.

If the Chinese were Tibetan, they would understand us, Yungyang says.

I wonder if Tenzin and Yungyang enter into discussions of identity when they are among their own families. They are where they have always been. There are no outsiders here and so they do not feel burdened by definitions and obligations of belonging or not belonging to one location. They have not met anyone in

Dhompa who speaks of belief in other religions and other deities. Perhaps identity will enter their thoughts in the future when more of their young leave, and people who are not known to them come to stay on their land.

Kunga, my town-born nephew, is ill at ease in Dhompa. At first he was excited to ride a horse but with each passing day he misses the common markers of a town: the flash of a television screen through a window, the cavernous Internet houses where the young gather to play video games all day, even the simple purring of a car. Dhompa is not a place for a seventeen-year-old town boy. Young men here cannot exchange books and music with him. The men of his age here have responsibilities he does not.

He categorizes Dhompa as one of the places that needs development. It is pretty, he says, but he misses his friends and does not know how to keep himself entertained among hills and cattle. His money cannot purchase the tokens he wants here: it is not yet a liveable place. He speaks of the cities of Tibet with approval— Lhasa, Chengdu, Shigatse, Ganze—and even though his hometown, Kyegu, has a long way to go before it could become one of those cities, he says it is preferable to the quaint existence of nomadic life.

Twice I see wisps of smoke rising from a patch of tall turnip plants and inhale the self-announcing smell of a cigarette. I tell him the turnip patch is a poor hiding place; whole fields are available if he wants to hide his smoking from his grandmother. He sleeps in late every morning, to while away the day I suspect. He has instant noodles for lunch. He differentiates himself from the nomads: his education, his ease with the Chinese language, his indifference to tsampa and Tibetan butter. He explains that this does not mean he is not Tibetan, he is simply a modern Tibetan. To prove his loyalty he tells me a story about a Chinese history teacher in his school. This teacher distorted facts, Kunga says. He was dismissive when he spoke about Tibetans and introduced the Nangchen king in one sentence, "The Nangchen king was a bad man who thought only of himself."

This introduction did not fare well with the students, most of them from Nangchen. Kunga and his classmates took the teacher into the bathroom and beat him up after the lesson. He narrates the story with pride and says many students carried and still carry knives to school and will not hesitate to use them if their pride and honor are smudged. This is not what I expect from students in a small town in Tibet. He is disappointed by my lackluster response.

He reminds me that knives are a part of the khampa's dress. Even his grandmother has a knife hanging from her belt. "We are khampas," he states. For now, for this day, he has chosen to assert his roots.

Kunga's Tibet begins in 1950 after the successful liberation of the people. He studies the history of Tibet from Chinese text-books. Tibet required emancipation from ignorance and back-wardness, and from the gluttony of the lamas and chiefs who exploited and did nothing for the people, or so he has learned from books in school. He hears contrasting stories from family members—about famine, imprisonment, decades of hardship—but these are narrated so calmly and in such a matter-of-fact tone that he feels it must not have been so terrible. Besides, history is not his favorite subject—he prefers literature.

My Tibet ends with the Chinese invasion and with my mother's escape into Nepal in 1959. The world she referred to and belonged to—including its chieftains and lamas—was remembered as being benign and glorious. I tell Kunga that eighty thousand Tibetans escaped to India in 1959 and that they are now all over the world. We talk about our grandparents and many other relatives who lost their lives in labor camps. I tell him it is estimated that one and a half million Tibetans died under the Chinese.

Kunga has been taught in school that Dhompa chiefs are part of the inglorious past. I learned from my mother to believe they were of divine lineage. Yet ultimately for both of us the family lineage is a resource for understanding our history and our relationship to Tibet.

Tenzin reminds us the Dhompas are heirs to Sing Adhom, a general in King Gesar's court. King Gesar of divine origins, the hero of the Tibetan epic *Gesar of Ling*, was sent to redeem Tibet from a state of anarchy and from the rule of negative spirits and demons. He is a character so mesmerizing that people reportedly sit through the full week it takes for a singer to recite his story. To Kunga and I, the story of King Gesar is a legend so fantastic—Gesar singing to his mother from the womb; Gesar growing to the size of a one-year-old child immediately after his birth; Gesar conquering three demon birds at the age of three; Gesar understanding the birds and the animals so well that he is able to provide food for his mother when they are banished into the wild—that we cannot seriously believe he was a living person.

For Tenzin, Gesar is no fanciful tale. He tells us Gesar was a poor herder's son born not so far from where we are and not too different from us. He points to the field below us and says the general Si Dhungmo of Gesar's court camped there with his men on his way to a battle many, many years ago.

We look down at the field where Si Dhungmo camped. It is full of flowers. It is not difficult to imagine an army resting there. Perhaps they went to the river to wash the blood off, perhaps they killed a yak and feasted late into the night. Perhaps they won the war.

This land makes me believe anything is possible. Here lies a gift unraveled as was meant to be: within its many folds are humans, animals, insects, and plants. The green goes on and on in relentless beauty. As I look at the land I am heartbroken thinking of the future when I will not be here and when this place, too, will be something else. Here in the boundless field, with no other person in sight, I understand how a nomad might understand the universe. I wonder what it takes for a nomad to feel part of the world when he is sitting on the back of a horse measuring distance and the day's labor by the hour.

Tashi and I lie on our backs. The drama of the sky unfurls above us and it is the blue of turquoise braided into a woman's hair. In the evening the clouds are sometimes bandages for the sky's scars. Perhaps it is my nostalgia for this place that gives the sky such grandness. I view the sky as though it belongs only to this location. In this, I am completely unreasonable.

I form long thin ropes with the soft kneaded flour, then roll them into marble-sized balls, which, one at a time, I press into the center of my cupped left palm with the right thumb. Small conch-shaped balls of dough fall into the pot of boiling broth. Tenzin and Yungyang entertain me as I cook dinner. They do not recognize any condiments. They cannot advise me if the soup is too salty or if it needs more vegetables. Taste and delicacy are not a priority. When Tenzin is alone he survives on tsampa, yogurt, and milk, and every once in a while he eats a packet of instant noodles. They have not put their imagination to innovative use when it comes to food.

We are good eaters and we waste nothing. If there is extra milk, Tenzin makes yogurt. When the yogurt gets too sour for us, he makes *churtsa*, a sour tsampa soup. He stirs water into the yogurt and brings it to a boil. The aroma takes over the room. He adds dry cheese, salt, meat, and tsampa to the boiling yogurt and keeps stirring the mixture until the broth is thick and creamy. Each mouthful is a sour benediction. On hot summer days we pray for yogurt to sour.

For fuel we use the yak manure Tenzin has collected from the hills around us where the animals graze. A good year is measured, he informs me, by the height of the dung piled outside a nomad's house or tent. He has built a manure stupa on the meadow outside the house that towers over us and gives us confidence in his preparedness for the coming winter. Some nomads prefer to plaster flat cakes of manure on the low mud walls that encircle their winter base, while others spread a thin paste on the grass. When dry, these are torn off the walls or the ground and are stored in the kitchen.

Our drinking water comes from a spring half a mile away from the house. It is to this place the Dhompas have gone for water for over sixty years. When it rains, the water contains little granules of stones. Tenzin tells me the history behind the spring. (The hole in the ground is munificent just as the word "spring" is to its size.) He cannot guess a date but says Neten Chokling Rinpoche, a renowned lama of the region and the family's spiritual teacher who visited Tingsikha often, was responsible for bringing water from the ground. On one of his visits Chokling Rinpoche was requested by my grandfather to strike water for the family since the helpers had to walk a considerable distance down to the river to fetch water. Chokling Rinpoche gave instructions to dig a hole halfway down the hill. Though its smallness of size caused skepticism it continues to offer water.

Our bathroom outdoors stretches out as far as the eyes can bear. Every time I go among the turnip leaves, I fear I will encoun-

ter someone but I am never exposed except to the three-legged
dog who knows my habits and appears in front of me every single
time with a silly grin on his face. On days when it rains, I drink
less water. The pleasure I take in my walk through the thicket of
grass and flowers that dampens the ends of my clothes is subdued.
I do not enjoy the cold raindrops that slide down my bottom and
I still have to answer to the hope in the eyes of the mangy wet dog
who appears in front of me. There is no escape from the indignity
of constantly being found by him, but in the rain I feel it more
keenly.

News from the outside world and messages from town come days
and even weeks late. A phone in the regional government office
works at will and weeks go by without it making any sound; the
books I see are school workbooks, tattered from the rough han-
dling of little children over many years, or Buddhist texts written in exquisite calligraphy and wrapped in red or yellow cloth
in the bags of monks; the only newspaper I find is a newsletter
published by a monastery in Chobdrak, at least a full day's journey away from us. It seems apposite that the news here reflects on
the whereabouts of Buddhist masters and the musings of young
monks on compassion and impermanence in the forms of elegies,
essays, and poems. A monk had brought the newsletter to me
upon hearing of my poetry. He was eager to show me how there
were poets in Nangchen too. He asked if I wrote as they did. He
offered me the names of writers and poets in Kham who wrote
in Tibetan and in Chinese, a list far more comprehensive than
Tibetan writers I know of in exile.

This land has been home to the family of Dhompas for over two
hundred years. It was the imaginary home I grew up in through

my mother's stories and her insistence that it be remembered as home. It is more beautiful than I imagined. The land is vast and unhindered by trees, highways, electric poles, or tall buildings. There are few distractions other than what is offered by the imagination. But this will not last for long.

The one television in the center of the village is capable of slowly changing everything. And the young are ready for change.

CHAPTER TEN

Mother

It was never clear to me if I was born on the sixth or the seventh of March. My school documents stated March sixth but somehow I had adopted the seventh as my birthday. My mother's equivocation did not help clarify the confusion. It could have been the sixth or the seventh. What difference does it make, she would counter to my query.

Birthday celebrations outside of the Tibetan New Year, a day when all Tibetans turn a year older, are possible for those of us born in exile but even then a nervous caution is our best measure, for it is clear our parents—who may have given birth to us at home—were not paying attention when they registered us in school, and converted the Tibetan months and weeks into the Gregorian calendar.

Each March my mother sent me a birthday card extolling in cursive print the joys of having a daughter, and of love, that love of a mother for her child not as I had known from her but as the greeting cards made known in florid language. Even though individual birthdays were a new concept to her she learned about greeting cards and gifts and said she did not want me to feel excluded from the customs of my time. Her own date of birth was unknown. For official purposes she had set it at 11 November.

When I received a card from Mother I tried to picture her entering the gift shop and searching through racks for the perfect one. It was not something I could imagine easily because I never saw her send cards to anyone else. How had she found the store? I panicked for her: What if she had felt uncertain in the shop? It wasn't that I underestimated her ability to complete a shopping transaction. It was a discomfort at the thought of the one I loved dearly being in an unfamiliar place and suffering a small inconvenience. As certain as she was in her world, I did not know how much at ease she was in places she did not frequent: the new shops in town that rang up purchases instead of calculating on a little notebook, the fast-food restaurants with their menus on the wall, the disorienting shopping malls with neon signs and escalators. I worried for her if she had to order pizza from impatient twenty-year-olds, or purchase ice cream from the parlors in the city where new flavors put infrequent customers at odds with their usually easy choice of the stalwart vanilla. I wanted to be there to protect her just as she protected me where I faltered.

I continue to worry for my mother today because I know she is somewhere in the world in her new life.

The cultures and languages of India and Nepal came effortlessly to those of us born in exile, and many Tibetan children became interpreters for their parents or grandparents in marketplaces, offices, or in their own schools. We learned to be the buttress for the elders whose gaze remained on Tibet and who adjusted slowly and reluctantly to life in exile.

As a daughter I looked to my mother for guidance and for the groundedness and equanimity she possessed in abundance. I followed her cues when we went to monasteries to visit lamas or when we were with elders. I learned to arrange the altar and memorize my prayers from her. She fretted that I was not steeped in Tibetan culture and specifically in Buddhism, and often articulated her regret for having taken me out of a Tibetan school at the age of seven. She had sent me to a Christian boarding school instead, with the financial help of an American sponsor, Dr. Melvin Shaffer, who became a surrogate father to me. She worried I spent too much time reading English fiction and would offer to pay me to read *The Songs of Milarepa*.

She did not fret over my future nor did she abet ambition for material acquisition; instead she put her entire focus on showing me the value of deep-rooted Buddhist knowledge and practice to ride the difficulties of life. She was afraid I would forget to say my prayers, that I would marry a non-Tibetan and drift away from my roots. She feared we would not be able to return to Tibet within her lifetime. She was afraid her death would leave me alone in the world and so for all these reasons and more, she prayed for me and for my happiness every single day.

When there are just two of you in the world, you carry the fear that if one of the two should go, there will be just one left; you are two against the idea of time, death, and happiness. I am not ashamed to declare I was a child who drank from my mother's breasts until I was four. It is not necessary to tell you the extent to which our love for each other shaped our lives.

Mother never spoke much of her escape from Tibet, but listening to the escape stories of elders around me, I developed the notion that she had been in Lhasa in March 1959 and that she had been part of the large exodus of Tibetans who left soon after the Dalai Lama's escape. In notes she had begun writing at my request, she mentions being hungry for days and that her group had to exchange gunfire with Chinese soldiers more than twice or thrice. In the winter of 2008 while working on this book I traveled to Bir, a Tibetan refugee settlement near Dharamshala in northern India, where my mother had lived while she was still married and where many elders who were with her on the journey from Tibet continue to live. The elders pointed out soon after our meeting that I was not as beautiful as she had been at my age. But their eyes filled up with tears when I laughed. They remarked that I had my mother's manner of gazing dreamily into the distance or tilting my head as though embarrassed.

I said three months was a long time to be walking. They said three months would have been wonderful. It had taken them three years.

I assumed I had misheard. Was it possible they were exaggerating? Had it really taken that long? Three years?

My mother's friends, now in their late sixties and early seventies, have lived their exiled lives in the same refugee settlement. They say their memories have been assaulted by the medications they have had to take over the years for their physical troubles but those three years are indelible. They were not part of Kham's guerrilla army but for three years they fought the Chinese at every step of the way to exile. Three years, they said, was a long time to evade the Chinese army.

I realized early that despite her gregarious and inherently buoyant disposition, a certain sadness resided in my mother. Even I, her only child, whom she loved more than anything in the world, could do little to soothe the sorrow that had taken root with the separation from her parents, her two sisters, and her brother. The contrast in the life my mother experienced before and after leaving Tibet was so extreme, it must have been impossible for her to make sense of her life and to escape the inexhaustible longing for the past. Caring for me on her own inside crowded rooms of tenement buildings in towns and cities, she must have felt she had dreamed her past or that she was dreaming her present existence.

Mother

The places and residences we lived in were never quite home to her and led her to cling, more tenaciously, to the past. My mother had guarded her past sorrows from me because she knew me well enough to sense I would carry her grief as my own. Still, how had she managed to hide such an integral journey of her life from me?

My mother had left her husband's village in early 1959 to be with her mother for the birth of her first child. She had a difficult pregnancy and had been confined to bed. The Chinese entered Nangchen just as my mother's health deteriorated, and she lost the twin boys soon after giving birth to them. My mother's husband had made the decision to flee to India with his people and he came with a few aides to coax my mother to make the journey with him.

My mother's friends say it was a difficult time. There was nothing to be done.

Mother had been too sick to grieve and too disoriented to bid a proper farewell to her mother and family, who promised to follow her into exile. The Chinese were said to be approaching so she joined her husband and his people out of Dhompa. She had never spoken to me of her firstborns. I heard of the babies from someone else when I was in my early teens.

She left her home with five hundred men, women, and children. Their journey was blighted from the very beginning. Every route they chose led them to encampments where the Chinese army waited. It took the group a long time to get out of Nangchen. They hid in the mountains during the day and walked when it was nearing dusk. Almost all men carried guns. The group had their biggest encounter with the Chinese near Nagchukha, according to my mother's friends. They lost a few men but managed to kill quite a few Chinese soldiers. The two men I interviewed were not certain how many Chinese they were able to take down but they remembered hearing different numbers even then: a hundred, fifty, twenty-five. It was never clear because they were always on the move and nobody was counting. One of the men said the Chinese soldiers were bedraggled. They wore boots that gaped open and shirts without sleeves. They had been fighting for a long time in a strange, hostile land.

My mother's party was ambushed eight times on their escape to Nepal. By and by, they lost their horses and yaks, they ran out of food, water, and bullets. The elders remembered walking for three or four days without food.

"We were so thirsty," my mother's friends said. They sucked greedily on pieces of ice when they got to mountain passes. They were compelled to raid other nomads for food. Sometimes they forced Tibetan farmers to give them food or shoes for the exchange of an ornament. One elder forced a farmer to buy his sword in exchange for a horse so my mother, who had not yet regained her health from her difficult childbirth, could rest her feet.

The Chinese did not make it easy to escape. The group had no idea where Nepal or India was and more often it was the Chinese who determined which direction they took and where they went. Every time they were ambushed, they lost direction, they lost a few more animals, more people, and more belongings. Once my mother and two other people were separated from the group. A few days later they found each other at a mountain pass and for a brief moment they forgot where they were in their happiness at finding each other.

How is it possible to protect your loved ones from old heartaches? I can do nothing now for the nineteen-year-old woman who had to experience the loss of her two babies, her entire family, and her country in a journey to a freedom she would experience in exile. It is too late for me to comfort my mother.

My mother's friends recalled observing two Tibetan new years on the way. The third year they reached the borders of Lo Monthang in Nepal like hungry stray dogs. Sixty-five men and women survived from the five hundred that had set off. My mother's shoes had barely covered her feet, her clothes were frayed. She took shelter in the monastery in Lo Gekar, Mustang, for a year and then gathered the energy and nerve to make her way toward India.

Her friends had laughed at the memory of little things while telling me stories about their journey to a new life. They marveled they were able to travel in Nepal and India without knowing anything of the land or the ways of the land. They had paid their way to the Indian border by selling their remaining rifles to Nepali traders in Kathmandu. Once in India, they pushed their way into trains and buses shouting "Namaste, Dharamshala," and "Namaste, Dalai Lama."

My mother mentions in her notes how she had heard that Indians respected women and would not strike them, so it was the women who pushed into the trains ahead of their men. My mother's friends did not remember how long it had taken them to reach Dharamshala from the India-Nepal border. They suspect they had gone back and forth on the same rail route a few times in their confusion. The names "Dalai Lama" and "Dharamshala" were their only codes into the new country. Every time Indian passengers and ticket collectors pushed them out of the trains, they fought their way back in. I am certain that Indian railway officials did not try to push them out of trains very often for these were khampas still wearing long hair and their knives, and their desperation might have lent them a menacing air.

They knew they were in Dharamshala when they encountered hundreds of Tibetans wandering like spectral figures. In Dharamshala they were able to get work as road laborers in the mountains of Garsha and Spiti in the summer and in Manali in the winter. My mother's notes record a severe snowstorm that killed many Tibetans one winter in northern India:

> While in Chotta Dhara, it snowed for many days and there was an avalanche which nearly covered all of us. There was nowhere to run and I was scared beyond speech. All of us gathered together day and night and prayed with our hands folded and eyes closed. There was nothing to eat and drink. The brave can face the Chinese, fight, run and escape but with nature as enemy one can only sit and pray for protection. Many of us were frostbitten and could not walk. Our belongings were buried under snow making us refugees again.

In exile my mother had to learn what she never thought would be required of her: to make fire, prepare tea, and dig the hard ground in the Indian Himalayas.

She said she was often overtaken by great sadness. During those times she would remind herself to be grateful for being alive. Sometimes she wondered if it would have been better to have remained in her village and shared a common fate with her loved ones. She prayed every day for her family. She felt alone even though she was with her husband. In this way my mother's life began in exile.

Eight years later I was born in a crowded train while Mother was passing through a dusty little town in India. She had wondered if this time she would die. After thirteen years of marriage, she had chosen to separate from her husband a few months before my birth. She told me that she had not been an agreeable wife. She had spent most of her brief time as a married woman hiding from her husband: living two years in the Sri Aurobindo Ashram in Pondicherry to learn to read and write English and get a basic education, then choosing to work as a teacher in an orphanage for Tibetan children far from the refugee settlement where her husband lived. She spent her vacations with friends, allowing only a short time for her husband. She had treated her marriage and her husband like a health clinic. Perhaps on one such visit I was conceived.

When I was born, I was not given a dog's name even though I followed twin boys who had not survived birth. I was named Tsering—"long life"—Wangmo—"blessings" or "powerful woman."

CHAPTER ELEVEN

A Woman's World

The August sun seduces flowers, grass, and earth to an agreeable temperature. Lassitude overtakes all of us, including Tenzin, who adopts a languorous pace in the evenings. The yaks are desultory eaters: What would be the purpose of quickening their gait when the field stretches beyond their vision into eternity?

Tashi and visiting elders speak of how the sun makes the body forget its pains. They speak of the sorrows of old age when they are together: how their bones have knotted into stiff bolts, their blood thickened to run sluggishly in their veins, how their bodies revolt against the mind's desires.

Clouds come and go. The world swivels unhurriedly. I slip away for a walk on a warm afternoon and am surprised by a fit of ill-humored downpour. The rain falls furious and hard and I run for the nearest tent.

Pema, my host, invites me to sit on a small carpet, the best seat in the tent. It is dark, warm, and smoky inside. Her tent is approximately thirty feet by twenty feet and cozy for her family of eight. The tent is as black as her hair; she has woven it herself from yak wool. A few strings of prayer flags flutter on the outside. Her family owns two wooden cylinders for making butter tea, three homemade leather boxes, a small altar containing photos of lamas from Nangchen, and a radio. A box of instant noodles rests behind the radio. Several blankets propped against the periphery of the tent serve as a backrest. The mattresses are made of yak skin and fur.

Everything they own is layered in dust and smoke. Animal hair settles in the milk, yogurt, and butter. Pema is twenty-seven and has six children between the ages of nine and one. Her one-year-old sits on a blanket of sheepskin sipping milk from a plastic Pepsi bottle. He wears a necklace of medallions with portraits of the Dalai Lama, the Karmapa, and the Khenpo of Serta. His mother hopes these lamas will protect him from unknown disasters.

Pema hovers over the stove of mud positioned close to the tent's entrance and directly beneath a hole in the roof that serves as the chimney. When her family vacates this spot, she will destroy the stove, leaving behind a blackened lump of mud as the only trace of her family's long summer encampment. She turns the handles on a small metal machine resembling an old gramophone. I see strings of pale yellow butter drip from a small spout attached to the machine. These she rolls into small balls and soaks in cold water. Gone are the days when she had to shake a leather pouch of milk continuously for several hours to make butter. The women have options now; Pema's neighbor finds it easier to shake a plastic container typically used to store water or kerosene. Pema prefers the machine, which she calls a milk-grinding machine, from which butter is formed quickly and without much effort. She tells me of nomads who have relocated to town and who profess to love the washing machine best of all the goods produced by China. The blades of the washing machine are very effective in making butter. A lot of butter can be made in one washing machine, she says wistfully. She admits she cannot dream of making butter in a washing machine when she has yet to experience the daily conveniences of electricity.

Pema goes back and forth from the butter machine to a pot of milk boiling over a low fire. Raindrops fall into the milk through the chimney. Her eyes are red from the smoke trapped in the tent and her hands are blackened with work. She stirs the milk until the solids separate from the water. When she is satisfied, she drains the liquid and lays out the crumbled milk on a plastic sheet. She will dry these solids in the sun until they harden to become dried cheese, *chura*. The cheese is used to garnish tsampa or is eaten as a snack. Tucked into its pores are rain, soot, and yak hair. On days when she hankers for a treat, Pema tells me, she makes *thi*, a cholesterol boost of dried cheese, butter, and sugar.

Her hands are marked with scars and they look as though they are made entirely of muscles; they speak of the endless grind. I imagine she is adept at skinning an animal and removing specks from her children's eyes. It is this adaptability—this capacity to perform delicate tasks and take on the burdensome ones—that make her and most nomadic women seem incredible. Yet they are invisible and for the most part undocumented, even in their own stories about the land and people. Pema says she is incessantly busy: milking the goat and the female yak before dawn, making butter and cheese, tending to the children, sometimes doing all of these at the same time. She tells me it is a hard lot to be a woman in the nomad country.

More than a few women have told me they think it is easier to live as a yak than it is to be a woman in these mountains. Pema is a decade younger than me but her face wears the anxieties and travails of her daily life in deep furrows. She is shocked to find out I am much older than her. "My life is hard, it ages us," she explains. There is a lot she would like to escape from. She does not like the task of milking female yaks in the morning. (Every day the female yak must be coaxed into giving milk by allowing the baby yaks to suckle first, otherwise the animal will not give milk. And it is work to tear the baby away.) She does not enjoy collecting water from the stream a mile from her tent, and she does not like the long winters when the animals are so miserable and hungry.

"The chores never end," she sighs.

Pema was born in a neighboring herding community. She met her husband when he came to her village to purchase a horse. When he left, she went with him. She and her husband do not have many animals and they are able to survive by taking care of the animals belonging to relatives who have moved to Kyegu. Some days she thinks about leaving for the town too but she is not literate and neither is her husband. What could they do there? She has no skills of use to town life. She tells me of a family who signed up to resettle in the town of Nangchen. Within a year they were penniless, the children fell ill, they wanted to return but they had already given up their land. They regret having moved, she says. There are some stories of success but these are few compared to the majority whose misfortunes serve to caution against a migration to town.

She has not rested for a single day in her adult life. I think of the treats I give myself—a morning relaxing in bed, a run in the park, a swim, a hike, a day spent in the kitchen cooking for pleasure—I do not know what it is to work unceasingly. She has the long night ahead of her and she is so tired she can only think of sleep. "Sometimes I am too tired to find the energy to sleep," she confesses with a shy smile.

Pema's family survives on what the animals provide them. She does not have money to purchase necessities such as new clothes, flour, tsampa, and oil. Thankfully, in the past few years nomads have been exempt from paying tax for the use of land and for the size of their herd.

I ask her if she has collected any caterpillar fungus this year. She hasn't.

What about her husband?

He has poor vision.

Her children?

They are too young. Maybe in a few years they will be able to help and then they can make some money, she says.

She'd be happy if she could find a handful of the fungus—even that would bring money. There is nothing predictable about the fungus. There are days when a person returns without so much as one and then there are days when he finds as many as fifteen. Pema says her time for wealth is never in sight while just a few hills away the nomads of Karjung and the nomads of Zatou have prospered.

Could she go to Zatou to harvest fungus?

She cannot afford the fees. She says the land gives Tibetans everything they need but it is the government who makes the rules and dictates how they must live. She can pick fungus in Dhompa but must pay collection fees as high as four thousand yuan to pick from neighboring lands. The increase in migrant Chinese and Tibetans seeking to join in the trade leads to several disputes each summer. Nomads see these migrant collectors as poachers and feel no kinship with them partly because nomads don't get any portion of the collection fee taken by the government.

In 2006 there was a big fight between the nomads of Zatou and migrant collectors. The nomads brought out guns hidden in their tents and fired into the crowd preparing to enter their land. One person was fatally wounded. The outsiders came armed with slingshots and stones. The army was ultimately brought in to restore order but not before a few people were killed and many injured. Stores in the town of Zatou were ransacked.

Even Dhompa's close-knit community has not proven impervi-ous to tensions over the fungus. Three years ago herders destroyed a bridge in their determination to stop neighbors—herders known and related to them—from crossing the bridge to pick from their hills. Now, both parties must walk a few miles to another bridge just so they can cross the river and take their animals to their grazing grounds. The herders have been asking for a new bridge but local government officials say they can hardly petition the offices in Xining to replace a bridge that was destroyed by its own people.

It is not very difficult to spot the families who have benefited from a good year of fungus sales. A motorbike, a solar panel, and new clothes decorate their tents. During my visit, cousins of my cousins from Zatou carried the money they made from their sale of fungus straight to a land cruiser dealer in Xining where they paid in cash for a jeep. They drove the jeep on a month-and-a-half-long pilgrimage to Mount Kailash in western Tibet. It was money well spent, the elder of the family said upon his return. They were able to light butter lamps, give money to monks, and make three circumambulations of the holy mountain.

Pema thinks it is unwise to pick fungus every year. The fungus is a living creature. Killing so many of them saddens the deities, she says.

In June when hail as large as tennis balls fell on the land, the elders collected details of the damages: thirty lambs had holes in their bodies, two jeeps were dented, ten men suffered bruises on their heads and foreheads. Pema kept her younger children inside the tent that day. Such hail had not fallen on the land for three decades.

She wondered if the hail was an indication that people had offended the divinities. It had to be the fungus that people sought so greedily.

Pema keeps an eye on her youngest child as she works. Three other children—a girl of seven, a boy of four, and a girl of five—are out with the herd; the latter two tend to the goats and sheep and the elder daughter is with the yaks. They will return at sundown. She fears her children will never be able to walk in town with confidence; they will not be able to read the signs on stores or on office buildings, or comprehend the regulations they will agree to follow. At the same time, Pema has little faith in village schools, where children study for a few years and then find themselves with no access to higher education. Her oldest child is in school and she has her doubts about his ability to prosper. She suspects he is not a keen student. She fears he will be useless once he graduates from school, good enough neither for town nor for the land. He never did enjoy the task of bringing the baby yaks to their mothers early in the morning, she says with a grin. The baby yak, so strong and three times his size, would kick, stamp, and drag him each morning. Her seven-year-old daughter is very bright, but Pema is reluctant to send her away to school because she's very good at milking the female yaks and is a big help at home.

I tell her the school in Dhompa runs through up to the seventh grade.

In recent years the government has waived school fees for nomadic children, but the schools will have to improve drastically in order to win parents over. Parents such as Pema admit to frightening their children into discipline with the threatening words, "If you don't behave, I will send you to school!" She would prefer to send one or two children to attend school from her brood of six.* Every nomad is now obliged to send their children to school. There are many complaints from parents: children must huddle together and sleep on mud floors, and teachers—often recent graduates from teaching schools unprepared for the harshness of nomadic life—do not stay in the schools for the full school term. The fact is very little money is available for schools and teachers barely earn enough to cover their food rations. The Chinese government is making education their priority but many small

---

*Exempt from the one-child policy, most nomads have an average of three to six children.

schools in nomadic villages do not have the resources for teachers to teach and for students to learn.

Pema and I are swaddled by layers of mountains with no other tent in sight. If one of us were to break a limb or to eat a poisonous mushroom, her husband would have to borrow a bike and ride for an hour to the nearest Tibetan doctor who may or may not have medicine to treat us. If it is a serious illness there will be no recourse but to visit the lamas and offer prayers.

I ask of her husband's whereabouts, expecting her to say he is loitering in downtown Dhompa. But he is out putting up the new fence around their grazing territory. The government has ordered the nomads to fence their land.

The Tibetan grasslands is one of the most vital grazing eco-systems in the world, and as the source of three of Asia's major rivers, it is believed to indirectly or directly support and influence a significant portion of the world's population. Recent interest in Tibet's environment has brought a number of new policies that purport to protect the ecology and biodiversity of the grasslands. But Tibetans worry the policies take no equal consideration of the culture and traditions that have preserved the land for hundreds of years. Herders say they cannot keep up with the names and objectives of the numerous reforms they have been subjected to; it is uncertain if these methods will indeed prove more sustainable in the long run. According to Tenzin, the new policies encourage a more sedentary and restrictive livestock system, contrasting sharply with their traditional peripatetic ways.

I ask Pema what she thinks of the fence.

"The Chinese must know what they are doing," she says with a shrug of her shoulders. The previous day I had met a group of young Tibetan officials from the town of Nangchen who were in Dhompa to supervise the fencing initiative. They had been to colleges in China; they were warm and frank about their discomfort in camping in the remote land. They acknowledged the beauty of the land in praising the fish they had caught from the river. They explained the concerns of the government: overgrazing, overstocking of animals, increasing nomad population on the land, and deterioration of the grasslands, but they had not gone into the details.

"We are doing our job," one of the young officers had said. He wished for the nomads to get to the fences quickly so he could return to his family.

Pema points to one section of the land and says she is not to let the animals graze in that section. She is to let it rest for a year. She repeats the lines as though she is memorizing a puzzle. It is easier to round up the herd when their movements are restricted. "It will be like living in the town without too much work," she adds with a laugh.

She does not have a vocabulary for the preservation practices inherent in her herding life because she has never had to explain them to anyone. Why would she ignore the land when it is the land that provides the only means of livelihood to her and her family? She keeps the health of the grasslands in mind as her forefathers have. She says nomads do have a system of ensuring that the land is protected. I wonder if nomads have any input in the discussions over grassland degradation and in the government's sustainable reforms aimed at slowing the overgrazing process, or if the rules are envisioned by experts who have never lived as herders on this land.

In any case, the government has decreed that nomads must install the fences or they will be fined. So the men of Dhompa balance bales of steel wire behind them and take their motorbikes as far as they can to the tops of the mountains. When the machines can no longer climb, they carry the heavy bales on their backs and fence themselves in.

A long scar zigzags along the ridges of mountains across from us. The herd cannot wander aimlessly anymore.

Perhaps the yaks will knock the fences down; perhaps the steel is of poor quality and will rust and break, I say.

Pema says the fences will not last forever. She hopes it will keep predatory wild dogs or wolves away for a while.

National strategies are not easily understood, least of all by me and by Pema who, as I suspected, cannot pronounce the titles of the programs she is expected to follow. She cannot read the announcements or explain what each new policy stands for. In recent years she has had many to follow. Pema says it all sounds complicated to her. I can barely follow the intentions of the policies translated to me from Chinese into Tibetan and then into English.

The idea behind the fence reforms is to allow the grasslands a rest so that the land can restore itself. Another solution has been to encourage herders to move away from their land. Under such initiatives nomads are persuaded, or forced in some regions, to give up their animals and to move to towns where they are put into cement rooms and left to fend for themselves. It is believed that as many as two hundred families have moved from Dhompa to settlements in Kyegu and Nangchen. The prudent among them have left some family members on their land so that they have a home to return to if they cannot survive in their new environments.

I have noticed even townspeople who begrudge the onslaught of nomads in their domain admit pity for the resettled nomads. The settlements are located on the outskirts of the town where transportation is unreliable. The people of Kyegu and Nangchen view these settlements as potential ghettos and crime communities and they stay away as though ill luck will befall them should they stray into the sad colonies.

Pema lingers in my mind long after I leave.

The sky is pink when I reach Tingsikha. Yungyang and Tashi have been talking all evening, Tenzin announces when I enter the kitchen. They talk at the same time and over each other's monologues. Somehow, they are heard. Yungyang is kneading a strip of sheepskin. The stiff leather is softening under her insistent hands. Tashi wants to make jackets out of the skin.

Tashi asks if I had crossed the bridge to go to the other side of the river. I tell her I had walked alongside the plateau and then climbed the hill on the east side. She picks her nose as I talk, and after a disinterested look at the content, brings it flat on her sleeves with a delicate flick of her fingers. She tells me what I would have seen from where I was: the panoply of flowers, the black of the rocks, and the sudden gradient of the hill with views of a steep drop into the river. "You were near Pema's summer grazing land," she tells me. The land is imprinted in her memory.

Tashi loves this land. She was not born here but as the elder of the Dhompa family, she is the representative of the family and of the region. Yungyang was born in this land but she had to work as soon as she was able to walk. She knows the land through practical inquiries: the hillsides favoring wild garlic or where mushrooms can be picked by the handful.

Tashi confesses she had never considered Yungyang's troubles as a young woman. She knew Yungyang was poor and that therefore she was working for the Dhompa family; Tashi understood poverty and suffering when the Chinese stripped her of her family riches, land, house, and animals. She had to work from dawn to sundown in the fields and there were many days when she had nothing to feed her seven children. She understood then what it was to be absolutely destitute.

"It is very difficult to be hungry and to know there is nothing to eat and it is worse when you see your children hungry and you have nothing to give them." She hastens to add she was not totally abject because everybody else was in the same condition. That knowledge protected her from despair. "It is different now," she says. "Some are poor and some are rich, so you feel any deprivation more acutely."

Tashi was born in Zasep, now in Zatou county, five hours away if you ride in a sturdy jeep and don't stop to drink tea and yogurt along the way. Her father was the chieftain of Zasep and also a lama. He had the means to educate his three daughters but he neglected teaching them to read and write. Instead, he got his daughters married off before they turned fifteen. He had his reasons: he was not blessed with a son so he depended on the men that his daughters would marry to protect his territory and people. He was a successful matchmaker: his oldest daughter married the son of the chief of Upper Gerji, the middle daughter went as a bride to the son of the chief of Kyegu at fifteen, and his youngest daughter, Tashi, came to Dhompa to be my uncle's bride at twelve.

"I had the most beautiful pair of red brocade shoes for the wedding," Tashi remembers. How she loved those shoes! She had to be held upright by two people on either side, so heavy were the amber, turquoise, and coral beaded into her hair on her wedding day. She had a dress of brocade. Several chieftains from Nangchen attended the wedding bearing gifts of tiger skin, leather, horses, yaks, and bags and bags of dried cheese, butter, and meat. The men wore sumptuous brocade chubas and silk shirts and were flanked by retinues of servants. My grandfather was a generous man and he sent each chieftain home with twice what they brought: sixty yaks for thirty presented, ten horses for five horses, four *dris* for two *dris*.

Poor guests offered wool stretched out in thin strips to serve as a scarf.

"Your uncle was the most handsome man I had ever seen," Tashi says with a giggle. She remembers the wedding day even though she was a child and did not understand where her life would take her. She had her first child at fifteen. One of her grandchildren is fifteen today. She cannot imagine sending the young girl to be a wife to a man. "She's only a child," Tashi says.

When Tashi was young, girls from notable families were betrothed while they were children and without regard for their consent. Marriage alliances were often engineered by third parties—relatives, chiefs, or lamas—and sealed when the boy's family made a formal request for the girl's hand in a meeting where they offered gifts of tea, guns, and fabric to the family of the future bride. Once these formalities were completed a wedding date was picked in consultation with a lama.

Tashi remembers crying for many days after she came to Dhompa. She missed her mother very much. She had been raised to respect her parents and had never considered rebelling against her father's decision to marry her off to a stranger. My grandmother had been kind and shown her tenderness. She had wanted Tashi to feel comfortable with her husband and her new family. She had instructed my uncle not to touch his child-bride for almost two years.

A month after her wedding, Tashi was sent to her father's house in keeping with the tradition known as *rang-kor*—"a visit to one's own"—where brides went back to their parents' home to pay homage to them after a month of married life. My grandfather sent a few maids and male relatives as chaperones. He offered tea, brocade, jewels, and clothes for all her family members. Tashi still remembers the blue brocade dress she carried for her mother and the striking yellow brocade with dragons extending from the shoulders to the navel, a dress her father donned immediately.

Tashi had longed to linger with her parents, but she had

returned to Dhompa after four weeks. It was not uncommon, however, for some new brides to linger for as long as four months, or even a year with their parents. Every so often there would be a recalcitrant bride who refused to return to her husband's house, as one of my grandaunts did. Tashi's father sent her back to Dhompa with gifts for my grandparents: a hundred male yaks, forty female yaks, a hundred sheep and horses. (My mother took with her a hundred young female yaks, male yaks, sheep and horses, and swathes of silk and brocade to her husband's family when she returned from her visit home after her wedding a few years later.)

In some nomadic villages of Nangchen, a new bride was not permitted to feed or offer food to anyone for three days after being received into her husband's home. The bride's old name was discarded and she was given a new name to live her married life. (My mother was named Tashi Dolkar when she married and went on to become a Bongba.) The horse used by the bride was not permitted to enter the premises of the new house, and properties of the horse—the saddle, the horse blanket—remained outside for five days. This act was believed to keep bad luck, if attached to the bride, from entering the house with her. Tashi thinks the rituals might have also been influenced by a belief that a woman's purity was sullied by her first sexual experience with a man.

It is a strange contradiction that a man should make a woman impure, and yet he be deemed superior in all practical ways, I tell her.

Tashi says farmers and people living in the plains were not as superstitious as nomads in the high mountains. In the past it was believed the deity of the kitchen or the stove felt stifled in the presence of women, so only men were employed to cook in the Dhompa home. So sensitive was the deity of the kitchen that women who were not family members were forbidden from entering the kitchen, a tradition that is not enforced today. Still, there are a few women, even today, who will not visit the kitchen in Dhompa despite my invitations to them to do so. In the old days, women who were not related to the household did not walk the grounds of the house, for it was held that they would bring illness or misfortune to the family. Tenzin believes it was the reverse: that visitors feared they would fall sick if they angered the deities of the household. I am surprised to hear that even my mother's own playmates had to wait for her across the hill from Tingsikha when they met to play.

I had assumed large and frequent gatherings were common between nomads. I had assumed they depended on each other. Yungyang does not remember socializing with or visiting the tents of other nomads as a child.

Tashi points out that nomads lived far from each other and had so much to do. They did not have days off from their chores and the great distances from each other made it possible for them to cling to their beliefs and superstitions without anybody challenging or upsetting them.

I point out the contradictions in permitting women to milk the female yaks and goats when their very being is feared to contaminate the aristocrats. Tenzin and Dorje are amused. I explain myself: if women brought ill luck with their mere presence, how was it nobody fell ill drinking the milk they handled?

Tenzin laughs and says I do make a good point. He says nomads are like yaks because they don't think.

The men call their wives *nahmo*: "female whose place is inside the home." Women are also called *kyimen*, more commonly translated as "one who is of lesser birth." Tenzin says the word "men" also refers to medicine; *kyimen* also implies one who has properties of medicine and can heal others. There were others in the society who suffered worse prejudices: butchers, metalsmiths, and people who killed marmots. A butcher remained a butcher all his life and his descendants took on the profession. There was little escape from the stigma and a butcher could not enter the main dwelling area in most regions of Kham. The only exception I know to this is Gerji, a nomadic community not too far from Dhompa, where nomads celebrated the birth of a son by stating the family would not have to hire an outside butcher. Butchers were not looked down upon in this nomadic community because the sons were expected to kill the animals for the family's needs.

It is summer and the people of Dhompa send word to us that they would like to honor the deities of the land with a ceremony on Dhompa's sacred mountain, Ghoye Ruma. Tashi reminds me I will not be invited to join the rituals. Perhaps she fears I will insist on going to the top of the mountain with the men. "We can have tea, we can watch the men look more and more like crows as they move further up the mountain." The men will offer prayers and leave Ghoye dressed in new prayer flags, she tells me excitedly.

The men will return elated and happy, assured that the deities of the land will look after them, she continues. After the ceremony the people of the land wait for the deities to show their pleasure and deities do so with a lavish display of rain.

Her face relaxes when I tell her that I have no desire to challenge the practices of the land. I will not insist on going with the men, I assure her.

I am, however, curious to understand the origin of such beliefs. Tashi tells me that a very long time ago one of the wives of the chief insisted on going to the top of the sacred mountain to witness the mountain honoring ceremony, despite gentle reminders from lamas on the unconventionality and danger of the journey. The chief had not objected to his wife's decision and the men, being of the ilk who put their faith in their chief's wisdom, had not protested either. The chief's wife had not made it very far down the mountain after the ceremony for she was immobilized suddenly and was dead within hours. No woman has accompanied the men to the top of the mountain since then, Tashi says.

"Not everything we do and believe in has to be proved," she says, when I suggest that this might be a fabricated story.

I ask Tenzin why women are prohibited from walking to the top of certain mountains, from entering specific protector shrines, or from participating in certain religious rituals.

He does not know why these beliefs exist; he suggests I take my questions to the lamas. He offers a chagrined acknowledgment of the unjust treatment of women in Kham and says he has heard women in towns now lead a better life. He says the women in Lhasa were known to partake in prayers forbidden to women in Nangchen and they enjoyed more privileges even in the old days. He has heard, because men are meek in Lhasa, it is the women who dominate the household.

I am intrigued by superstitions; some of them seem particular to Dhompa, and I ask the women who visit me what they think of the prejudices against our sex.

The women who visit Tingsikha shrug their shoulders and say they haven't given it much thought; they've got plenty to take care of. I am acquainted with the deference to males in my community. Male relatives are usually served food before the women unless the elders in the family are women. Boys are readily excused for any lapse of cultural etiquette whereas it is important for young girls to be cognizant of proprieties. It was in the attitudes toward sexuality that the hypocrisy seemed most brazen: men are just being men if they fooled around but a woman is tainted or shamed if she enjoyed the same liberties. With age comes respect for women and a certain power not accorded in their youth.

My own mother had not adhered to the role scripted for women. She had separated from her husband right before I was born, despite admonitions and recriminations from friends and family members who could not understand her decision; it was not common for a woman to divorce her husband and to bring up a child on her own, especially as a refugee in a new country.

My mother was the first woman elected to represent her constituency of Kham in the Assembly of Tibetan People's Deputies when the government-in-exile was in its formative years. She was never the mother who sat in the kitchen slicing onions and making noodles while the men carried on with their conversations in another room. She did not sew, knit, or readily offer to cook like the mothers in my neighborhood. Every evening, from the age of thirteen, I waited with a thermos of hot tea for her to return from work. I bought curtains for the house, purchased matching plates, planted jasmine to cover the walls in the garden, and learned to cook. She marveled at my skills around the house. She confessed to me once that a lama had told her I was her mother's reincarnation when she went to see him during her pregnancy. Every now and then she had to remind me that she was the mother and I was the child, when I scolded her to eat her vegetables or to dress warmly when she stepped out for her early morning prayers around the stupa in Kathmandu.

We had monks and men visiting our house to seek her opinion on various political or social matters. It is only now that I can appreciate the unique position she held within our community and it is only now, being in the society and knowing how difficult it still is to gain a voice, that I understand she was not like most women of her time.

She was not one to make rules. She made me feel she had complete faith in me. When I wanted to experience what it would be like to get drunk in my early teens, she asked a relative to procure a mug of Tibetan rice beer. She helped me to bed when I was decidedly satiated and sick from the drink. When I was fifteen and she was to go to Tibet for most of the year she spoke to me of love and sex in a way that made it seem imminent. She told me I was no longer a child and that I would have to prepare for the possibility of falling in love. She said love or infatuation would come, and that it would come even if I resisted it.

I was shocked at her silliness. I had no intention of acquiring a boyfriend!

"If you fall in love and have sex with a man and get pregnant I want you to wait for me to return. Do not harm yourself. Send a message to me and wait for me. We will handle the matter together," my mother had said to me. She said it would be a disappointment if I were to get pregnant but she would be heartbroken if I were to get an abortion or harm myself. "Anything can happen in life," and quite often, unsuspecting girls were the ones to fall in trouble, she said. Because of her I was fortunate to have been protected from the scrutiny and pressure to conform to the guidelines of being a "good" girl, although my predilection for books kept me indoors and therefore quite good in the eyes of the elders.

But even my mother never thought to walk to the top of sacred mountains. For all her progressive personal decisions and ideas, my mother was deeply rooted in her Buddhist faith. She offered money to monasteries every time I had an exam and when I did well she would say it was the prayers that had made the difference. She consulted lamas for divination on important decisions, and had she lived longer she might have chosen me a husband with a lama's help. She tried to teach me to have the kind of Buddhist faith she had, the kind many elders have, which I will never obtain, for I have a faith that wavers and selects its places of confidence.

During my stay in Dhompa I persist in asking lamas, elders, women, and men why women are considered inferior to men. No one could point to a specific Buddhist text that suggests so. One young lama tells me women may have been considered inferior for one task and then the idea might have been accepted as a norm. Women were more powerful than men during certain times of our history, he tells me. Maybe sometime in the future women will be more prominent again, he says.

A nomad believed he could give me a reason for the privileges afforded to men. He said that a long time ago while Guru Padmasambhava, the great Indian master, was traveling through Tibet he was invited into a humble farmer's house and asked to bless the family. Guru Rinpoche stepped into the main room and performed a blessing. The farmer's wife was hiding behind the door and missed the blessing. That is why women are inferior, the nomad said.

Inferior, or unlucky at that particular moment, I asked.

It amounts to the same thing. To miss a blessing from Guru Rinpoche is a great misfortune.

As an afterthought, he said it was karma.

I asked him if he tells his daughters they are inferior.

He thought for a while and said he teaches them there are some things that do not change.

Like what?

He teaches them not to walk on sacred hills and not to harm living beings.

In the old days women did not dance; it was the men who danced to the songs their women sang. In the old days a gong would sound at dusk and all women in the precincts of monasteries would leave. I recognize this was necessary to keep the sanctity of the monastery and to keep the monks from breaking their vows of celibacy.

Tenzin often has answers to everything, so I ask him if he has any thoughts on why the deities of the land are so repulsed by women. Why did they take offense when women danced or when unknown women entered the area where they were said to live? Tenzin answers my question with a silent shrug.

Earlier in the month, Tashi and I had stopped at a monastery to see a lama. The lama had been in retreat, but when he heard we were visiting he had stepped out to see us. He had invited us into the area typically forbidden to those not in retreat, and naturally, to women. Tashi and I had thanked him and asked if we could instead sit out on the roof to talk to him. A short burst of showers had interrupted our talk. The lama had packed our bags, instructed a monk to bring incense, and after reciting prayers, he insisted we follow him into the retreat hall. I do not like rules broken for me and had apologized to the lama, but I had not wanted to offend him either by protesting too much. A group of ten monks with long hair and long nails—they were still halfway into their three-year retreat—had quietly observed our entry. One monk had presented me with a hundred yuan; my mother had helped him years ago when he had visited her in Kathmandu. We sat there while the lama ran in and out looking for food to feed us. I had found it difficult to bear the burden of his generosity. The monks displayed no signs of weariness for having their routine disturbed. Every now and then the lama came over to me and held my palm against his cheek. He had known my mother well.

He confessed he had not seen many people apart from the monks in retreat. He was not well, he explained. He returned with a bag of dried cheese and a bag of sheepskin for me. "It is all I have to offer."

I narrate this incident to Tenzin. I have slept in monasteries in Dhompa and I have entered the sacred room of retreatants. What negative impact would this have on my karma?

"You are a member of the Dhompa family. You can go anywhere. The lama and the chief are different from other people," he responds.

I remark I am a woman.

He says I am of good bone.

I ask why my blood or bone, as it is called here, would make me different from other women.

He says because that is how it is.

It is not fair. I remind him that the time of the chieftains is over.

He thinks I ask too many questions. He says faith demands agility in surrendering one's cynicism and fear. He says some things don't make sense but they are what they are.

I do not understand but sense that such an understanding is not relevant to him. Tradition is. I am living a contradiction. I am not the Tibetan woman his sisters and nieces are—unattached past the age of thirty, a writer in a community where not one among the hundreds of ancient texts he reads is attributed to a woman; these deviations from the norm are ignored because I am my mother's daughter and I am Thutop Gombo Dhompa's granddaughter.

In the nomadic community of Dhompa, I am often the only woman besides Tashi sitting with the lamas and asking questions to the men. This is accepted because I am an outsider and because my mother and my grandmother were also not unlike me. But even for the two women, recognition had come with age and marriage. A "better" birth had not protected my mother from being coerced into marriage at the age of seventeen. She had been given no choice in denying her people their wish when it was announced that she was to marry the son of her father's foe to keep peace between the two clans. As a daughter it had been her duty to follow her parent's wishes.

I tell Tenzin that just as he cannot view me as a traditional Tibetan woman, I am not seen as an American in America. I tell him I was faulted by a boss at a nonprofit organization for not being "proactive" and asking questions. I was made to feel I was in bondage to tradition because I was not free from cultural ties and obligations. An assimilated Asian American, I am not. I tell him of my misery at work on days when my boss was cruel to me.

"How could anyone mistreat you? Don't they know who you are?" he asks in surprise.

His guilelessness makes me smile. I tell him I am just another exile in the United States.

Tenzin does not provide answers for my life outside Tibet. He tells me Buddhism is what he knows and believes in. There is no reason for people to mistreat another human being, he says. He slips into a time when he was young and would follow my mother into the barn where they would steal the horses belonging to guests. My mother's friend who is called upon to build monasteries from wood and stones has tears in his eyes remembering the days when he rode unfettered in fields now in our view.

He has hot water ready for me each morning when I walk down the steps of the main house toward the kitchen. He warms the milk while I brush my teeth. He is not like this with his sister or his wife, of that I am certain. To my own surprise, some of the most tender gestures I have experienced come from Tibetan men like Tenzin, Dorje, and the men in my family who are otherwise brusque. I have not observed them reciprocate the small gestures their sisters and wives make toward them every day—cleaning their shoes for them, preparing their breakfast, replenishing their mugs with hot water—yet they show great consideration toward me.

I also observe that although the young women in my family are strong and independent, they readily take the role of caretaker when the extended family gathers together. They often defer to the men when asked questions. The men order daughters, sisters, and wives to tend to them. I realize it comes easily to me, too, as it does to my female relatives, to take care of others regardless of whether the person is a man or a woman. And it must be said that it is largely women who do the housework even while working full-time.

There are codes of behavior I follow instinctively when dealing with those of the opposite sex. In the company of men not related by blood, my female relatives launch into raunchy jokes. The stories they tell of the inhabitants of the town makes it seem as though every street has become an eye. Mothers are often the most lewd, because they consider themselves mothers and therefore in some way above reproach and shame. However, when it comes to men from our own family, we are deferential or shy to enter into any form of conversation that broaches sex.

It took me a while to realize it was discomfort and not lack of interest that made a cousin brother leave the room every time I mentioned men. In Kyegu, he scurried out of the room when a man and a woman made a gesture toward each other on the television screen. I asked his wife why he bolted each time the couples on screen moved toward each other. She explained he was a traditional man. He was not comfortable watching a love scene or talking about amorous relations with a female family member. It is through wives and daughters that my male relatives enter my personal life.

The women beseech me not to marry a "foreigner." They ask: How will the family in Tibet speak with him? How will the foreigner understand who you are and what your family history is? What will your children become? How will the man know how to care for you? A cousin advises me to have a child. She tells me she will be retiring in a year and she will have nothing to occupy her time. "I am going to tell myself that next year I will have your baby to care for, it will keep me excited," she tells me. I am yet to find the man to father a child, I say. She is certain there is a man; I just have to accept him. I tell her I will do my best and she is appeased. I am keenly aware of considering my own happiness when I am in Tibet because my family wishes for it deeply. They say they cannot keep their anxieties at bay when they think of me living all alone and so far away.

"A human being is not meant to live alone. Unless of course, you are a nun," they tell me.

I am referred to as a "child." I realize it has to do with my marital status. Having a husband and being a mother are signs of maturity. We are captured in samsara once we are embroiled with another. We are unerringly on the path of suffering, and of joy.

It is this suffering my mother tried to warn me of while I was young and it this suffering Tashi tries to acquaint me to while I am with her. She tells me life will present many more sorrows, as though by warning me all misfortunes will be recognizable and easier to accept. She tells me a child and a husband will bring me comfort in my old age.

An unkind husband or a difficult child might bring me more anguish, I remind her.

She had not considered that possibility.

I am happy in my solitude for now, I explain to her.

She has seven children and countless grandchildren and yet loneliness still finds her. When she was young she was happy, but she didn't realize she was happy because even then there was something or the other that interrupted the happiness. Now she looks back and can see how good those times were. She has lived through several skins. While telling me stories of her past she alternates between tears and laughter.

"People say you can die of unhappiness and of heartbreak, but you do not die," she tells me often. "You do not die even if you wish for it."

Of happiness and of the past, we speak often. I tell her I have lost my mother; everything else is easier to live through. The worst is over, I tell her.

"There is," she says, "always something more to lose. It is a woman's way. We are made to suffer."

These are words spoken by one who has survived many hardships. I wonder if she takes any credit for her strength or if she gives it all to fate and gender.

CHAPTER TWELVE

Miracles of the West

A little girl collects wildflowers in a field called Lha Cham Sa ("where the gods dance"), named appropriately for its spread of colors. The boy with her, probably her brother, points to a bell-shaped yellow flower and announces it is poisonous. She contests its use as panacea for headaches. They argue over its name. Valerian, elephant's head, bistort, and aster grow around their ankles and brush against the ends of their trousers, with their own Tibetan names, their own purposes. The achingly small pink flowers, a favorite food of lambs, is especially abundant here. It crushes easily under my shoes. My mother's paradise is faultless in its summer splendor.

I spend afternoons with visitors who knew my mother, or my grandfather, or who come to see me because they are passing through. Rarely do they introduce themselves to me. If Tashi is beside me, I beg her in a low voice or a nudge to explain who the visitors are. If she is absent, I mask my ignorance with questions hoping that in the course of our conversation their identity will be revealed to me. I ask if their family is well, if they were able to collect fungus this summer, if their lama (if they are monks) is well. I wait to discover them as they unravel with their answers.

Quite often people come with specific questions: Might I happen to have news of a certain person who left six years ago and now resides in Nepal or India? A first name or a family name is offered and they are not able to give me the name of the town or city the person lives in. They are surprised when I do not have an answer. They know everyone who lives here. Elders ask if I can diagnose a sickness. They trust I know the answers to many questions, at the very least those pertaining to the body.

I tell them I do not know of diseases and their cures.

They ask me if I know other things: for instance, how to fix a solar panel or radio?

I explain to them I do not know much of anything.

They want to know what school of knowledge I carry in me. They have heard I spent many years studying.

I write, I say sheepishly, feeling the inadequacy of the answer as the words leave my mouth.

A visitor remarks the United States must be very powerful to be able to stay in darkness when Tibetans are eating and walking in sunlight. He is young and the question is posed timidly.

I open my mouth to run down the names of the planets and the positions of the sun and the moon and the movement of the earth, and manage to stop myself from doing so. I imagine him telling his mother it is night in the United States while she stirs milk in the midmorning light.

How do they make that happen, she asks.

It is America. They can do anything, he explains.

I can tell him that Americans fly when they don't want to walk and he will believe me. The real and the unreal have permeable borders. Almost all nomads here have grown up with tales of lamas who covered the distance from Lhasa to Dhompa in an hour and whose bodies deliquesced into air to become a rainbow at their death.

Tenzin tells me of the powers of the lamas and monks in his monastery of Lachengonpa, where for decades they have astonished worshippers at special rituals. Most recently, symbols of the prayer OM MANI PADME HUNG floated in the air while the monks recited their prayers. It was as though the words had turned into matter right before their eyes, he says. There are people who witnessed this feat, he assures me on seeing my quizzical look. Then last year, he hastens to add, when the monks were at prayer to make the *mendup*—the sour blessings compounded of many medicinal herbs—that lamas give to people, the *mendup* transformed into small molds of the deity Tara.

Years ago, Tenzin says—and we could fall into a long debate on the exact year by calculating the reincarnations of lamas and adding up their years, but he is stricken by horror and malaise at the task so we settle for the concept of amassed years . . . so therefore, years ago, he says—when the monastery's prayer hall was being built the head lama did not have the funds to purchase gold for the wall murals.

What did they do then?

The lama was famous for his clairvoyance, Tenzin says. One night the protector of the region, a deity who lived in the river nearby, appeared in the lama's dream and instructed him to send a monk to the riverbank. The lama summoned a monk in the morning and asked him to go to the river and search for unusual objects along the riverbed. The monk walked along the river and saw a dead fish on the shore. He returned to the lama and told him there was nothing but a dead fish. The lama sent him back and the monk looked everywhere but found nothing. He returned to the lama with the same answer. The lama then asked for the fish to be brought to him. The monk picked up the small fish from the sand and walked toward the monastery. As he drew closer to the monastery the fish got heavier and heavier until the monk's strength could only afford to drag it. He dropped the fish at the feet of the lama in befuddlement. The lama opened the belly of the fish to behold slabs of gold. This is the same gold that covers the face of one of the deities painted on the walls of the inner shrines of the monastery, Tenzin tells me. Such a preposterous story, but one, I must admit, I find quite plausible.

That painting is held to be the only mural in Dhompa to have survived the Cultural Revolution. The monks were clever enough to disguise the paintings under a coat of mud before the Chinese soldiers stormed into the monastery. The soldiers used the monastery as their base and the prayer hall became a storage room so it was spared total destruction. Decades later when monks began returning to the monastery they washed the mud away. Specks of gold now flash from the wall as though fireflies are playing hide-and-seek. This is the gold that came from the belly of a fish.

The nomads seek to establish a common ground with unknown lands. Amrika. Nepol. They say the names slowly and carefully as though the land will cease to exist if they throw the words out carelessly from their lips. Katchamanadu. The name falls out like a pebble. What must this Amrika be? They would like me to show them this strange country with people wearing eyes of the sky and hair of autumn grass.

I tell the nomads of the microwave that warms food up within minutes, of email, of phones and GPS systems that tell you where you are and how you can get to your destination.

A young man flashes his mobile phone at me. There is no coverage in Dhompa but he makes use of his phone when he goes to Nangchen. The elders who have not been to Nangchen or Kyegu are fascinated. Who is this creature who lives in the gadgets and knows everything? An elder asks if people with blue eyes can see as well as those of us with black eyes. Do Americans have yaks? Do they believe in Buddha? Do they eat yogurt? Do they speak Tibetan?

Each response is a validation of how the United States cannot be as wonderful or as devastating as their own land. I struggle to explain the everyday to them and find my life is circumscribed by speech. Our lives are so different! I do not have words in my dialect for the ordinary: How do I speak of a donut or coffee? If I were to describe a round sweet bread with a hole in the middle, they might ask what the hole is meant for. I cannot explain how the Internet works because they live without electricity and many have never set eyes on a computer.

I wake up early in the morning and work all day, I explain. This, they understand. I am relieved they do not follow up with more questions. How would I explain the work I do? I do not have names for the subway train, elevator . . . and what of the photocopier, the three-hole punch, and the stapler?

Most often it is men who gather around Tashi and me when we go to a monastery or to a public place. I feel their eyes fall on me like windows over a crowded street. Young men stand with their hips pushed forward in a careless pose, and when they move they do so with a swagger. They are careful to mask their age but their quickness to laugh at small pranks gives them away. Their cheeks are the color of coffee. Their haircuts are fanciful. I suspect they were shorn with blunt scissors or with knives. They look like the original punks. Their hands are cracked, their nails full of dust and dirt. To clean them would be to defeat the purpose of living in such a place I suppose. They keep the nail to the little finger long so they can dig their ears and their nose, and have a tool should they be in need.

Sometimes I move my shoulders as though to shrug their gaze off. They talk about me in front of me. They turn to each other and say, "She speaks the dialect. She wears pants like a Chinese woman." When they have a question for me, they turn to address

Tashi: What does she do? How old is she? How much is her monthly salary?

I resist the impulse to silence my aunt and answer the questions myself, but it is a relief not to have to introduce or explain myself. Tashi says something as simple as, "She likes our milk and tsampa," and they turn to me and nod with pleasure as though I have achieved something remarkable. Yes, of course, they say. She is a Dhompa. They say my mother was no ordinary woman.

Over and over, the connection is made to the past and to the achievements of parents and grandparents. The elders say I resemble my mother and speak with her voice. My hair is black and straight. I am brown like them. Very often they tell me about my mother as though I am yet to meet her. One man tells me my mother was notable and wise. He talks as though it is his responsibility to introduce her to me.

Do you know how great and good she was?

Yes, I do, I tell him. I ask if he knew her.

He says he remembers her from his youth. He spoke at length with her when she visited Dhompa.

Do you think you can be better than her?

I tell him I cannot be better than her.

"Yes, that is true," he says thoughtfully. "You cannot be better than her but you are her daughter."

The nomads count the number of people from Dhompa who have escaped to India or Nepal. They say there are three men from Dhompa who live in New York. They ask if I have seen them. One of them calls me every so often to tell me where he is and how he is doing, I tell them. He asks if I need anything. He says the markets in New York are so full of things and he will be happy to send me something.

The young and old know the names of the places in Nepal and India they would like to visit on pilgrimage: Lumbini, where the Buddha was born; Bodh Gaya, where the Buddha was enlightened; Sarnath, where the Buddha gave his first sermon; and Dharamshala, where the Dalai Lama and the Karmapa live. India is the holy land. They dream of a pilgrimage and for their eyes to fall on the blessing that is Gyalwa Rinpoche's face. A monk asks if I have a leaf from the Bodhi tree under which the Buddha discovered the four noble truths of life.

I describe how the tree spreads its limbs out like a giant octopus. Monks meditate below it and every now and then leaves fall into the laps of people sitting beneath the tree. The nomads laugh at the wonder of the whole thing. Imagine sitting where the Buddha once meditated!

A young monk tells me a scarf fell off the statue of Jowo Shakyamuni and landed on his neck when he was praying in the holy Jokhang temple in Lhasa. He presented the scarf to his mother. The nomads around us speak of their dream of seeing the face of Jowo once before they die.

I explain the schism of exhilaration and despair in me when I am in Lhasa. I cannot bear to see the Chinese soldiers at every corner of the city, I explain.

The monk understands. Last year a friend was arrested in Lhasa simply for being a khampa monk. He says the Chinese arrested all pilgrims from Kham.

No surface in Lhasa feels safe to me, I continue. I sense a slight rigidity to every physical form. Perhaps it is the presence of soldiers around the city that makes me perceive this gravity. Perhaps it is my expectation that it be so. A despondency rises in me when I am in Lhasa.

I think of the concrete street stretching all the way from the Potala to the Jokhang. All along the main streets there are beauty salons, karaoke bars, and clothing stores run by young Chinese women who have come to save money so some time in the future they can return to the places they call home and to a better life amongst their own. At night the streets are lit by pulsating bright electric signs. Music clogs the air. I describe the Potala, the winter palace of the Dalai Lama, and how it comes into view from many streets and rooftops. It has an inexpressible becalming influence on me. When I feel forlorn among the new, shiny buildings of the city I look for the Potala and fasten my eyes on it. I tell them how the ruins of monasteries like Ganden and Sera carry a medieval melancholia distracting less-informed tourists into feeling like they are looking at natural ruins and not orchestrated cultural destruction.

The elders say they would like to have their eyes fall just once on the Potala. They would like to prostrate at the Potala and the Jokhang. Then they will be happy to die.

I tell them I love Dhompa best. When I am here, I imagine I am looking into my mother's childhood, even as I understand the place has changed. The nomads in Dhompa live on the land they were born in and they follow the ways of those who came before them. They believe everything is impermanent, even the calm that settles momentarily on their grasslands. They are most at home with their animals and in the mountains. One young man tells me his feet hurt when he walks on the concrete streets of Kyegu or Nangchen. He says he can walk all day in the mountains and this pain does not visit him. He does not feel at home in Kyegu. People make him feel ignorant. I understood what he said. Family and friends in Kyegu have told me they have no trouble identifying the nomads in town: the jauntiness with which they saunter about in the marketplace with their left hand out of the jacket sleeve that is left flapping at the side like a ladies' purse; the oddly pronounced Chinese word forced here and there in sentences; the sweaters that hang limply on their shoulders; the gold capping on their tooth; the crimson stains on the cheeks of women.

In towns, the nomads remain outsiders for a while. They become a class divorced from their occupation as herders. They are called *drokpa* in an undertone that indicates an unsophisticated, uneducated person, a person still in progress. In their own villages they are known to everyone for their horsemanship, their ability to round cattle, their weaving skills, for being a good child to their parents, or simply for their ability to make good yogurt and dried cheese.

A part-time monk, who is on his way to see his sister's family in Bagsikha, says more than anything he would like to go to India, but he already has too many problems to deal with. The monk explains how he moves like a ghost between his two lives of being a family man and a monk. He tells me he did not intend to marry and have a family but he was forced to leave the monastery as a teenager when the Chinese army destroyed it. He worked in a labor camp for many years and when he returned to Dhompa the monastery was still shut. In the 1980s the monastery was permitted to engage in a few traditional rituals and he rejoined as a monk. He lives with his wife and children in a tent all summer and in a house close to the monastery during the winter. It is the best he can do to honor his duty to both his family and his teacher, he says.

The practice of allowing men to be monks and family men at the same time is specific to a few monasteries in Dhompa. It was the only way of accommodating monks who had faced a situation that led them to give up their robes. Here in this small nomadic community a concession has been made by an established religious order to adapt to the circumstances of its people. Present-day monks are not granted this special lifestyle and they are expected to adhere to a celibate life like the monks who live in exile. If they should break their vow they must give up their robes and leave the monastery.

Our visitor tells a tale of sorrow involving the women in his life. His eldest daughter had been very sick five years ago and has never been the same again. She was in bed for months while he cared for her. Her face, he says, aged before his eyes. His own grief rests in his eyes. He says he has tried everything. He took her to traditional doctors and lamas but nothing worked. Even as he studied about impermanence as a monk, as a father, death was not an option.

Across from him one of our guests uproots the hair from his nostrils with his fingers; he is casual and so insistent in his task.

The monk continues with his story. His second daughter has been ruined by love. At the age of sixteen she ran away to Lhasa with a married man from a neighboring nomadic village. As though to lessen the impact of her foolhardiness, and to cover his shame, he names all the other young women who eloped or returned home pregnant and alone. He thinks it is not love that makes them run away, it is the fear of work and a desire to escape the monotony of tending to animals and grass. The young, he says, confuse desire with love, and they end up hurting everyone around them. They do not understand cause and effect. This monk who is a father cannot bear to think of his daughter's suffering. He never liked the man of his daughter's choice but because of his own love for her and his exceeding fears for her well-being, he had begged them to return home. Now, two years later, the daughter and her little child live with him and his wife. The young man abandoned his daughter without offering a penny toward the baby's future. The monk says in the old days, the young father would have had to give his daughter at least one horse and one female yak capable of giving milk for the infant.

"Old parents are looking after their children and grandchildren. It should not be this way," he says. "It is the young who should be taking care of the old."

His face wears the blows delivered by life. Half his pain lies in what he omits from his story; the other half sits on his face with a tenebrous weight. I am struck by the thought that we live the life we have and then that of those we love, so that at all times we are aware of either existing suffering or imminent suffering. Even in these far-away mountains, despair is still despair.

Our nose-picking guest nods his head and proceeds to pluck out hair from his chin. His lower lip is tucked under his teeth to tighten the area. He plucks with great precision. He pauses his grooming to announce that he has just purchased a metal butter churner and a solar panel. The monk's face lights up and he enters into a eulogy on the benefits of electricity. For five years he has used solar panels and still delights in calling light from a mere flick of fingers. Now, he says, he can continue living his diurnal life, even when it becomes night. For a few minutes all of us forget our small despairs. A dogged forgetfulness we Tibetans are so blessed with.

"It is a miracle, these glasses with eyes," he says.

Our part-time monk is reminded of his duty. He would like to reach his destination before nightfall. If he were young he'd have ridden a motorbike and made the journey in less than half the time it takes on his horse, he says. I escort him to the wooden gate where his horse is tied. He walks ahead of me and without warning adroitly lifts his robes and begins urinating. He continues conversing with me, turning his head back to look at me even as

I shuffle and lean away from his gaze. I am not sure how to handle this scene before me of a man—and more specifically, a monk—pissing as he talks to me. He does not squat as monks typically do. His ankles gleam white as the flour that comes from China. His robes flop around his knees. He continues to talk. After a while, I lose my discomfort.

Tashi is unperturbed when she walks up beside me to find him urinating. "I am getting old," she says.

He agrees. He is too.

Tashi sits down to rest a few steps from him. This short walk to the gate has exhausted her knees. Robes now safely covering his legs, the monk turns to free his horse. He says something to soothe my aunt as we say goodbye. We watch him take the path down the hill.

So much happens in a quiet land. Even without phones, email, and a postal service, and even though distances are far on foot and horseback, everyone knows everything. Some have heard I work in a telegraph office, some have heard I fix airplanes for a living, and that I work for a radio station. I do not know how they come to such conclusions.

Two representatives from an elected body governing the cluster of villages in Dhompa ask if I can help them acquire funds to bring electricity for the school, the monastery, and the community living in the vicinity. They say there is a dip in the river Kyichu where the force of the water is mighty. They have heard of a monastery, far, far up in the mountains of western Nangchen, that has been able to generate electricity from a river. I tell them I know nothing of hydroelectricity. They say perhaps one of them could visit the monastery and learn how it is done. As they discuss, they keep enlarging their area of demand so that by the end of the conversation they have moved from speaking of two or three regions to covering almost the whole of Dhompa in light. I tell them it would take a government to bring electricity to the whole of Dhompa. I do not have the knowledge to help them nor the finances. I feel useless and helpless against their needs.

In San Francisco I live alone, I work full-time, and I pursue my writing after work; my life is contained and predictable. Since the age of twenty-four I have taken care of myself and it has made me insular, solitary, and more attentive to my needs. More selfish is how a Tibetan might describe it. In Dhompa I am nudged into seeing myself simply as my mother's daughter and the niece of the Dhompa family; everything else I may have accomplished pales beside this fact. Rarely am I addressed here by my given name. The nomads assume it is natural I listen to their needs and they expect me to help them.

For now, I am accepted even though they know I am ill-equipped to do what they can do. My years of education are inadequate to support me here. Not one person can read what I scribble into my notebook. I cannot milk the female yak; I cannot make butter or hear the faint shuffle of cattle at night and read their intention to wander away. I do not assume all nomads are happy with their lives; some of them probably dream of another lifestyle. I think of my friends far away in the West whose lives are haunted by fear. In Dhompa, we observe daily the sky, the approaching winter, the river, the mountains, and the temperamental deities that exist all around us. It is as though I am living my mother's past and my own present simultaneously.

On my walks I come across men sleeping beside the river with half their bodies in shade and the other half in the sun. I expect them to be young boys from the way their bodies recline languorously in the meadow and the carefree ease with which they twirl blades of grass in their mouths, but most often these are grown men. They appear to be neither in the present time nor entirely of my imagination. When I see them this way I am not sure what they represent to me, but I sense I have already created a scene of a carefree pastoral idyll that may not complement the reality of their lives.

Men wear hand-stitched yak leather boots. They line the soles of the traditional boots with rubber. It is an odd but accepted coexistence of the old and the new. They do not worry over the incongruity in appearance. A few wear their hair long and in braids around their heads.

Glass windows have arrived in the one shop in Dhompa. Young men wear suits and though they are ill-fitting and almost certain to be in shades of blue, the suits make them walk with a song in their gait. They kick up dust with their heels so that a ring encircles the ankles of their trousers. A suit is a statement of style, and of money. A suit proclaims the man has tasted a life other than that of the mountains, the rivers, outside their herds. A suit is part of the world they will inevitably meet.

CHAPTER THIRTEEN

Faith

Magpies appear in autumn. The white of their feathers contrasts sharply against the black, and my errant imagination sees them as penguins or crows. It is possible they have been present all summer long and were overlooked because my attention has been monopolized by the mountains, the yaks, the grotesque contortions of juniper, and the flower-decked hills. It is not just me though—those who belong here are equally besotted. The nomads in Dhompa love Ghoye Ruma, the sacred mountain of Dhompa, the best. Ghoye is man, he is mountain, and sometimes he is wolf. He has the archetypical build of my childhood drawings of a mountain, a broad base that tapers to form a slightly unhandsome pyramid. As god of the locale, or *yul lha*, Ghoye has many responsibilities: he is deity, warrior god, pillar of the sky, peg of the earth. He provides the people of Dhompa an ancestry and an identity that roots them in this particular land.

Ghoye is a warrior. He is crimson in complexion, his left incisor protrudes midway to his chin, his lips purse downward in an angry pout, and he wears an expression that in the mildest terms is of infuriation. His hair—a huge halo of red dreadlocks—is knotted at the back of his nape in a big bun. He wears a red brocade coat and carries three weapons on him: a knife, a spear, and a bow. In his left hand he drags a naked man by his head in a noose. Ghoye comes with a retinue of red birds, red dogs, and red wolves.

Black clouds hang above him, a panoply of deafening thunder, lightning, and hail.

I can describe him with such certainty and specificity thanks to his portrayal in three different songs of praise and supplication written by lamas over the years. The first prayer was written seventy to eighty years ago by Tenzin Rapgay, a lama from Lachen monastery, after Ghoye appeared to him when he was returning from a pilgrimage to western Tibet. Tenzin Rapgay's vision matched that of two other lamas of Dhompa and they collaborated to compile a meticulous profile of Ghoye that was delineated by artists.

People of Dhompa speak of Ghoye as ubiquitous. They point to his favorite spots as though they have seen him and personally know his proclivities. He likes to feed on meat and he enjoys the taste of blood. He is believed to frequent the fields behind our family home because he likes to tie his horse to a particular juniper tree. A young boy told me a woman had been jettisoned off the tree while attempting to cut off one of the branches. He said he has heard from the elders that the woman went rolling down the hill like a pebble. Older nomads point to a deep stain visible along the ridges of mountains neighboring Ghoye, and say it is a path Ghoye travels to reach his consort, a broad-bosomed, rust-hued mountain in Bongba; it is the same region that welcomed my mother as a bride to their chief. Ghoye's bride is said to come from Kawa Karpo, a sacred mountain in Dechen in the Yunnan prefecture, and to allay her homesickness she grows on her summit stubby shrubs, native to her home and foreign to this part of eastern Tibet.

Ghoye's greatness, secured in songs and prayers, makes us great. Elders in Dhompa know for instance that it was Ghoye who surprised the great lama Tenzin Rapgay en route from a year-long

trip to Kailash in western Tibet. The lama, at first not recogniz-
ing the bedraggled stranger who asked if all was well, realized as
soon as he left that Ghoye had come to check on him. The following morning, the story continues, Ghoye appeared to a nomad
in Dhompa. The nomad, judging Ghoye to be a pilgrim, asked
him where he was journeying from. Ghoye told the nomad he was
coming from Ngari. The nomad inquired whether he had seen or
heard of their lama Tenzin Rapgay in Ngari. Ghoye replied he had
indeed met the lama the previous day and that the lama would
arrive in a few months. After Ghoye left, the nomad pondered the
stranger's words and realized there were only a few beings, Ghoye
among them, who could make the long journey from Ngari in a
matter of hours.

Tenzin says Ghoye is a benevolent parent who watches over his
people. He tells me it is Ghoye who was seen covering my mother
in a veil when she left Dhompa. It is he who kept her alive on her
long journey to exile.

Does Ghoye watch over me when I am far away?

Indeed, he says. Ghoye watches over all the people from
Dhompa, wherever they are.

Eleven years ago, an elder told people he saw in his dream deities
racing in the fields near Bir Sakya monastery. He noticed some
were on horses while others were on motorbikes. The deities on
motorbikes sped past those on horses. The elder was very upset
and warned his friends that in the near future horses would be
sent to graze high in the mountains and nomads would ride
motorbikes. Younger herders ridiculed him. This was a time when
horses were prized all over Tibet; nobody imagined they would
give up riding. Now, as men replace their horses with motorbikes,

people narrate the elder's dream to each other and say the old man was right. The horses blissfully graze on high pastures, let off from all labor and responsibility.

Powerful deities, for all their strength, are very much like humans. They are subject to periods of despair and are not free from the crippling consequences of emotions. For over two decades Tibetans were forbidden from holding any religious ceremonies or prayers. No prayer flags, incense, or ceremonies were offered to the deities and demigods of the region. This neglect broke their hearts and they became bedraggled and weak.

In recent years, monasteries all over Kham have again begun honoring the local deities with traditional annual ceremonies comprising elaborate rituals and offerings of new dresses (prayer flags), music, incense, and sumptuous feasts. The lamas and monks thank the deities for taking care of the people and ask for their constant and continued guardianship. They also make offerings so that all human assaults against the land, past and present, are forgiven. The ritual mollifies the deities and helps them feel attractive and powerful, Tenzin says, and the land and its people are once again happy. Such rituals linking man and nature are a feature of Tibetan religious life indicative of the belief that both the natural world and humans are psychological and moral beings dependent on each other for their survival.

Tibetans know their regional and local deities and they also know the names and locations of famous national *neris*—permanent or temporary abodes of deities—such as Khang Rinpoche in western Tibet, and Kawa Karpo and Amye Machen in eastern Tibet. There is a difference in the believer's relationship to and expectation from the two categories of deities. For instance, the nomads of Dhompa feel more familial toward Ghoye and look to him for daily succor while they view the *neris* as dream destinations from which they can accumulate merit for themselves or for others. (You can dedicate your merit to someone else who cannot make a kora.) The people of Dhompa pray to Ghoye every day—however, they do not necessarily make a kora around him.

Ghoye is just and benevolent, my guide Dorje says, for did he not sacrifice the two most elegant mountains of the region for the stability of the land and the safety of the beasts? Speaking as though he were a witness to a great historical battle, Dorje says that a tall and stately mountain, the Palace of Glass, and his neighbor, the Mountain of Pearls, did not get along. Had one of them been plain they might have loved each other like siblings, he reasons. Day by day, their animosity toward each other grew until the air around them was also corrupted. Fearing a war, Ghoye summoned the two mountains to his residence and attempted to make peace between them but they would not stop their bickering. Exasperated, Ghoye struck the glass mountain and shattered him to pieces. When Dorje finds shards of crystal on the ground he shows them to me as evidence of the once-resplendent Palace of Glass and repeats the story.

"There's the doctor," Dorje says pointing to a slender mountain. "And next to him is his mother." He advises me to look at mountains as humans, for like us they are subject to anger, jealousy, and sadness, and they are just as easily appeased with gifts and praise. He has stories of sacred mountains that roamed the land in the guise of handsome men and impregnated women herders. Their offspring were recognized as being of divine origin because they were tall, handsome, and superior to all others. Their sons sent many Chinese soldiers to their deaths in 1959, he tells me.

I wonder out loud about the ratio of male and female mountains in Dhompa. Dorje does not know the answer. I have heard that in places where there are more male deities, the men are strong and fearless, and in places where the mountains are gently sloped and filled with female deities, the women of the land are beautiful and gracious.

The hills we walk on must be young girls for they are white with the thick growth of bistorts who nod good-naturedly in the wind. I know them because they were my mother's favorite flowers and every summer she would long to see them. I grew to love the flower for her sake and on seeing it, for its own.

"It is the *tsi metok*," Dorje says. It is built like a bottlebrush. He tells me its root can be roasted, ground into flour, and made into flat bread. He has not tasted it for a long time, now that white flour is plentiful. He digs one flower out of the ground, cleans it up, and reveals a root half the size of my pinkie finger. He drops the plant in his pocket and says although it is too little to be of any use it is a perfect gift for Tashi.

It will remind her of the old days, he says.

The flowers stir up Dorje's memories. He says people died a hand's breadth away from plants they could have eaten. Chinese soldiers struck starving women and men who were caught reaching for the *tsi* flower during the famine years. Dorje plucks wild garlic, two different varieties that grow here, and tells me we can add them to our noodle soup. He learned about plants from his father.

Here and there we come upon the blackened stones of an erstwhile stove—the residues of a summer home. Nomads build nothing else on the grasslands where they live all summer long. Sometimes we see one or two deer in the distance. Dorje recalls a time when the whole mountain was brown and red with deer. Now they too are gone. The juniper trees of this area were chopped for fuel by the Chinese army. It takes fifty years for some of them to grow to the height of my waist. On the other side of the hills facing us, nuns desperate for winter fuel have felled trees surrounding their nunnery, rendering a ragged view. I see hills covered in scabs. It will take another fifty years for the stumps to grow a few feet, if they ever do. The trees were so thick when Dorje was a boy that they hid the yaks grazing in them. It takes very long for the land to gather what it has lost, he says mournfully.

Dorje carries the land in his body. He remembers the rocks he played on and the trees he hid behind. He points to the mountains in front of us and says he can no longer see the big rock that sat on the shoulder of a particular ridge. He looked and looked the other day for the boulder but could not locate it. "It is gone," he says with sadness, as though stones are at will to relocate. He knows the treasures of the land: gold, silver, stone. He says lamas have known for decades of the precious metals buried in the soil. It is the duty of the people to keep the treasures inside the land. If we take them out, what will the deities wear?

Such a culture of beliefs does not build empires or evolve industrial nations. It does not even allow for the taking back of our country—not in the immediate future—but it has protected the mountains, the rivers, and the animals thus far. It comforts the elders and as long as they are alive, they apply it to avert injury or death to others. They protest against all forms of mining on their land, fish leap in rivers without fear of being caught, flies are plucked to safety from tea cups, rats roam freely, lizards multiply without shame, and stray dogs could form a colony of their own.

But this country we love is not ours to protect. Not too far from Tingsikha a group of Chinese men are performing tests on the soil in an area that has been cordoned off. The nomads don't know what is buried in the ground but they think it must be valuable because the Chinese are at the site day and night. A few elders had gone to question the local government representative to learn if it were indeed true that a mining company had been contacted to send agents to Dhompa. The nomads were reprimanded and told not to agitate. They were told the orders for the tests had come from "very far up" in the system and could not be contested. They were warned against protesting or asking questions. So the people watch silently, afraid of the changes that will befall them; they know nothing good follows any scrutiny of their land. They have only to recall the stories from Chumaleb and from other parts of Kham, where the Chinese forced the wealth out of the ground, and then left the land scorched, to know their fears are well grounded.

In Chumaleb, Dorje tells me, long stretches of land were mined for gold. Huge hills were blasted and plundered and none of the profits from the gold, estimated at 130 trillion yuan—the number varied from nomad to nomad—went to the people. The land has never been the same. There is no water—this in a region where the Yellow River begins—and people in the town of Chumaleb have to buy water by the bucket. The grass does not grow well anymore and the herds have shrunk.

The story is repeated by many nomads: a regional Tibetan officer in Chumaleb received orders from a supervising Chinese officer in Xining to give the mining rights to a Chinese business-man from Xining. Within a year, the men stole mountains of gold and made mountains of money, including the local Tibetan officer, while the animals and the people were left to drink muddy water for a decade.

Chumaleb is an ailing land. For generations, people of the region had known there was gold in the belly of their land, and they believed it to be an ornament and offering that kept their deities well and prosperous. It is no longer so. The deities of the land are naked without their jewelry and the region has lost its confidence and courage. Chumaleb is now one of the poorest counties in Yushu. The nomads of Dhompa relay this and similar stories to gird themselves against a similar fate should their land be dug up to make China prosperous.

I have always envied older Tibetans for their capacity for faith. They require no proof to believe in divinities and the spectral protectors of the land. In addition to sacred places and deities of the land, they place their faith in innumerable reincarnate lamas. My family members, even those of my age, consult with lamas when making decisions much like people might seek a consultant's expertise in the West. Business ventures are undertaken, marriages are forged, medical treatments are decided, travel dates are set—at the outcome of a lama's divination. Nothing deters their faith, not even when the decision proves to be unfortunate, as happens sometimes. I think many would gladly offer their last penny to their spiritual teacher.

Perhaps this belief in Buddhism comes from their experience of impermanence and suffering. Perhaps it comes from having lived in isolation from the rest of the world, where belief in external temporal powers is crucial in order to survive. With this faith comes an acceptance of all the adversaries in their lives and around them, an acceptance that seems all too remarkable, all too simple. What astounds me is that these beliefs survived two decades of Chinese reeducation programs meant to stultify and kill Buddhist thought and culture.

Lamas and Buddhist teachers have been able, in recent years, to reclaim their place in the community. Four lamas, of the twenty-two who resided in the eleven monasteries under the Dhompa chief's patronage, survived the Cultural Revolution. During my mother's first visit to Tibet, she took the names of all the lamas who had been killed in prison and whose monasteries were await-ing their reincarnates and she approached a senior lama in exile who was able to locate all of them. Now the people of Dhompa can go to the lamas to ask for names, to divert obstacles, and to bless their sick and dying.

I meet a few reincarnate young lamas at a prayer festival in the monastery. They have a lot to live up to, as their predecessors were much revered by the people. One young lama promises to stop by to visit Tashi before he returns to his monastery. A few days later we see him alight from his horse; we know our visitor is a lama from the conical shape of his yellow hat. Tashi and I walk toward him and bow our heads. Instead of putting his hand on our heads as blessing, the young lama takes his hat off and touches our bowed heads with his forehead.

The lama is reticent in front of his teacher but an attendant tells us later that the young lama has a quick sense of humor. From the age of six the lama has adhered to the rigid traditional cur-riculum and responsibilities of his lineage. He is also pressed to follow Chinese dictates, which stipulate, for example, that his enthronement can only be official when he is recognized by the Chinese government. A certificate from the Communist regime will authenticate his divinity. The people of the land believe in him and feel delight when they see him. When they look at his face they see his previous incarnation and the incarnations who preceded him.

He is gentle with a young girl who approaches him for his bless-ing. The girl bows her head when he blesses her. I am not sure how he really feels about these responsibilities but he performs these actions confidently, kindly, and with an air of resolution. As long as he remains in Dhompa, follows all the rules, and is apolitical, he will be able to practice his faith and teach his people.

A mother brings her one-year-old son to him. The baby has been crying all day; the mother is not sure what ails him. The young lama blows into the baby's face and recites a prayer.

"Perhaps you should take your baby to a doctor," I catch up to the mother. She nods with a smile.

I understand her nod conveys that she is content for now with the lama's blessing. The lama is her doctor as well as her spiritual teacher. She has inherited this aptitude for faith and because there is nobody here to contradict her, she is happy in her decision. The young mother cannot explain why she trusts the lama but she has no reason to disbelieve him. She believes him even if she cannot read or understand the Buddhist texts from which the lama quotes.

"I cannot have faith in lamas as these women do," I confide in Dorje.

He agrees it is not possible anymore to always remember and follow our beliefs. There was a time when nobody ate fish even when they were dying but now people who live in towns do eat fish for the pleasant taste of its flesh. Then, there was a time when people did not guard their grass so fiercely from each other, and there was a time when people left the fungus in the grass.

Dorje points at a small creature scurrying ahead of us into its hole and says even the pika is testing people's patience and faith. Pikas are related to rabbits and hares but are much smaller in build and have shorter ears. They are pests for they exist in such astonishing numbers here and have overturned the land with their burrowing. Not long ago, government officials offered poison to kill them. When nomads voiced their hesitation to kill on such a massive scale, the government offered money as incentive. Then the nomads left poison at the openings of the holes and they were pained to see the bodies of hundreds of pikas the next day. In some cases, a yak or a sheep got poisoned. Dorje says two pikas came for every one that was killed, and now there's an even greater population of them. He says the morning after a mass poison operation, surviving animals were seen peeping into the holes to check if other family members were alive. The survivors were lonely and sick. There is great sorrow in his voice as Dorje tells the story. "The pikas were like humans looking for their loved ones."

He believes the poison now lies in the grass and in the ground. How can that be good for people and for the cattle?

There were always pikas but never in such large numbers that they had to resort to killing them in this manner. The birds, the foxes, and other larger mammals ate them and the lamas prayed to keep the numbers low. Now there are too many of them and not even the lamas have any control over them. He believes nomads know they were wrong to kill the animals but there were so many of them; the nomads are wrong to dig the fungus but they are poor. He says it is hard to adhere to our customs when the strain of staying alive takes up so much energy.

I tell him about the time when my mother located three mice under the kitchen sink in our house in Kathmandu. She wrapped them in a towel and headed toward the neighboring fields. Twenty minutes later, she reappeared at the door with the mice. She had not been able to leave them in the fields to die. She had not been able to bear the thought of the mother's anguish on finding her babies gone. I rarely felt the pain of the cockroaches and would ask my mother if I could annihilate them. She would tell me to be patient: their lifespan was brief and besides, winter would take them.

One morning I had pressed my thumb into a mosquito. When I turned around, I saw my mother standing behind me with tears dribbling down her cheeks.

"How is it you feel nothing when you kill the insect?" she asked. I felt sad observing her sorrow.

The people take to heart the suffering that marks the living beings around them, but they are also quick to embrace customs and fads that contradict their Buddhist beliefs. Some years ago, many people in Kyegu and Nangchen paid dearly to decorate their chuba with a strip of tiger, leopard, or otter skin to wear at public festivals. The fur trade flourished as families traded in their savings to ensure at least one member in the family would have such a dress. But just as quickly as they embraced the trend, they were inspired to abandon it, upon hearing the Dalai Lama advise Tibetans to refrain from buying, using, or selling animal parts as ornamentation during his address to devotees at the Kalachakra blessing in January 2006 in India. His Holiness said he was ashamed when he saw pictures of Tibetans wearing skin and fur. Within days of his talk, there were photographs on the Internet of Tibetans inside Tibet setting ablaze in public their valuable chubas.

For decades Indian, Chinese, and international animal rights activists have been working to stop the trafficking of fur and animal skin. All it took was one appeal from the Dalai Lama to cripple the business in Tibet. This was a reminder to the Chinese that for Tibetans, devotion to His Holiness still precedes everything material. It was also a powerful example to me of how Tibetans inside Tibet feel about their lamas and how quickly they are able to reverse their actions and desires to accommodate their faith.

Over the summer I attend several festivals in Nangchen, Chumaleb, and Kyegu and in all these regions there were but a handful of people wearing clothing lined with fur. These were officials, who, people were quick to point out, were under duress to wear them. Most families, mine included, had simply packed away these clothes. They lie in suitcases, wrapped in naphthalene balls, inching toward ruination. My cousins say they will not wear their fur and some have sold their dresses at a big loss to traders who buy them in hope that there will be a time in the future when fur will be fashionable again. If the young betray any inclination toward stepping out in their fur clothes—after all, they have paid a lot to have them—the elders intervene to stop them.

The elders are the sentinels of place and tradition. In Dhompa they are often found sitting in a row a few feet from the entrance to the monastery. They look like they have dug their way out of a sandstorm. Their hair is matted and their faces tanned to a brown-purple tint. They sit still amidst a flurry of movements with prayer wheels in their right hand and prayer beads in their left. Even from a distance, I see their lips form the prayers OM MANI PADME HUNG or OM AH HUNG BENZA GURU PEMA SIDDHI HUNG.

The elders see everyone who enters the one shop. Three years ago the sale of beer and cigarettes bolstered profit in sales, but these are no longer sold in Dhompa. A young monk studying in a Buddhist school in Golog had inspired most of the men to give up alcohol and cigarettes after his address to the public. He is said to have so eloquently linked their struggles and their sorrows—the sad wives, the neglected children, and the poverty—to the wasteful habits of drinking, smoking, and gambling. A few young men are unhappy—the only indulgence they had is gone, they say— but they do not think of opening their own liquor shops nor do they resist or question the wishes of the elders. A bottle of beer, a pack of cigarettes, or a bottle of whisky now and then make way into their hands. The elders hear of even these transactions.

The elders have had their share of suffering. When they sit in a group—many of them deaf, many with cataracts in their eyes, half of them severely stricken with gout—they are amazed they still get around as much as they do. They give all credit to the deities and to their past deeds and say nothing can help them but prayers. So they allow prayer wheels to push them forward into an ever-present preoccupation with coming death.

They say they are out of step with the Chinese date and the Chinese time. They eat when they are hungry and when they have food, and they sleep when it turns dark. A few of them have no homes so they huddle in damp rooms near the monastery. These elders who are the memory of our recent history, the guides to our culture, and whose lives have been determined by the changing policies of the Chinese, have never been able to benefit from political decisions.

Did they know happiness? Of life without strife?

They point to incidents of their youth. One recalls the thrill of that brief instant when his tongue collided with a girl's the summer he licked yogurt off the rocks with her. She was a good rider and before her marriage to a lama at the age of fifteen she would spend whole afternoons galloping by the river. The elders recall the excitement of the long days of picnics and horse races during the summer festival in the fields in front of the Bagsigon monastery. They remember their mothers and their fathers.

A nun who was my mother's chaperone spent many hours riding with my mother. She had tried to escape to India in 1959 but her horse was shot under her and she did not make it very far on foot. She said she was showered with bullets one day, and when she had taken her clothes off to sleep, bullets had fallen from her clothes. She thinks her prayers and her faith in the lamas saved her that day. Her husband and parents were not so fortunate. Her eyes moisten and then she smiles as her mind returns to the days when she rode in the fields we now stand on.

She complains the young in Dhompa have all but abandoned the use of horses. Five years ago, horses were prized possessions;

now they roam the fields with no work to do and cannot be sold. Only the elders continue to ride them; they are too scared to ride the angry metal beast. She is suspicious of a moving vehicle for she gets nauseous as soon as she sits in one. She sees trucks and tractors usher in goods and lead the young out and fears that in time the way of life she knows will be erased.

The elders register the changes in their people when they return from a visit to the town. In a land where milk and yogurt are fresh from animals that graze some of the world's most magnificent pastures, town-dwelling Tibetans drink milk from plastic bags produced in Inner Mongolia. The townspeople do not see the great impunity or the contradiction in this. They only see the efficiency: that kind of milk can be stored for a long time. It is the elders and the nomads who feel that in addition to losing their land, they are gradually losing their young. They remark that the young in towns keep their face hidden from the sun for fear of being burned and brown like the nomads. The nomads say young Tibetans want to be slim, and they only want Tibetan dress and traditional jewelry for the days when they show off their Tibetanness.

Chinese companies are making instant Tibetan tea, a miracle never thought possible. Tibetans who prefer making their own tea are abandoning the traditional tea churner for electric blenders. Women say the job gets done quickly. You can get instant tsampa meals I hear, much like oatmeal, but this hasn't entered Kyegu yet. I witness the onslaught of China's modernization and am surprised that younger Tibetans feel they are Tibetan and Buddhist at all. How is it possible for the young to hold steadfast to the traditions of their parents when the world is transforming so rapidly in their lifetime? It is a wonder they speak the dialect.

Even though blind faith does not come easily to the young and even though they cannot suspend their disbelief, most young

Tibetans firmly consider themselves Buddhists. What of the many Tibetans voicing their desire for *rangzen*, for independence from the Chinese? It is largely the young—the educated, the monks and nuns in towns and in rural Tibet—who are writing, painting, and singing about being Tibetan. It is they who are finding ways to speak about what it means to be a Tibetan and about life under the Chinese without karma as a contingent.

The elders argue it is not just the young: even the lamas who go abroad are never the same when they return to their monasteries. Even the best change when they attain wealth, the elders complain. It is as though after the lamas taste the water from foreign taps, they cannot live as before. They forget their devotees, they discover pleasure in women, they buy houses in the towns and slowly relocate.

In turn, I have heard lamas state that from a distance they are able to see the pettiness. They say our people are small-minded and demanding. They cannot be happy to see someone else prosper. They must tear each other apart.

And so we, who see and understand each other best, see the worst in each other too.

Mothers send their daughters into the mountains to tend to their yaks and sheep while the young men of Dhompa dawdle before restaurants. War and action movies are popular with them. Perhaps the young men see their own lives as devoid of any opportunity for the heroisms of the past or what they see on screen. They follow a routine dictated by the pattern of seasons within which they keep themselves and their cattle alive. They are surrounded by never-changing mountains and rivers and never-alleviating hardships. They do not envision any tangible reward in this life.

As far as they know all the singers, leaders, and heroes are in cities and towns.

More and more young herders inch toward towns. They want a life that has more to offer than cattle and tents, and in a place where it is possible for them to be more than herders and fathers of herders. They want a place where heroism is inevitable and where women are without shame.

CHAPTER FOURTEEN

Song of Suffering

A song penetrates the silence of the afternoon hour. I follow the sound to the kitchen and find two elders with their prayer texts held at arm's length. Between memory and effort they reach the words. They look like crows in their black chubas and white blouses. I am lulled into a sense of peace by the low and melodious timbre of their voices, even though it is sorrow that underlies the song. They are singing the songs of Milarepa, Tibet's beloved poet and yogi. How can we, their eyes seem to say, talk of suffering when here is a man who has borne so much more.

Milarepa was born into a wealthy family and his parents lived in harmony with each other and with their extended families. After his father died, however, Mila's once-loving uncle robbed Mila and his mother of all their wealth and turned them out of their own home. Brokenhearted and embittered by this experience, Mila's mother urged Mila to take up the study of black magic and seek revenge. Mila excelled in his studies and was successful in applying his knowledge to destroy his uncle's family. At his first attempt, he sent a giant scorpion to disrupt the feast his uncle and aunt were hosting to celebrate their son's impending wedding. The scorpion demolished his uncle's home and killed thirty-five guests. Mila then conjured a hailstorm that ruined the crops on which the villagers subsisted.

He had expected to feel relief at destroying his enemies but instead a deep sorrow took hold of him. Mila was unable to shake

off the feeling that he had caused himself great harm. He set out
to understand this strange uneasiness and thus began the second
transformation in his life. Mila found his master, a renowned
teacher called Marpa, and studying under him for many years
became a great Buddhist practitioner and attained enlightenment
during his lifetime.

This man, who suffered much, also wrote some of the sweetest
Tibetan songs and taught us kindness, the two elder women say.
"We who have experienced so little pain must learn from him,"
they add. Yet again the elders find a way not to bewail their own
losses.

It is past eight. The hills before me are bathed in a gentle light that
falls like sleep on weary eyes. Everything is soft and undefined.
This is the hour Kham is most appealing to my sentimental self.
There is no aggression in the air, just a drowsy stillness. This is
the time of the day when people are immersed in the mundane
actions of preparing for the night: gathering the yaks, feeding the
dogs, rounding up their cattle so the goats and the *dris* face each
other and are in the right position to be milked in the morning.
A time when people are deciding whether they should take their
clothes off or lie in them. A time when night is already evident in
the way people light candles.

I cook handmade noodles with spinach picked from our garden. After dinner we sit in the dark kitchen recalling select images
from the day: the coral around a visitor's neck; the brief shower
of rain that plucked Yungyang from her nap on the grass and sent
her running into the dark kitchen, only to sit on another elder
because she couldn't see in the dark; the river that had turned yellow as amber. And then when the day cannot be revived any more,

Tashi and Yungyang announce they are sleepy old women who need to go to the bathroom. The three of us walk out and away from the house and its grounds with rows of turnips and rows of spinach. We walk under the open sky and squat in the dark, close enough to each other to imagine we are looking into each other's eyes.

Beside us, our dog with his three good legs howls for the moon and howls for a lover.

I can hear Yungyang, "the wealth of turnips," struggle to lift herself from her squatting position. The grass makes a sound as it straightens after her weight is lifted off it. I want to help her stand up but she is already grinning in my direction like a beam of light shooting out from a torch.

Soon, all the animals will settle to their posts and close in to each other. Fires will be left to extinguish and adults will lay their tired bodies to the ground and drift into sleep with prayers on their lips. Soon, I think to myself, a young nomad will turn toward his lover in the lambent light. He will convince her he is adept with horses and motorbikes. She will pretend to write on his back with her fingers. She will notice how his back is berry purple and smooth like the rocks on the banks of the Kyichu. She will observe his muscles flex under his skin like lightning limning the sky.

Something burns with a soft light in a tent across the river. And just like that, as it often happens with those of us who live with aging heartaches, I think of my mother who is no more. I feel all at once, once again, the enormity of her absence.

CHAPTER FIFTEEN

Two of Us

My mother wrote me a letter for every week I was apart from her in boarding school from the age of seven. In her weekly letters she would remind me to say my prayers every night. At the end of her letters she would draw a picture of the two of us. Sometimes we were rowing a boat on a lake, sometimes we were walking hand in hand on a hill, sometimes sitting in a garden of flowers. The drawings were of stick figures but I could always see myself in the smaller figure and I could see her in the mother figure. In this way, she reminded me she was always with me and I was always on her mind while she was on her own far away from me. I wrote to her every week from school and when I returned home for the long winter holidays we would pile our letters and burn them because we were together again.

I imagined I knew my mother as well as she knew herself. I could read the slightest movement of her features and had a sense of her as I do of my own self. I believed that nobody else in my life would love me unconditionally and absolutely as she did. When she died, I told myself I was fortunate to have had her love for twenty-three years. I believe still what I felt then: her love will see me through my lifetime, perhaps even a few more lifetimes.

She was a good teacher. When I was not yet five, she freed a bar of chocolate from its wrapper and gave me a piece. After the first square she asked me if the chocolate was delicious.

I said it was very good.

She gave me a second piece. She asked if it was good. I replied with a yes.

So she gave me the third piece.

She asked the same question and I gave the same answer and so she gave me another piece. After we had done this for a while and the chocolate bar had diminished substantially, she asked if the chocolate tasted any better. I responded it remained the same in taste.

So what difference does it make if you eat one piece or twenty? It will taste the same whether you eat it alone or share it with others, she said.

That is one of the first lessons I remember.

It is not easy to continue with lessons I learned as a Buddhist child—to believe in karma, to be kind, to attend to the happiness of others before myself—when I live in a world where the self functions on the premise of being an isolated entity. It is not easy to remember that this life is the basis for the next life when the words "happiness" and "success" are so often tied to material ambition and achievements.

I continue to worry about my mother. I pray for her on her prayer beads every day because she is somewhere in the world in her new life.

If I close my eyes I can see her dancing in the living room. She is wearing an ill-fitting white cotton nightdress decorated with small pink flowers, and she is looking at me with a look that is both ridiculous and delightful. She is suppressing a giggle because she is trying to dance before me to her favorite disco tune, "Jungle Boy." Her hands move up and down while her feet march in one spot. The disco music is a little too gregarious for her. She is dancing and marching like a three-year-old does to music. I stand before her, as I often did, telling her to behave herself.

Two of Us

Talcum powder floats down her body. It is as though she is composed of light and fragrance. We are, once again, stricken with laughter.

CHAPTER SIXTEEN

Free Tibet

Mist, thin as cotton gauze, glides over the mountains. It is far too cold for a day in late August. There are women singing on the other side of the Kyichu. Their voices enter the quiet of the afternoon. The air is musical.

To know the past I rely on the memory and the experiences of those who have lived here. Tibetans, I forewarn you, and this I have ascertained after years of questioning, are uneasy managers of their memories in their reluctance to speak of themselves and of those who are deceased. This is particularly true of the people in Dhompa. After all, when I asked her about her parents, my mother described them as each having a nose, two eyes, and a mouth. Tibetans inside Tibet held their tongue from referring to the past for fear of retribution from the Chinese, and even now they remain cautious. Those who attempt to speak of their lives before 1959, out of deference to my wishes, do so with reticence. It is apparent they find it unsettling to focus such attention entirely on the self. They take a circuitous route where diversions—a horse they loved as a child, an exceptionally harsh winter, winding descriptions of mountains—allow for an entry into their lives.

This year I have come with a strategy. I do not ask people about their lives; I ask for stories about other people. The results are more satisfying. There are those, however, whose diffidence cannot be penetrated. They will not tell the story I would like to hear. And here is the dilemma—as a Tibetan who has lived outside of Tibet,

I gravitate toward particular aspects of a life or history of place that do not always seem pertinent to the narrator in the understanding of his life. The details I want to hear—whether they are stories he heard as a child or novel items introduced during her childhood, or memories of thieves being publicly punished—are not those they choose to remember as significant. The story that ultimately emerges is often after a laborious effort and a sort of collaboration between the narrator and me.

My questions are intermittently answered with remarks on how they are stupid people, dumb like their yaks or their sheep because they cannot recall details. I think of Heinrich Harrer for he too mentions, "One constantly hears Tibetans saying, 'We know nothing. We are so stupid!' But of course the fact that they say so proves the contrary."

Unlike Harrer, I begin to think perhaps the nomads are right. Why else would they meet my simple questions with obdurate silence? Is their reticence to speak the result of Chinese colonization or is it because they were rendered mute by the lamas and chiefs of the land before the Chinese came? Perhaps they are ignorant like their animals—they are illiterate, they have not traveled beyond their nomadic environs, all day they are with animals or immersed in work.

Such thoughts arise when I wait for answers that will help me understand our history. As I wait for narrators to unveil why and how we became who we are.

While listening to a group of men speak of the difficulties of keeping their herd alive, I ask about the politics of herders. How has the fence affected their relationship to the land or with their neighbors? What will they do if the Chinese mine on their land?

They look at me askance and when they see that I am waiting for some response, they nod their heads cautiously. "Yes, maybe," they say.

These are not the passionate responses I expect to hear from khampas. I persist. How do they feel about their history? The upheaval of the past? What of the future? Do they think of rangzen? The word *rangzen*, translated as "self-power" or "independence" in Tibetan, came into the Tibetan lexicon much later, along with words like "capitalism," "socialism," and "exploitation." It is our word for freedom. The word, once used infrequently in Tibet, is now a catchphrase for younger Tibetans.

What would a free Tibet mean to the elders? Would it change their lives?

They do not say anything. I do not know if I ought to repeat my questions. After considerable silence one elder says he is happy as long as he can say his prayers, and he is happy as long as his herd has good grass to eat. The others nod their heads in agreement.

Freedom, as I have been taught to understand as a political being in exile—to be protected by law, to be able to live my life as I choose, absent from tyranny and persecution—is perhaps not the foremost aspiration here in Dhompa's pastoral and nomadic world. There, I have made that assumption and spelled it out.

The elders tell me they equate freedom with the right to live as Buddhists, which entails being able to perform their rituals, have access to lamas and to monasteries, and be able to participate in retreats and studies. They might even refer to an aspired state of mind: to be free of attachment, anger, stupidity, jealousy, and arrogance. To be released from fear and, perhaps, even from their attachment to the past.

How can the nomads here define freedom as I do when they are rarely offered any protection or consideration by any law or government? Their land is their security and protection; it is the land that has provided them and their herd with everything they have. Their struggles are devoted to finding a way to survive on this land without any amenities or assurances of outside support.

My politics is not their concern. It is not their way to make meaning of everything that happens in a day or in a year. There are lamas and politicians for that. They understand this life of the grass and the life of work. They get up early, they take their herd to the grazing land, they watch the grass grow, they make predictions for the day, the weather, the health of their herd, one day at a time. They follow the Tibetan lunar time, two months behind and 127 years ahead of the calendar followed by the Chinese government and the rest of the world respectively. They live so far from the cities where people make the rules and dispatch new officers every few years. They don't feel they can even understand or articulate what it is that their lives represent to others.

Yungyang says, again and again, the times are better because she can say her prayers now. She asks about the health of Gyalwa Rinpoche, the Dalai Lama. She is happy to hear he is well. If he is well, then she is well, she declares. It is an acceptance and understanding of life that I cannot quite translate into words.

I do not want this way of life of the nomads—as they live and understand it—to disappear. Such thoughts come to me when I am with them. Sometimes I am filled with admiration for them, and sometimes with disbelief at the ease with which they appear to live through their difficulties. I know I am naive in seeking to simplify the varied and complicated life of a human being into sentences that present one way of looking at a person as though people do not change, and will not change. I am wrong to want to stumble on one or two key discoveries that will alter my way of seeing the world or the way Tibetans are perceived. This is not how it works. Whole afternoons vanish in silence with nothing to account for. I begin to think that abstract questions on existence would be inconsistent with the average nomad's life. He deems such things to the domain of the inexplicable, like fate. He is more forthcoming talking about poverty and the difficulties of herding, and he attempts predictions for the immediate future based on these problems. He does not make anyone accountable for such struggles. And the past, what can he say of the past except to list the names of the dead—the father, the mother, the uncle, the aunt—and to point to the land as though the land, in having accepted the dead, will speak for him.

Sometimes I wonder if they live in a state of apathy or ignorance, or if they are passive, but when I consider what continues to exist inside Tibet, even after such violent upheaval, it is resistance that comes to mind, not inaction. I have come to equate concrete action as resistance. It is harder to define their quiet refusal to change, and their resilience, because I have not been taught to acknowledge what comes without manifestations in word or action.

Every day for over two decades Tibetans were killed, persecuted, and indoctrinated against their own people, against their own culture, against Buddhism. Anger and denial would have been an easier path. It would be beneficial for them to believe in what the Chinese insist upon, and yet many of them choose to have faith and they continue with their prayers to the deities of the land.

A young man who has recently returned from the Tibetan refugee camp of Bylakuppe in South India, where he lived as a monk for two years, is able to understand some of my dilemmas. He could not acclimatize to the weather and to the food in India, he tells me. He fell gravely ill and he returned to Dhompa to die in his country and with his family around him. He has experienced life as a free Tibetan in India, he says, and having returned (and in good health now), he understands how it is to live within a shell. He complains the nomads of Dhompa do not understand politics. They accept the Dalai Lama is in exile and they are here in their country; he says they listen to the news and they accept what they hear. He bemoans that Tibetans in general are not capable of achieving anything big or successful. He is not certain why. He gives the example of the nomads who collect fungus and then spend the rest of the year happy, celebrating in the meadows.

What is it about us, that we cannot achieve greatness, that we cannot make money from money like the Chinese, he asks.

There are businessmen who do well in Nepal and there are a handful of businessmen from Dhompa who have moved to Lhasa and are thriving, I tell him.

He says he learned a lot in two years, enough for him to see how little he knows. "Tell me what is happening in the world," he asks eagerly.

⸙

Every afternoon I sit with a group of men or women who do not know the name of the premier of China, but they can tell me who my great-grandfather was, they can name the lamas of the thirteen monasteries in Dhompa, and they can estimate the total number of livestock of most of the herders in the region. If I ask them to go back further in our history, as far back as they know, they say we descended from a male monkey and a mountain ogress. The monkey, an incarnation of the compassionate spirit, Avalokitesvara, met and married a mountain ogress. Their union produced six children and from these six, the people of Tibet followed. Tenzin says we can trace our characteristics to the forefathers: those of us who are more compassionate, intelligent, and contemplative inherit our nature from Avalokitesvara while those of us who are ruddy-faced, stubborn, and lustful resemble the mountain ogress.

The river Kyichu flows nearby and across from us stretches the field of Yigi Thang: "the field of letters." It is shaped like an open book, its pages cut in neat quarters by the road built in recent years by young Chinese laborers. At the base of the plateau is Babjang Khang—"the tent"—where Si Dhungmo, a general in King Gesar's army, put up his tent one afternoon to rest. The Chinese play no role in our stories.

When I am with my mother's people, I inspect myself as an outsider and as an insider. Coming to Tibet is a form of exercising my privilege as a transnational body. I have a passport in my own possession and can travel at will as long as I have the means. I have also been stateless and without citizenship for half of my life, but even then, I had the flexibility to move freely within certain borders. In Dhompa, I experience another form of freedom in the obvious release from habitual routine. Unencumbered by the shrill advocacies of television, the reliance on electricity, the credit card, the tyranny of a boss at work, I can pretend that in this bucolic life is a carefree existence. In the quiet happiness of being here, my thoughts often turn to my life in the United States. I do not tell the elders I had ended an engagement. Only my aunt is privy to my personal life and she asks why I had decided against marriage.

I tell her the man was not kind to me.

"If a human being understands karma, he will naturally lean toward kindness," she says. She says I made the right decision to leave the relationship behind.

I tell her I had not expected love to be so contrary, for it to be so easily unmoored.

She suggests I marry a kind Tibetan man, someone known to the family.

I tell her I want to love the man I marry.

She says love will come on its own.

She married my uncle at twelve when she would have had no power to break an engagement. Tashi remembers her life with my

uncle with great longing. She says he was a good man. You learn
to love the person you marry. It happens, she says.

Here in Dhompa, far from the city and from the offices of the
government, it is easy to think nomads are free from Chinese
oppression and free of the demands and desires of modern con-
sumerist life because they are far from the bazaars. Yet here too
there are pressures. The people of Dhompa live at the bidding of
the sun, the wind, and the rain. And always, there is the shadow
of poverty. What is freedom when you have not been given the
choice to reject anything?

The nomads have few other places or professions to escape
to. It would be difficult for them to get a passport to leave for
a new country. I think of the time my grandfather presided in
Dhompa—the people deferred to him, they paid taxes in kind.
There were no laws protecting anyone against the decisions made
by my grandfather. What was their freedom then?

Some of the young nomads say the herding life is impossible
and they want to move to the city where they can become something else and where life can improve financially. Within these
expectations, the notion of personal liberty is exercised.

I tell the nomads of the many Westerners who persist on our
behalf, how many of them feel committed to fighting for Tibetans to have basic rights and for Tibet to have its independence. I
tell them of the protest marches outside the Chinese embassies all
over the world and the slogans of "Free Tibet" greeting visiting
Chinese dignitaries.

It is unimaginable to them that they can be freed through
protests. "How are they punished?" they ask. I explain that there
are no punishments if you get prior consent from the city. They
cannot believe you can apply for permission to the very same
government you seek to protest against. They narrate incidents
that have taken place in Lithang and Golog, even in Nangchen,

in recent years, where individuals have disappeared into Chinese prison systems simply for raising a Tibetan flag or uttering the word *rangzen* or praising the Dalai Lama in public. No protests have taken place in Dhompa, not during the days when my grandfather was alive, and not since. The elders say they pray for those brave people who speak for Tibet and for Gyalwa Rinpoche. They say they will do what they know: they will pray, they will live on their land, and they will teach their children what they know.

Tenzin asks if the protests bring results.

I think of the brief lightness in my heart on days when people honk their car horns in support or wave while I am standing with a small group of Tibet supporters in front of the Chinese Embassy in San Francisco. For that brief moment I have hope that it matters, that Tibet matters, and that something, even then I am not sure what exactly, will change for us as a nation and a people. And then I go home and the event becomes just another episode in a long day. Does anything change? What are the results? I have never felt at ease at the marches, never certain what I stand for and what I hope for. I go because I would like to be there for those who believe more assuredly than I do that Tibet will be independent of the Chinese.

My hope is unsteady because I have been to Tibet and I have seen just how entrenched the Chinese are in my country. It is hard to imagine the Chinese will give up what they have sought to destroy and then to build in the last five decades. Within this anomaly and within these complexities, hope for a free Tibet seems a punitive effort. But to give up hope would signify worse: the end of all possibilities for a different future.

When I am with my mother's people, I realize I have a lot to unlearn. I look to them to uncomplicate my notions of Tibet and Tibetans. They know where they are from; they live on the land. This assurance does not come in the same way to those of us in exile who experience a lack of certainty, for is it not from the land that we get a sense of stability? Those of us born in exile inherit Tibet by inhabiting the memories of our elders.

I understand what the elders mean when they speak of the old days, for it feels as though we are still somewhere deep in the past. I can see why my mother could not forget the land. It is the land that surrounds us and nothing else: the mountains we climb with great effort, the rivers we cannot wade through during the summer months, the long winters that make the road so icy that it neglects its purpose and traps all living beings. It is the land that envelops us like a womb. And on this land there are sacred deities of mountains and rivers known by many names: *yul lha*, protectors of the region; *gzhi-bdag*, owners of the place; *gtsan*, strong wrathful spirits who have both beneficial and malevolent tendencies and who if wronged bring painful illnesses to the people. There are regional divinities known as *klu*, and serpent spirits, or *nagas*, who dwell in streams and springs. There are a variety of demons who are recalled in stories for their past rampages to devour human flesh, to cause disunity among people, to cause death, hail, and lightning. These were once-powerful humans who transformed into harmful deities due to a proclivity for anger and destructive behavior. They were finally subdued and converted by Guru Padmasambhava, the eighth-century Indian Buddhist master, to protect the land and its people, but because they are not yet enlightened, they can get absorbed in their own emotions and forget their duties toward the land. Therefore, offerings are made to them, to appease them and remind them of their promise to do good and to protect the people.

I ask the elders in Dhompa if it is possible we will be free from the Chinese. I ask them again and again how is it they have no anger or resentment toward the Chinese. In the late afternoons when the sun is warm, and we are lying on the grass under the shade of a floorless canvas tent that serves as our daytime living room, I think to myself that they will reveal themselves to me.

Tenzin seldom rests. He is either collecting yak dung from the fields behind the house, carrying water from the spring, or sewing, but every now and then he sits with us. He says there was a time he resented his own people, those who joined the Communist cadres—and there were many from Dhompa who did so—but he understood their actions as desperate measures to survive. How much can one body bear?

"It was difficult to feel angry because everybody was suffering. You cannot feel bad for yourself when others around you are going through the same experience," he says.

And the Chinese?

"They do not know about karma." He has just remembered he needs to put the solar panels out in the sun so he can read his prayers at night. He dusts his pants and runs off, shooting a smile in my direction.

Tashi tells us Tenzin's story in his absence. Tenzin was fourteen when his father was taken to prison with other adult men in Dhompa. Only women and children were left in Dhompa and so Tenzin worked with his mother and eight siblings on the communal farm. He never saw his father again. The families' entire personal food stock had been confiscated and all their livestock had been led to another county, where efforts were made for collective rearing. The Chinese army had no knowledge of caring for yaks and sheep and most of the cattle had died of hunger. So many humans too followed their animals into death, Tashi says.

Tenzin returns with a jacket and with his sewing kit. Two buttons are coming loose, and he says he'll sit on the grass with the women while he finishes his work. He tells us how the army set up a collective farm near the monastery in Bagsikha and young children and women were made to work there all day with brief intervals for meals. There was never much to eat, and never enough.

"I ate grass because I was so hungry and needed to chew on something," Tenzin says. He remembers the army bringing grain all the way from Xining, not to feed the famished, but to put the seeds in the hands of the hungry for them to scatter it on the infertile ground.

His account is echoed in many other parts of Tibet where Mao Zedong's orders to grow more wheat in place of barley, which was the traditional Tibetan staple, led to terrible waste and to many deaths from starvation. Long after the policies of the Great Leap Forward were stopped elsewhere in China, it continued inside Tibet. When Tibetans recovered from this long season of hunger they were thrown into the even more tumultuous ride of the Cultural Revolution.

If the Chinese had only asked, even the simplest of nomads could have told them that the soil was not good for wheat, Tenzin says. But voicing an opinion could have got them killed, so weak and hungry as they were, they fed grain to the earth that would not accept it. "Nothing grew. People ate what they could: grass, leaves, tree bark."

I look at Tenzin and try to capture something about his nature that explains or reveals the unique relation he is able to adopt to his own suffering, and yet I am also learning from him not to make too much meaning of words. When Tenzin and the nomads tell me about their lives they do not track specific moments, or stop at one or two experiences to make sudden denouements or to declare epiphanies. They do not tear their experiences into isolated parts to define themselves or their trajectories. They tell their stories as a series of events that unfold over time so that the process of understanding a life takes a lifetime.

Tenzin wears his suffering with the same acceptance as he wears his old clothes. He says his prayers, thinking, I am certain, of the dead, not of himself. If I were to ask him for one incident that transformed his life, I doubt he would understand the question or its relevance.

He smiles kindly at me when I remark his life has been fraught with suffering and that he should tell his stories to his children.

Every human being suffers, he reminds me.

I think of the glut of memoirs that are published each year in the West and how a small personal trial or achievement is met with extraordinary reception. Tenzin does not think he has arrived at any discovery of his own self or of his life. His life—the life of one person—is but a point in a cycle of ceaseless lifetimes. There are no sudden beginnings and endings, there are no isolated moments of significance. Time unravels what happens within time. His story is not extraordinary: everyone around him suffered, he reminds me often. My mother never spoke of her painful past and losses as particular to her life either. When I was younger I found her philosophy of fate and acceptance meaningless; it seemed like an easy way to end all discussions. I understood her lack of protest and injury to be fatalistic, but more and more I begin to see the psychological and mental benefits of such acceptance. It does not make the suffering go away but it is a tool and a strength that helps maintain some equanimity toward the self and its place in the world.

Tenzin and Dorje were young boys in 1959. Everything that was familiar and beloved to them in Dhompa was within the reach of their horses. "Suddenly our lives were turned upside down," Tenzin says. The only assaults he had known before the Chinese came were the skirmishes the adults had with neighboring nomads, or the dramatic enactments of the wars in the stories of Gesar of Ling. These were wars fought to protect Buddhism and to subdue the evil demons of the land who brought suffering to Tibetans: such as the famous war against the man-eating demon Klub Tsan of the north or the war with Hor after Gesar's wife was kidnapped by the king of Hor.

Why did the Chinese think they knew what was best for Tibetans? Dorje and Tenzin still do not understand why the Chinese, total strangers to them, had come all the way to Dhompa to make them suffer. They had not known they needed to be freed from their own people and lives. Tenzin says there was such chaos and rumors when the Chinese came: the nomads had believed the Chinese would leave after they completed whatever it was they came for.

Some women boiled the leather of their shoes so that there was some taste to the water they drank for dinner. Mothers were told to kill sons, sons were made to spit on lamas, daughters had to dance on the bodies of their fathers, nuns were forced to have sex with monks, and men and women were coerced to trample on sacred statues. The limbs of deities lay in the dust like the severed limbs of babies. Tenzin can still picture hundreds of texts written in gold fluttering in the air like a band of butterflies. His eyes have seen what his mind could never have imagined, and he cannot recall in simple sentences the small and big injustices he has lived through.

Dorje was thirteen when the invasion happened. He remembers hanging out with friends in the meadows discussing news of the advent of the Chinese army. He had never seen soldiers. He was unprepared for their numbers and for their brutality. "So many people died of starvation over there," he says, pointing toward the outline of buildings at Bagsikha.

"Why didn't you eat fish?" I ask. The Kyichu has a bounty of fish.

Dorje's eyes crinkle with laughter. The Chinese ask them often,

"Why didn't you eat the fish?" It simply never occurred to the Tibetans; they would not have known how to cook it, he says. For decades, the nomads have left the fish alone and they continue to do so. The calculation is simple: one yak feeds a family for three to six months and one fish feeds a man for one meal. It does not make sense to kill one life to barely nourish one life.

I think of the fish in the river and long to eat one. It would make a delicious meal but I don't express my thoughts out loud. No man or woman in my family has ever fished from the river below the house. I do not want to be remembered for breaking this tradition.

Months after these exchanges with Tenzin, Dorje, and other nomads of Dhompa, when I am no longer in Tibet, I search in libraries and on the Internet for research articles illuminating the period mentioned by Tenzin and Dorje. I am verifying their stories in papers written by people who are scholars, but who are not Tibetan and who did not live through the Cultural Revolution in Tibet. The irony is painful. And this, when they have not revealed the worst they have seen and been through, and when they have accepted my stories without judgment. If Tenzin and Dorje were scholars, would I have doubted their memory, and the chronological veracity of their stories?

There are nomads in the small villages of Kham and Amdo who remember the unnerving silence that muffled their land after the animals and the men had been killed. Bones covered the land for years, they say.

The nomads in Dhompa watch their cattle graze and say times are better. They cannot protest or speak freely, they cannot move uninhibited as they wish, but in comparison to the harsh days they have experienced, they feel the relief of a lighter incarceration. To have suffered so long and for so many years under the Chinese and to still emerge from the bad times with some kind of gratitude toward any leniency is an attitude I find astounding, but they do not see anything extraordinary in their response.

How can we free our country with our propensity to accept even macabre injustices as outcomes of our own karma? As Buddhists, Tibetans believe in nonviolence but it is hard to believe that nonviolence will bring us to our independence in the near future. And how will violence set free a population of six million people with no army? It is enough, if you travel the highways between Shigatse and Lhasa, and Nagchukha and Lhasa, and catch a glimpse of the convoy of Chinese army trucks crawling along the road, to suffer the realization that we do not have the capacity to overthrow such a giant with our hopes and prayers. Each day, there are unaccountable numbers of Chinese coming into Tibet. It is estimated there are easily over six million Chinese in Tibetan areas. How do we persist in our hope for independence or even autonomy with such knowledge? How do we keep such knowledge from driving us insane or from making us act in violence?

What will become of us when the nomad cannot say, "If the Dalai Lama is well, then I am well." How, then, will we measure our well-being?

As a displaced community, Tibetans often speak of learning to look to the future without forsaking tradition. And as Tibetans continue their flight from Tibet to India or Nepal and then scatter farther and farther away from the physical land of Tibet, the conversations on identity and culture become more crucial and complex. As the distance increases so does the desperation about keeping Tibet as an eventual home, our aspired home. Yet it is the loss of Tibet and its very distance that also awakens us to view patriotism and identity in new ways that are not guided solely by Buddhist philosophy. Self-assertion—an approach avoided in the past because of the Buddhist aspiration to prevent focus on the self—enters our identity as Tibetans.

Secrets are teased out on the long days when we tell stories to entertain each other. On a warm, lazy afternoon we come to know that Dorje was once jailed after being caught with a stolen artifact. He did not know it was stolen, he explains. He lost his heart for business after that experience. On another occasion, it is revealed that Tashi and my mother made a hole in the chamber pot belonging to one of the ministers in Dhompa, and that when he woke up and put his feet on the floor he stepped into a pool of his own urine.

Tashi tells me my mother was so distraught at the news of her arranged marriage to the chief of Bongba's son that she cried for a whole day and emerged with a plan to escape on her horse. An hour after she rode off, she returned, saying she could not bear to hurt her mother. I come to know that one of my mother's cousins had small clay pots delivered to him every day, and all morning there would be a cacophony of crashes from his room. He was only a child then; when he was old enough to know about treachery, he led a Chinese soldier to the secret spot where my aunt, his first cousin, had hidden her jewels.

I also get to hear that Yungyang had one of the most coveted jobs during the Cultural Revolution: she was the one who blew the whistle to alert Tibetans to attend the reeducation meetings in the mornings and evenings.

This job, granted to her because she was *clean*, coming from a poor background, spared her the punishment others received. She witnessed their singing and their beatings. Tenzin remembers how sharp and serious she was about her whistle-blowing duty. She denies having had the job, but Tenzin whispers to me that he can hardly be mistaken in her identity when he stood in front of her for weeks. She was strict, he adds. Those days of terror when people were forced to renounce their loved ones and commit heartbreaking acts—slapping or kicking their loved ones—are now regaled over tea and dried meat.

My friends speak the words to the songs they were taught to sing. Their voices quiver, their pronunciation so Tibetan, even to me.

Long live Mao. A thousand years to Mao.

I teasingly tell them their Chinese hasn't improved. Indeed, it is the only Chinese they speak. It was unreasonable, Tashi says, to expect people to remember words in a language they did not know, and especially after hearing it just once or twice. They were forbidden from saying their prayers. Mao was the focus of their devotion and they sang to him in his language. So many beatings they received, Tashi says, because their silly heads wouldn't keep the words in order. Tenzin explains that some people visualized a deity instead of the picture of Mao and so they sang willingly to their deities.

The words are garbled but they emerge out of the years of hibernation. It is almost another language.

It is not easy to imprison the mind. Even in the midst of such madness, my mother's friends survived without becoming broken, bitter, and vanquished. In the face of their endurance and impassivity, it is hard not to feel a loss with regard to young Tibetans—even those of my age—who may not develop this incredible acceptance, resistance, and strength.

My nephew Kunga reads in Chinese, watches Chinese movies, and reckons learning Tibetan will not get him very far. He will not find a job if he is not firmly grounded in the Chinese language, he explains. He is eager to tease Tenzin with a joke. He has already tested it on other visitors.

A nomad comes to the city and tries to eat *momos* with chopsticks but he has a hard time grasping the slippery *momos*, Kunga begins. The nomad gives up and uses his fingers. On his next trip to the city, when he is offered a plate of *momos*, he grabs one with his fingers and says, "I couldn't get your cousin last time. I am going to make sure I get you."

Tenzin breaks into loud laughter and says the joke makes no sense. Besides, he has heard it before from Kunga. He thinks it is silly how the town people use chopsticks when fingers would do the job more easily. He says the joke is on the people who live in town. Kunga says the joke sounds better in Chinese. The word "nomad" in Tibetan does not carry the layer of ridicule necessary for the joke to be funny. Tenzin reminds Kunga that for all his town manners and style, the Chinese see him as a nomad by virtue of his being a Tibetan.

Kunga is silenced by that thought. "I am a Tibetan," he says.

Dorje is stitching a jacket for me. He sews with the needle pointed toward his body. I sew with the needle pointed away from me.

"You sew like the Chinese." Three years ago, he had said the same words to me.

What does he mean by that?

He says the Chinese sew with the needle pointed away from the body because they are superstitious about pointing the needle toward themselves. He says he cannot sew that way.

I ask him if he has tried.

He hasn't. He says his fingers would not know how. He asserts this small distinction between the Chinese and Tibetans.

China is present in the clothes Kunga wears, the writing on the gates of his school, the language in which he studies. He forgets why the Chinese are in Tibet. That he is a Tibetan living in Qinghai, China, and not Kham, Tibet, is not as conflicting a matter to him as it is to me. He would, he says, prefer it if the Chinese left him alone, but since that is unlikely, he doesn't see any other recourse available to him but to resign himself to the situation and make the best of it.

There are many who cannot endure life in Tibet, who escape to Nepal and India, but Kunga cannot imagine leaving his entire family and going elsewhere. I suppose in the same way some elders have moved from a sense of loss to a state of repose. The loss was due to their karma and so the Chinese are part of that karma. It is hard to fight with such beliefs. This too is the history of the Tibetan people. Acceptance and fate explain everything, while memory, our illusionary accomplice, hobbles at our side like a shadow.

My upbringing and life in exile makes me view China as the force that denies Tibetans the right to live as Tibetans in Tibet. It is China, not fate, that sent my mother into exile and made her an orphan at the age of eighteen. It is because of the Chinese invasion that I grew up without my grandparents, aunts, uncles, and cousins. I understand Tibet's history through images of loss. My only comfort comes from acknowledging—from a specifically Buddhist perspective—that the last fifty years are but a very brief moment in the whole of time. In time, everything changes. But this is a solace that does not alter the present or promise a desired future.

All afternoon Kunga reads *Don Quixote* in Chinese. The world is topsy-turvy. I realize how insular I have become to feel shocked at a non-English translation. I see the world around me through English. Everything is slower and newer when I try to think in Tibetan. Thoughts stumble and remain fragmented.

Only in English can I make sense of it all. Only in Chinese can Kunga make sense of it all.

CHAPTER SEVENTEEN

Maladies of the Self

Tashi loves the autumn months best when the milk is creamy, the yogurt tastes of flowers, and the grass squanders its fragrance wantonly to the wind. "The fall manure smells sweet," she eulogizes.

She tells me how my grandmother instructed herders to store the fall manure separately to be used when lamas and chieftains visited. She raises her nose in the air as though she is trapping the smells inside her nostrils for odorless winter days.

She loved, too, the round and silken contours of the horses during this season. It was a delight to slide off their backs, she says. They were good-humored, their coat was thick, and their well-fleshed bodies made riding so pleasurable. She interrupts herself then, astonished she remembers so much. "How does memory survive, despite everything?"

Her memory allows for small pleasures. When she is sad she tells me sad stories often to conclude with a reference to Gotami. In the days of the Buddha lived a woman called Gotami who had one child. When her only son died young she became almost crazy with grief. Her friends advised her to go to the man called the Buddha who was known to have great powers. Perhaps he would find a way to bring her son back to life. Gotami found the Buddha, and holding the body of her child before him, she begged him to return her son to her.

The Buddha agreed to help Gotami but only if she could find a mustard seed from a house untouched by death. Gotami rushed out in joy. She knocked on the door to one home and the woman happily gave her a mustard seed but informed Gotami that her husband had died the previous year. In the next house, too, death had paid a visit. From house to house went Gotami and everywhere she heard the same story: a son, a brother, a father, a mother, had died.

Gotami realized death was every human being's destination. When she understood this reality, she was able to accept her son's death. Tashi has returned to this story several times in her life.

As a young girl I understood Gotami's story as a parable of a mother's love for her child. The pain of losing a child was immeasurable, I was told by mothers. I often thought of my mother when I heard this story and I wondered if she thought of her firstborns when she looked at me. I wondered if she had grieved for them and wept for them like Gotami. My mother told me Gotami's story many times, referring obliquely perhaps to the day when she would not be with me. She would follow the story with lessons: do not gossip about anyone, do not lie, do not steal, try to give more than you take, do not be too friendly with your friends' husbands. This last advice always irked me. I would argue with her and tell her it made no sense because I was a child and had no husband. I now realize my mother was preparing me for her death from the time I was a young girl. The nightly stories and lessons were to be my crutches when she was no longer alive to guide me.

When there are just two of you, you try to prepare for that time when there will be just one, even if it is not possible to guard against such a sorrow.

As a teenager I would tell my mother that I could survive everything in life but her death. She would assure me she would be with me for a long time. When she died, it troubled me that days passed one after another despite my desire for time to dissolve in one place. I could not understand how the demands of a day remained the same when desolation filled my heart.

People tried to comfort me, saying in time the heart would not hurt so much. That has not been entirely true for me. In time I have found a way to carry the pain as a part of my body much like the scar on my forehead. I have come to understand that every single human being, from the unknown to the most celebrated, suffers the same loss. Death of a beloved is not my unique experience and yet that does not stop me from thinking that my love for my mother was different, that I loved her more than any daughter has loved her mother.

Tibetan elders speak often of their own end; it is as though once they turn fifty they are close enough to see death. They prepare for death with prayers, with circumambulations around the stupa. Death is the vehicle to their new journey. They hope to be reborn as a human being. They say their happiness will be complete if they return as a Tibetan.

"Human life is precious," Tashi tells me. She narrates the story of a solitary blind turtle who lives in the oceans of the world and who comes up for air through a small ring. It takes the turtle a hundred, even a thousand, years to locate the ring and come up for air. That is how difficult it is to come back as a human.

Despite this body, this life of suffering, the feckless manner in which the Chinese kill Tibetans, we are fortunate to be humans and to be Tibetans, Tashi believes.

The elders carry their ailments and their age with a touch of honor. Age is prestigious because as Buddhists they understand that life is impermanent. They love to provide details of the amount of medicines they take, of the shapes and colors of these pills, of the regularity with which they are consumed. The sick in town walk in the courtyard of the hospital and even on the main street with a needle taped to one hand while they hold the IV bottle steady in their other hand. I have even seen several women seated behind on motorbikes with one hand raised in the air, grasping an IV bottle. They do not hide in hospitals or clinics while they are being treated. Sickness and death is no mystery to them; they know it comes to all without exception. Sickness is an indication of life.

I am old, I am old, I need to say my prayers and get ready for death, the elders in my family say.

The word "old" carries no weighty burden but that of the inevitability of time. It sets them apart from those who came after 1959, and the older they are the more they have seen. Oh, the reversals of life they have known! While the West celebrates youth, I sense Tibetan elders know how to use their age to their advantage. In San Francisco, I have many close friends, older than I, who despite our closeness never reveal their age. Here in Dhompa, age is not a secret or sensitive matter; it is often the first question asked of a stranger. Age is a way to understand where we are in our lives in our relation to the other. We know our responsibilities once we establish whether we are younger or older than the other person.

Tashi was the youngest in her family while growing up; now she is the elder of the Dhompa family. Every morning she declares her illness as though she, by necessity, ails. The blood pressure is a little high, she will say. Or, the liver is acting up. It is as though she is observing someone else's body attached to her for caretaking. A little tremor in her system takes her toward the study of mortality. She is, after all, sixty-seven. Time is up, she says quite merrily.

I tell her I have friends who are eighty and sprightly.

She marvels at the health and optimism of the West. She reasons it is the climate and the food. She decides my eighty-year-old friends have not suffered much in their lifetime, as she has. If Tashi has milk and yogurt for breakfast, she reads an emergence of *rlung*, the element of air in her body, and she will set the matter right by eating meat or butter at lunch. If she has had too much meat for lunch, she will complain of *tripa*, the emergence of bile, and she will settle for a light dinner.

Some days it is her knees, some days it is her back, her blood pressure, or her heart that causes discomfort. It is as though being sixty-seven, she must naturally be beset by at least one physical trial every single day.

She chooses the antidote to her troubles from a bag filled with Tibetan and Western medicines: if it is a muscle or bone ache she settles for Western medicine; if it is something subtle like a disturbance in her blood or heartbeat she takes Tibetan medicine. She never complains of any adverse effects from the medicines and often I see her eating pills handed to her by other self-proclaimed physicians.

When a discomfort persists that she has not been able to shrug off even after two days of self-medication, she reckons a trip to the doctor is necessary. We visit Dhompa's only doctor in his house. The doctor takes Tashi's pulse and announces the color of her shirt is affecting her blood pressure.

Red, he tells her, is raising her blood pressure.

I point out she is wearing a purple shirt.

He says red, purple, and maroon are from the same family.

Red, Tashi announces, is not her color. Since she was wearing a white T-shirt under her shirt, she disappears into the next room and removes her purple blouse. She says she feels her blood pressure dropping as she returns to the room. She prescribes her own treatment of intravenous glucose, which the doctor obliges. She thinks glucose works best for her and for every ailing Tibetan in this region.

I sit across from her while she feels better and better. Her left hand is suspended in the air. She is impatient and wants to get up but she must wait until the bottle runs empty. In the meantime, she has decided to clean her ears with a key. She wets the key between her teeth as though the metal will be softened with her spit. She inspects the key when it exits her ear and cleans it on the ends of her chuba. I have seen her on other occasions use a stick or a little metal spoon that fits into her ear and quite efficiently scoops out what she refers to as ear shit.

The doctor wears the ubiquitous navy blue Mao suit and cap that many older men wear out of habit and comfort. He tells me he is not a learned doctor but he knows enough to take care of the sicknesses befalling people around him: arthritis, gout, high blood pressure, headaches, stomach problems. He is helpless against serious diseases. His clinic stores a small stock of painkillers and antibiotics; he cannot afford to have more. He does not have any medical equipment. It would be moot anyway; there is no electricity. He listens to the pulse of his patients, studies their urine to read their illness, and makes his medicine from herbs. He learned his trade under the tutelage of a monk. His patients are poor and some of them pay him with medicinal herbs or mushrooms they collect from the mountains.

Paper and plastic cover the mud walls of his house. I recognize the posters on his wall from my previous visit. There are two pictures of Mao in his living-cum-bedroom, and alongside them are a picture of the winter palace of the Dalai Lama, the Potala, and a poster of a plate filled with burgundy apples and pomegranates. The white of the plate is contrasted craftily so the red of each fruit is visible in its state of utmost ripeness. Posters of fruits and flowers in Tibetan homes are offerings to the deities. The pictures of Mao have been on the wall for a long time—he is not sure why he put them up in the first place but thinks he could have been pressed due to a state officer's visit to his village.

The kitchen walls are covered with pictures of young Chinese actresses and singers, and of kitchen appliances. Paper and plastic flowers choke narrow vases. The colors in his house attest to the theory I have of the aesthetics of Tibetan nomads in general and of Dhompa in particular: they have a propensity for the garish. All paper is deemed suitable as wall ornament. This malady is shared by many of my older relatives in exile, whose walls likewise are covered with posters of Indian film stars, horses, old calendars, and pages from newspapers and magazines.

The doctor has heard I have a taste for lamb. After advising Tashi to avoid lamb (it raises the blood pressure, he explains to me), he offers to "cut to the bone," a phrase used for a piece of meat from the thigh or between the shoulder and elbow. He cleans the meat off the bone after I decline his offer to do the honor. He breaks the bone in half. Tashi comments it is a good omen: he was able to break it neatly without cracks and splinters. The doctor smiles broadly. He uses a chopstick to dig out the marrow. He says the marrow from the upper part of the body is preferable to the marrow from the thigh.

Why?

The hand works a lot doing good deeds and bad deeds. The thigh, however, is only used for walking. It is the anterior limb. It only walks, he explains.

I ask him about his children. How many children does he have?

He uses a word in the dialect that allows for wide approximations, a word that suggests a number anywhere from eight to twenty. For instance, when I asked my cousin how many gifts I would need to buy to offer to people in Dhompa, he had indicated eight to twenty. When I pressed for a definite number, he finally said thirty.

I press the doctor for an exact number.

He begins to count on his fingers, draping each child's name on a finger, then going on to the next as though only through naming can he be assured of the number of children he has managed to sire in his house.

Nine, he announces. One boy died when he was still a baby.

I ask him how it is possible to be imprecise about the number of one's own children.

He lets out a big laugh. We have had this conversation before.

The doctor prepares medicine for Tashi. He looks through drawers, adding a pinch of small stones, three tiny conch shells—which he says are from the sacred lake Manasarovar—a few strips of plant stem, assorted leaves, and a chunk of black substance that could be a nut, a stone, or a piece of bone. I recognize the brilliant orange of marigold. These are crushed into a powder. He instructs Tashi to take a spoonful of the powder with warm water after her last meal of the day.

It is, he warns, extremely bitter to taste.

He asks if I can raise money to build a clinic in Dhompa. He will run it, he tells me, as we bend to touch our foreheads in a gesture of parting.

"We have lived another beautiful summer day," Tashi answers for me in response to his request. She says an old body feels everything more acutely.

"We Tibetans are lucky. We have our yaks, our rivers, and our mountains. What do the Chinese have? They have fields that do not yield what our fields bring us. As long as we have our yaks, we will not starve," she says.

Clouds take over the sky. It rains as we head home. We run into the kitchen and hide there until the rain abates. We have milk, we have yogurt, and our mud stove is glowering thanks to sweet-smelling fall manure. Our garden has spinach. Our herd is eating grass and wildflowers, now strengthened by rain, somewhere in the hills above our heads. The river has water. The roof keeps out most of the rain. Our world is small and complete for now.

CHAPTER EIGHTEEN

Imagined Country

The chieftain of Upper Gerji and the chieftain of Bongsar were not rich but they presided over their audience with a regal air and moved around their small, dark rooms in Kathmandu with a physical rectitude that intimated they were in command. In their presence I felt I ought to be deferential, for they were often surrounded by people of Nangchen, who, subdued by the decorum of the past, rarely spoke out of turn. The chiefs sat cross-legged in their beds, like lamas. They were different from other men in exile who worked to support their families. As far back as I remember, for my mother took me to see them every week, they were reliably home both late morning and midafternoon, a prayer book lying open in front of them. They wore their Tibetan chuba even in summer, braided their long hair, and rarely ventured out without their broad-brimmed hats. I never saw them light the stove, chop vegetables, or prepare tea for guests in their kitchens. They never wandered the streets and if they stepped out of their homes, it was toward the stupa for their early morning or late afternoon circumambulations. They spoke in the Nangchen dialect and never learned to speak the language of the host country, even though they lived more than half of their lives in exile. The people from Nangchen treated these erstwhile chiefs with respect, following a habit from the past of preserving their loyalty foremost to the lamas and chiefs of their old land before anyone else, perhaps even the government in exile.

My mother spoke to me in the dialect and encouraged me to maintain my identity as someone from Nangchen. This form of regional identification, I realized as I grew older, is more common among khampas in exile and is often bemoaned by government officials who have tried to create a common identity and feeling of nationalism in exile.

The elders in exile were always eager to talk about politics. They deliberated over who would help free Tibet—America, England, or the United Nations; it was clear we would need others to help us return home. Some of the elders had fought against the Chinese in the Chushi Gangdruk, the volunteer army formed in eastern Tibet independent of the Lhasa government. This army united people from Kham and Amdo to fight the Chinese under one banner from 1958 until 1974. When the Chushi Gangdruk was disbanded in 1974, many of its members left their base in Mustang, Nepal, and returned to life as civilian refugees. They learned to put their faith in the Tibetan government in exile, and year after year, they nurtured hope for rangzen, buoyed intermittently by the international recognition of our leader, the Dalai Lama. Many of these elders died alone and without recognition from the exile administration for their role in the fight for Tibet.

The elders focused their memories of Tibet on nostalgic peccadilloes they committed as children or the journeys they took to other regions within Tibet or on the beauty of the land. Their accounts rarely held anger against the Chinese. Since they did not possess anger themselves, they could bequeath no anger to me. They told stories of the old days so that when I returned to Tibet it would be familiar. I grew up, as perhaps many of my generation did, without anger for the fate of our country, just sadness and confusion.

When Indian classmates in school asked about my extended family, I explained I did not know where they were.

How was that possible?

My mother had been the only one in her family to escape from Tibet.

Why?

Because China invaded my country.

Why?

We didn't have a big army. It was our karma.

As a child I did not see my mother as belonging to another time, because most of my views and habits had been informed and shaped by her. I was more rooted in her past than in my own life. In school my friends found I was too quick to give my belongings away to them while at home my mother cautioned me against a materialism she saw in me. In school, I spoke in English and immersed myself in working toward future success; I won medals and studied for the highest grades. When I returned home for holidays, I spent my time with the old chiefs and monks and learned to adopt a less ambitious and more ambiguous notion of the future because I was not sure if that future was going to be in Tibet or in exile. In school I looked to the future; at home I clung to the past. The two worlds, so different in their pursuits, functioned independently for me—yet they held together because my mother was a strong and steadfast bridge.

In my mother's world my life was a success if I was literate in Tibetan, if I studied Buddhism, and if I grew to be a good and kind person. The rest, she said, would come and go. She gave away her possessions quite happily: there went a man wearing her jacket, and there was that woman with the precious amber stones my mother had loaned ten, fifteen, years ago and never claimed back. She would remind me often to put people before money, success, or a job. She had been parted from the wealth of her family and her life of comparative ease at the age of eighteen so she viewed material wealth as evanescent. Quite often she would exclaim we were rich even though we had very little.

"We have ten thousand rupees," she would say. "We are rich!"

She would show me where her money was hidden—usually in a handbag or in the cupboard under her chubas. She would show me the few jewels she owned and tell me they belonged to the two of us. Everything we owned, we shared. I was an undemanding child because I thought everything I needed was already within reach. I rarely coveted what other children had because I felt rooted in the bounty my mother managed to create in our small home. At least twice a week she returned home from work with half of a cookie or half of a fried chicken in her handbag. "It was so delicious I could not eat it without saving some for you," she would say.

She never spoke very much of the places we lived in and left: Clement Town, Dharamshala, Delhi, and, finally, Kathmandu. I don't think she ever felt she was in the right place. But for me, I think she would have returned to live with her family in Tibet. Home, to me, was any place by my mother's side. Since my mother's death, the idea of home has assumed many forms. I use the word loosely to refer to India, Nepal, and even Tibet when I am in San Francisco. When I am in Nepal or Tibet, I refer to San Francisco as home. Like my mother, more and more, I feel I am in many places and not quite in the right place. Home is a place that is always imminent but never present. Or maybe it is the very opposite—maybe I am at ease wherever I am, and the feeling of not belonging to any one place is a condition of being at home.

As a refugee in Nepal and India, I carried an uncertainty in me as though I were placed on the border of belonging and not belonging, law and lawlessness. I learned how to hide by learning from whom I needed to hide, and to whom I could safely reveal myself. I did not depend on schoolteachers or books to give me these lessons. I learned after encounters when the police stopped us on our way back from the market late in the evening to ask for our papers, or when I traveled to boarding school, and then later to university, and my documents were scrutinized by the immigration officers, or when Tibetans were prohibited from small protests outside the Chinese embassy, or when I saw that there were no laws protecting my mother. Tibetans living in Nepal and India feel vulnerable. We are guests who are reminded of our status through the documents we acquire with great trouble—the refugee travel permits, questionable Indian and Nepali passports and driver's licenses—that never give us the assurance of those who belong to a place.

We wear a cloak of culpability the moment we see a person of authority because we know we are without representation. We tell each other to lie low. We tell each other to walk the other way if we see a police officer. We believe it is easier to give money before we are questioned because we will naturally be at fault.

We learn we cannot form deep roots because we do not have the right to place and citizenship, and because we do not have citizenship to a place we do not have the right to a voice. We are alienated from our own past and from the future of the countries we live in. Where we are is the best we can hope for. We learn to be grateful.

We call each other *kyab chol pa*—"those who have taken refuge"—and after more than five decades of relief assistance, there are many of us who put our hands out more readily than we use them to work. As people in need of help, we are sought by nonprofit organizations whose representatives come to visit, and we sing and dance for them. When they suggest they know what is better for us than we do ourselves, we listen to them because they determine what we can have. In this way we are helped and we remain oppressed by our own helplessness and their generosity.

We call each other *dhu shor pa* or *yul shor pa*—one who has lost his land—or *sar jor pa*—one who has recently arrived. The Chinese government states that we are the people who forsook the land willingly. Amongst our own, we are distracted every now and then by regional and religious factionalisms. We cannot help ourselves from creating divisions based on our arrival dates. The new refugees who escape each winter from Tibet provoke ridicule, discrimination, and also our admiration, for they have lived in Tibet. They know the happiness of being born in our motherland.

We live in a condition of expectation: our hope not quite ours, our power not ours. We take to dreaming easily. We dream of returning to a country our young have never seen and for whom the notion of Tibet has come through the writings by early Western explorers, who, having succeeded in entering the sequestered country, wrote as if they could interpret the mumblings of red-skirted monks, wild-haired, butter-reeking men and women. Perhaps these explorers had never known such a land where it was incumbent on visitors to disguise themselves in order to be disregarded. It was those hardy Westerners who penetrated the land and emerged alive who committed Tibetans to words, and who presented to us the idea of our own country. They fueled the aura of mystique that was accepted and that continues to envelop the country, even to this day.

The idea of Tibet is where fable and fantasy coalesce for some people. Tibet with its gentle monks, horse-riding warriors, and reincarnate human-divinities is fantastic and far away, so much so that many people often forget it is an occupied country. This has proved problematic to Tibetans like me, born in exile, who still struggle to find a way to speak about Tibet without the influences of the past or prevailing perceptions coloring our description.

Tibet was forbidden to me as a child. It was a country to which I could not go because I was Tibetan. It was a land that carried much of my mother's nostalgia. The halcyon days of her life were spent in Tibet. It was an object of yearning and wonder for those who belonged and those who did not—all agreeing on the premise that there was nothing quite like Tibet.

Looking over my documents at the American Embassy in Kathmandu, the staff at the counter asked if I was Tibetan.

"No, I am a Nepali," I said, pointing toward my Nepali passport.

"It is okay to say you are Tibetan," the man responded in Tibetan. Overtaken by embarrassment—ours is a small community—I nodded self-consciously. A recollection of the exchange moves me deeply every time I think about it. The exchange encapsulates the vulnerability of life in exile. It is only a Tibetan who can reassure another Tibetan that it is all right to reveal that he or she is a Tibetan, because only a refugee recognizes, by virtue of confronting identity and politics on an everyday basis, the hesitations in revealing his or her identity.

Are we Tibetans fatalistic as a people? Are we passive and peace-loving? Are we immobilized due to our Buddhist inclination to leave everything to the will of the deities and our karma? Have we come to see ourselves solely through someone else's representation? These are questions I ask myself; I seldom have unambiguous answers. Quite often when I reveal myself as a Tibetan in San Francisco, strangers ask if I meditate, if I am a vegetarian, or if I possess innately the tranquillity that they find so difficult to achieve. They tell me with assurance that Tibetans are a gentle, peaceful people and when they announce that, I think of the place I belong to, the warriors I come from.

As Tibetan refugees we often applaud our own capacity to adjust. Put us in India and we'll be fine, take us to the United States and we'll adapt there too. Without a real home, any place is home-like. And those parts of me that I share with many Tibetans—the capacity for an unquestioning acceptance of circumstances, the reluctance to probe or to inspect beyond a certain degree—sometimes serve me well in my roving life. It is this same sanguine quality that enables many nomads to move from Dhompa to small towns. Some are abetted by poverty, some forced or lured by the government's resettlement plans. Others follow relatives without much deliberation or preparation. There are those who journey even farther, to India and Nepal. Maybe there is a better life out there. But it is not always desperation, political fear and repression, or ambition that drives them. Their move can be propelled by a simple idea followed by quick action: a woman can tell herself, "I must see the Dalai Lama before I die," and that will set her in motion; a man might say, "I must send my child to study Tibetan in India" or "I have killed a man and must escape." They do not learn phrases in preparation, they do not acclimatize their body to heat, nor does it occur to them to know the politics, the laws, or the geography of the countries to which they travel. They simply start moving.

Flight is inherent to the recent history of Tibet. My mother moved to Kathmandu from Delhi saying she wanted to be physically close to her land. I came to the United States to attend graduate school primarily because it was unbearable for me to live in Kathmandu after my mother's death. I thought distance and a new place would lessen the sadness of her absence: that was the extent of my ambition for a future. Now I feel I should return home even though I am not certain anymore what I mean by that. The flight continues: Tibetans in Tibet try to leave for India and Nepal, and Tibetans in India and Nepal try to leave for the

United States or some other Western shore. And having arrived, a longing arises to return, because we are nobody if we cannot hold the comfort of a country to which we can return. The imagined country never leaves us. It exists and is created to give us authority, identity, and a cause. Tibetans born in exile learn a language of desire, to be part of what is twice removed from us. We cannot claim the experience of parturition from home because we have never inhabited the home we seek to return to.

An imagined country has a tenacious grip, perhaps more so than a known one, for there are no disappointments or memories to contradict the ideal. The imagined country is an ideal, and within it, a perspective of the motherland gathers meaning. In this lies the irony of a refugee's state of mind, seeking to establish roots in a place that bears very little resemblance to what it becomes over time. Change or contemporaneity is often not consistent with such a state of mind. Time had in essence stopped for Tibetans when China drew a blanket of complete silence over Tibet—from 1959 through 1979—cleaving those called refugees-in-exile from those left behind in Tibet. Nobody knew of the other during this period.

Each year I receive news of the death of elders inside Tibet and a little more of our history vanishes with them. The elders in exile, watching more and more of their own die, speak less and less of going home. They joke that they have lived undisturbed for decades in exile next door to people they would have killed and stolen from in Tibet. Their stories of Tibet are the strongest link their children and grandchildren have to their country. Very few Tibetans born in exile have been to Tibet and it is uncertain whether they will ever have a chance to visit their country in their lifetime.

If the elders appear lost to their prayers, a large number of young Tibetans in exile seem to exist in a state of suspension between their dreams of rangzen and the disquietude in not finding their way into a living or a voice within our community in exile. The youth hold that the Dalai Lama is the symbol of Tibet, but they cannot allow the demise of the pursuit of rangzen. They cannot put their hopes in the deities of the land or in the conciliatory approaches of governments to fight for them. In time many of them are seen to put their efforts toward emigration, thinking that in America, Europe, or some other part of the world they will be able to undo the anxiety that comes from being dispossessed. In some other language they will be able to talk and fight for the freedom and future of Tibet.

I do not know yet how to fight for a country's independence— as some younger Tibetans hope for—nor can I put my entire faith in karma as the elders do. In this way, a struggle for my country continues.

CHAPTER NINETEEN

I Will Carry the Sky

When we—approximately sixty-six thousand speakers of the Nangchen language—meet, we lean a little toward each other, allow our foreheads to touch, and clasping each other's hands, we ask, *Ku wop jhi?*

Here *ku* is the honorific word for the body. The word is used for lamas and elders we want to differentiate from ourselves. Without the honorific, the greeting is less formal.

Wop jhi? Any inconvenience or trouble?

The language of this greeting—Has your body suffered any effort?—pays attention to the quotidian rhythms of the nomad's life where an arrival indicates a journey on foot or on horseback. And we ask, *Ka a thi?* Are you tired? The words allow an intimacy and a refinement so out of character with the khampa's rugged features and dusty clothing. It is a similar delicacy that prompts a host to bring tea, barley, and butter the moment a guest enters the house and takes a seat. A host in Dhompa does not place on the guest the onus of accepting or expressing gratitude by asking them if they would like refreshments.

This is no ordinary language. I imagine it to have been created by a nomad who tended sheep in summer and then renounced her herd to become a nun. I imagine she was a troglodyte for whom every little sound in her cave was an opportunity for exaggeration. When it rains we say the sky has come down. When it thunders, we say a dragon is speaking in the sky. When we lack a metaphor or a simile, we look toward the yak.

"We are content like our yaks," we say. "We are stupid like our yaks," we say. "We are dependable like our yaks."

There is no hello to establish a meeting, even if it comes after many years of separation; neither is there a word that strictly signifies a parting. We do not express our gratitude in words of "thank you" and "please" readily in this dialect. The words for "please" sound either childish or beseeching. They are typically used when speaking to lamas or those in higher authority. People nod or smile or say *tse ring* to show appreciation: "thank you" is a deferential tool. After a month in Tibet, I throw out my polite "thank you's" and "please's" along with other English words. A silent acceptance takes its place. Younger Tibetans in Tibet give thanks in Chinese and they teach their children to be familiar with etiquette and good manners. The elders say that the expression "thank you" comes in handy in a splintered community. It is a tool of the modern world.

We are also without words for new commodities: motorbike, cola, chewing gum, instant noodles, cell phone, electric cord. Although words have been created for such appliances and can be found in the new Tibetan dictionaries, they have not yet made it to Dhompa. Nomads use the Chinese terms for driver, television, motorbike, and beer, twisting the words charmingly to the sounds of the dialect, much like the way Tibetans in exile have adapted Anglo-Indian words: *gilas* for "glass," *mok* for "mug," *mota* for "automobile," and *tarik*, a Hindi word, for "date."

English is the language I use instinctively to express myself but it is the Nangchen language that brings me a visceral joy. I am unable, however, to use it to argue or to be ecstatic. I know no epithet in the dialect and tell myself that while I am among my people,

I must learn their language to show my pleasure as well as my displeasure. I ask a monk, who possesses a colorful tongue and whose sentences are accompanied by swear words, to explain some of them to me. He says he would like to abandon swear words but the words cleave to his tongue and will not leave. He repeats them one by one.

Dikpa khor or *dhig dhig khor.* (I will) carry all sins
Namkha khor. (I will) carry the sky
Zamling khor. (I will) carry the earth
Tse deb su thop. (I will) accomplish everything in this lifetime
Zamba ja. (I will) bear the sins of one hundred butchers

They are beautiful and sound more like benevolent wishes to me. He says they are big promises, boastful and insincere in nature. How can one person carry the world? How can one person carry all the sins of the world? How is it possible to speak of seeing a deity after death? These words are meant to burden the listener with empty assurances and false hope.

But the words themselves carry no ill will, I say. These are the words of a lover. I let them wander in my mouth.

Dhig dhig khor. Jamling khor. I will carry your sins. I will carry the world. How can such a phrase leave you unmoved?

The monk says the words are egotistical.

And then, there are the blessings. Every day my mother would kiss me and say, *Ame ga ga. Ga sho.* Mother's loved one. May you be happy. *Ame ga ga. Tse ring.* Mother's loved one. May you live long. She did not need to say she loved me.

We have not forgotten how to use our words in the grasslands, as well as in the towns.

When Dorje is exasperated, he says, *Khi mizuk kame kumen nagbur.* The dog has no option but to bark at a shadow (of a thief). The words indicate he is left with no option but to retaliate with force, anger, or some other unfavorable action. He also makes use of this line when he is upset with someone who repeatedly makes a fool out of him. In the old days this idiom was used to fight against an offender in court.

When Dorje can eat no more, he says, "I am full like the mountain." If someone is stingy with his food, Dorje advises the person, "Eat until you do not feel hunger."

What if you do not trust a person?

Why, he advises, then you smile sweetly and say, "Your feet are like ghosts."

I discover my favorites and write them down. If someone insists on bad-mouthing you, you might say, "The ground does not sink yet I walk lightly. The air is so high above yet I walk with my head bent low." This is to show that you, in contrast, are kindhearted and humble.

"If your mouth is silent, you will not have fights."

"If you cover your head, you will not break your neck."

I have come to love the dialect for its sounds and its courtesies. Dorje complains the young do not resort to these idioms. He states they prefer more direct ways of speaking.

I remind him the young still take leave of each other with traditional greetings: *Ku tse ring. Tse ring.* May your body live long. Live long.

Tse ring is a blessing used by strangers and well-wishers alike all over Shornda and other parts of eastern Tibet. It serves as "thank you" and "goodbye." Taxi drivers say it upon reaching destinations and shopkeepers say it when I leave their shops. The words make all simple pleasures identifiable. It gets to a state where I want to go to the market and buy from Tibetans, just to be blessed from the mouths of strangers.

CHAPTER TWENTY

Portrait of a Lama

At seventy-six, Ashang is my oldest relative in Tibet. He is also one of the oldest lamas alive in our region, so when I have questions related to family or to the practice of Buddhism in Dhompa, I turn to him.

The nunnery he supports and leads is tucked in the mountains not too far from the town of Nangchen, but for the past year, heeding medical advice, he has spent more months in town where he recently purchased a house. I head to the nunnery without checking with his attendant. A precarious road—created with sheer defiance by the two monks who carry supplies to the monastery on tractors and trucks—clings to the surface of the mountains. Our jeep tips dangerously close to the edge at each turn and I wonder if I will perish on the road, on my way to see him.

The only other inhabitants of this meadow are a family of nomads whose two tents establish the base of their summer grazing land. Nuns in shades of maroon, red, and yellow walk around a stupa as though this is a perfectly logical place to be. The main shrine, a new prayer hall, and a row of stupas are concentrated in one area while scattered tiny huts ornament the base of a hill. Extravagant flowers of summer bloom in the meadows surrounding the nunnery. It is believed that many decades earlier the king of Nangchen deemed this spot auspicious and moved to the valley to supervise the building of his palace. The king soon realized that the hill took all the light and cast huge shadows over the valley where he camped. Day by day his aversion toward this behemoth hill grew until one day he called his men and ordered them to cut its head off.

The men chosen for this task were aggrieved. To disobey the king would bring death upon them but so would an attempt to decimate the huge hill. They convened at dusk to deliberate on a plan. They were willing to carry out the task but couldn't imagine ever achieving it within their lifetime. It would be simpler to move to another location, but who among them would be able to make that suggestion to the king? While they were talking, an old woman who served in the king's household came into their midst and suggested they decapitate the king. The nomads believe she was a deity who came in the form of the old woman. She reminded them that many lives, notwithstanding theirs, would be lost over the years if they carried out the plot to kill the hill. Hers was a terrible suggestion, and yet it was a solution that made more and more sense as they pondered it.

The men gathered at sunrise and assassinated the king. Drops of blood from the king's severed head created sacred relics as soon as they touched the ground. There are no visible protuberances of relics to be seen today but a trail encircles the hill, and it has become a pilgrimage path Tibetans happily walk on as a means to attaining a more favorable rebirth. The king's family and ministers abandoned this land for the lower lands of Nangchen Gar, where they built their palace.

Ashang loves being far away in the mountains and far away from everyone, even his own relatives.

He is not there. I am told he is in Shornda. He left a day ago, a nun informs me. Who are you, she asks.

A visitor.

From outside?

Yes, from outside, I reply.

I make a circumambulation of the little stupa Ashang has built near the main shrine and begin the return journey, hurtling down toward Shornda. But he is not home either. I am told he is attending prayers for a man who died the night before and it will be hours before he returns. I sit in the veranda and wait for him. When he enters through the gate at dusk, I sense his fatigue but his eyes light up when he sees me. He peers into my face and when he is satisfied that I have not altered a great deal, he pats my head and leads me into his room.

I sit on the floor in front of him. An elaborate shrine takes up half of the room and his attendant tells me they had recently custom-ordered it from Chinese woodworkers. A plain wooden cot and chair serve as furniture. A thin lime-green carpet covers the floor and offers no protection from the cold concrete. He says he has his blankets and in the winter he has a heater. We inquire about each other's health and fall into a long silence. His fingers absently turn over the pages of his prayer book. I leave him alone to rest.

The next two days I wander in and out of his gaze. He sits in his room all day. I have been in his house for two days and he has not said much other than respond to my greetings whenever I peep into his room. He is unrepentant of all the time he spends in prayer even when I am visiting him from so far away. Cosmos and poppies bloom in a cement plant box in the front yard of his house.

Late in the evening on the third day he calls out to me. He says he is done praying for the day and he will eat his dinner with me. He looks at me and says, "Poor thing."

He says that quite often. I am uncertain if it is because I remind him of my mother who was his cousin or if it is a reference to my solitary existence. Or perhaps it is my foreignness that alienates him from me. I do not fulfill his expectations of how a woman should be. Not just any woman but a woman who is a niece of his family.

His hair is hoary and stands delicately on his head. He looks like a vagrant or a child who has just woken up from a nap. His expressions are mercurial. A dour expression takes prominence and I am not sure if I like him, but when he smiles at me I am full of love for him because he is my mother's only living cousin.

He feels great curiosity about my life. He asks me about the American "king" he has seen on television. He wants to know what Americans think of Tibetans. What is their opinion of the Chinese? What do ordinary Americans do for work? Do they raise yaks? Are they Buddhists? If not, to whom do they pray?

I take the opportunity to ask him the questions I often mean to ask lamas: What does it mean to be Tibetan? What is our future as Tibetans?

He says Tibetans are unique because we value the practice of Buddhism. He gives the example of Tibetan mothers who in the course of a day point repeatedly toward suffering. They tell their children: don't kill the ant, it will suffer; don't pour hot water on the soil, the earthworm will feel the sting and the heat will cause it great pain; don't pull the dog's tail so hard. We are told to think for the animals and insects who cannot voice their pain but for whom suffering is as acute as it is for humans. From a young age, he says, we are reminded that nobody is free from suffering.

I agree that my Tibetan friends are instinctively more likely to brush away flies or mosquitoes instead of crushing or swatting them. But why is compassion so important? What about our land, our independence? Will compassion free our land?

He says our language contains the essence of our beliefs and it is integral to preserving our culture. If we lose our language, we lose our identity. We will become like them. By "them," he means the Chinese. Very often, when he hears or sees young Tibetans speaking in Chinese, he says, "They are already Chinese, those young Tibetans." He insists young Tibetans are different from him. He fears Tibet will change.

I say maybe the Chinese will change.

It is more possible they will change us, he argues.

Tibetans are Tibetans because of Buddhism he states over and over to me for the remainder of my days with him. All day he sits cross-legged on his bed reading his prayers or nodding off to sleep in between. The only time he leaves his room is when his young attendant helps him to his feet and out into the yard where he stands, legs apart, to take a piss. His eyes are bloodshot. He cannot hear very well.

Once upon a time, he says, he had the keenest eyesight and he had a memory as dependable as the yak, but many years in prison have weakened him, and now, age.

I ask him if I disturb him by sitting in front of him.

He says this is his life, sleeping at his prayers, sitting alone on his bed all day. He assures me I can do as I like and will not disturb him. I sit for long hours watching him. Every now and then he returns my gaze and smiles.

My uncle becomes more sociable in the following days although he continues to end his conversations as abruptly as he begins them. I become adept at following his moods and strike in with questions when I think he is amiable. I ask him if he feels the loss of his youth and if he harbors anger toward the Chinese.

Ashang admits to surges of anger. He was angrier when he was young, but there was nothing he could do about it and he came to acknowledge the events of his life, especially the incomprehensible parts, as resulting from his past actions.

I ask him if this belief in karma renders us Tibetans pliant to conquest.

What would you have us do instead? How would anger change fate, he asks. Perhaps the younger Tibetans are who they are because they cannot accept the nature of cause and effect in their lives. He says he is losing faith in the young, especially those educated in the Chinese system and those working for the government.

How can a country of many people inherit one karma? How is that possible?

He says it is possible. I wait for him to explain, but he sits stubbornly in silence.

Perhaps he is embarrassed that I would ask such questions. He is nostalgic for the old world. He says people were kind then and considerate. He pines for the language of the old world, for its ordinary intimacies, and its poetic tendency of bestowing blessings on people. Where is the thought for such blessings in Chinese, he asks. He wants to know if the English language allows for such considerations and if we bless and pray for strangers. He says the young don't speak like the people of the old days.

I tell him they do. I do, when I speak in the dialect.

He is not convinced. In the old days a man was admired if he was a good Buddhist practitioner. Now a man is admired if he's rich and can lie convincingly.

How is it that lamas could not predict the future of Tibet? Can they pray for our futures and change our fate?

How can lamas change such big things, he bursts out in irritation.

But you are always praying, I add.

"Half of us are in Chinese hands," Ashang says. "We are already bought. There is nothing we can do."

He fears current government officials are perpetrators of many crimes: bribery, embezzlement, lies, and nepotism. He is frustrated that the laws restricting the movements of the average Tibetan seem to embolden the officials to do as they wish. He cites examples of people he knows who acquired jobs after bribing officials. He is torn between his presentiment of decay and his hope for renewal. Just as I do not follow his prototype of a woman, younger Tibetans are not the kind of practicing Buddhists he would wish them to be.

I tell him people of all nationalities bemoan the same deficiencies in their young.

He feels I do not understand because I was not in this world when Tibet was a different place.

Those who study Buddhist texts understand best what it means to be Tibetan, he states. Maybe teachers returning from Buddhist schools in Golog and Dege will be able to teach the good ways to the people, he hopes. A year ago, he tells me, a group of Chinese officials were brought on a tour to his nunnery. The officials roamed the grounds and were delighted when the nuns greeted them by singing in Tibetan.

Why were the nuns singing?

The lyrics to the song expressed their desire to be free of the Chinese. In the song the nuns asked the Chinese to leave their land. And all the while the officials smiled in pleasure and applauded. Ashang laughs in delight. His hands slap his thighs with gusto.

He too was rebellious once, he tells me. When he was in prison, he altered the words to the song they sang daily to Mao. Instead of praising Mao, he muttered, "die, die," under his breath. Ashang and the monk standing beside him were called into the jailor's office. The monk did not betray Ashang. Regardless, Ashang was put in solitary confinement for a month. The window to the cell was so tiny that even thin strips of light had trouble entering the room. A steam bun was all he got as the day's food. He had to urinate and defecate in a bucket and the bucket was his only companion. One month in that cell was a long time, he recalls.

He suddenly switches to another story. There was a lama who was assigned to knit socks for soldiers. He became very adept at knitting. Ashang was young and strong and was delegated to manual labor. Every morning the knitting crew received yarn and knitting needles and at the day's end they had to return them to the soldiers. Ashang requested the lama to make a rosary for his use. Of all the beautiful and valuable prayer beads he has used in his life, the wool thread with 108 knots was the most beautiful, he states.

One night in prison, he continues, he had a dream. He woke up in his dream to a sky of stars above him. A white horse idled beside him. He sat on the horse and the horse took him deep into a valley and toward a man who stood alone in an empty field. As Ashang came closer to the man he recognized him as Milarepa. (What happiness it was to see the face of Mila, even in a dream, Ashang says.) He got off his horse and kissed Milarepa's feet.

Milarepa commanded him to ride to the next valley. Ashang obeyed and came upon several squares of grass. He saw a small house on fire. When the fire died down, Ashang looked into the ruins of the house and saw Chairman Mao's body being devoured by insects. He said he felt giddy. His heart sang. He went closer to verify if it indeed was Chairman Mao. It was. He wept and quickly returned to where he had seen Milarepa. There was nobody there.

Ashang awoke to tears streaming down his cheeks. For days he carried the dream in his heart as a delicious secret.

Did Mao die soon after?

He did, Ashang says. He died a week or so after that dream.

And did Ashang feel the same happiness as in his dream?

He admits rejoicing in a person's death is not good, but yes, he did feel happy. He still feels a little giddy when he recalls that dream. He tells me he worries constantly about Tibet.

He is serious again. "The Chinese say they are a nation for peace. How can they be a nation for peace when they kill so many people? If they are a nation of peace, why do they need so many soldiers and so many guns?"

I ask him if it is possible to get what we want through prayers.

Prayers can remove obstacles, he tells me. But we are all tainted and therefore prayers are not so powerful anymore. "Our connection with the divine is impure. But we must pray anyway. What else is there?" He adds, "I am tired. Tired of living and seeing so much in this one lifetime."

Ashang reserves his highest disdain for the Tibetan officials who are members of the Communist party. "They are no good," he mutters. He is unable to compose himself. His equanimity is shattered. He stares at me, a look of bewilderment in his eyes before he returns quietly to his prayers. I wrap a blanket over his crossed legs and pat his feet gently. I leave him to his thoughts for he has slipped away.

***

I peep into Ashang's room the next day and he greets me with a beatific smile. His eyes crinkle into a line. His pupils sparkle. I beg him to tell me about my mother. What of the times when he would visit her in Dhompa as a young boy?

He says those were good days. He does not recall there being so many poor nomads as there are today. He admits he never really got around much then but still, he says, he did not hear of people dying of hunger. The poor were taken care of by the rich relatives, he says.

How does one teach a child to be compassionate, I ask him.

My dearest friend Val and I have many discussions on this subject. She would like her sons to be considerate and kind individuals. We wonder if kindness has to be taught just as parents toilet train their children or wean them from breast milk.

He says you teach by being kind. By telling a child repeatedly to be compassionate toward others, you teach her that it is natural and necessary to be so.

Just then his attendant, a monk who has tended to Ashang since he was a young boy, comes in through the door muttering angrily. He has just come back from shopping for lunch where some incident upset him. He withholds details of the altercation.

Ashang is now distracted by the subject of wayward Tibetans. "Money is destroying us. It is hard to live without money and hard to live with too much money," he bursts out.

"The land around us is rich and can feed us, but Tibetans sell the land or loan it to the Chinese and then we buy our food from them. We are paying to eat from our own land!" He takes the names of young men who have died in the past year. They made money from selling caterpillar fungus and they purchased cars and drove themselves straight to their deaths.

"We are stupid. People don't say their prayers anymore because they are busy worshipping their televisions and making money."

Surely it is not all lost, I tell myself, and surely he can see it is not all lost for he is beseeched by Tibetans all day long seeking his advice, seeking divinations, asking for blessings, asking him to remove their obstacles: the devotion to the lama has not changed. Some days he hides from people so he can say his prayers in peace. Strangely enough, the faith of these city people from whom he earns his livelihood, even the very officials he rails against, is not accepted as proof of the continuation of Buddhist culture. "They are killing me," he complains of the people and of the nomads who come for him from dawn to dusk. He says he gets no rest or

time to say his prayers. He thinks it is better for him to be alone
in the mountains. He sees a lot of things and his heart hurts, he
confides. He is convinced too much interaction with the world
disturbs his blood pressure.

The more time I spend with him, the more I come to realize
that the loss he speaks of has much to do with the Tibetan language and knowledge of Buddhism.

Ashang was recognized as a lama at the age of five and separated
from his family soon after to live in a monastery in Nangchen.
From a young age he lived with monks and underwent a rigorous
Buddhist education in preparation to be a spiritual teacher, but
just as he was on the brink of leading the monastery at nineteen
he was named a criminal, and taken to prison. He was released
after decades of incarceration, an old man with a head and heart
full of sorrow.

He remembers his monastery as a vibrant place of learning
where they had their own astrologers. He tells me proudly their
astrological calendars agreed with the one brought out by the
astrologers in Lhasa. Some monasteries still have knowledgeable
monks but they don't take the time to continue with their studies,
he complains. Again, it is the loss of tradition that troubles him.
For more than two decades, he says, Tibetans were not able to
teach or learn anything about their own culture, they just worked
to build Mao's dream for China. Many knowledgeable Tibetans
perished in prisons during that period.

I tell him it must anger the Chinese government to see Tibetan
elders persist in following their culture and Buddhist beliefs after
decades of reforms, reeducation programs, and punishment.

He believes the people of his generation, men and women who
were seven years and older in 1959, know the importance of culture precisely because of the suffering they lived through. It is the

young he fears for. He wonders who will speak of Tibet before 1959 once his generation is gone.

"You are like a Westerner. Poor thing," he says to me.

I know there's nothing I can say or do to make myself the Tibetan he would like me to be. If I wore a chuba and was able to recite all the prayers and talk about Buddhism with him, perhaps I would be more Tibetan. He asks if I know my mother's prayers.

I don't know what he means.

He laughs and pats me on the head. He explains that each person ought to know his mother's and his father's prayers.

He says the family of the Dhompas where my mother came from would have had a prayer. I tell him I don't know anything about that for my mother had never referred to such a thing. He chants his mother's prayer out loud; his mother who was also a daughter of the Dhompas. He tells me that being Tibetan I must know my heritage. The Dhompas, his mother's family and my mother's family, are his links to Nangchen's history and to the history of Tibet.

I tell him the world beyond Tibet, or even beyond Dhompa, does not care about the history of the Dhompa family.

He says I am mistaken. *Rupa*, one's bone, is important. The Dhompas are a race of good people. He makes this pronouncement as though it will lead us back into a place of happy memories—a place he cannot yet give up.

I tell Ashang about a photograph taken possibly in the summer of 1957 when my mother was fourteen and on a pilgrimage to Lhasa with her mother. For several months my mother had traveled with a party of sixty or so nomads. They would ride for a few hours in the morning and then camp in the afternoons. The photo was my mother's first and only image of her life inside Tibet. There is no indication whether the photographer was called to their room in Lhasa or whether they went to a photo studio. There are no belongings betraying the identity of the room. The two young girls, my mother and Tashi, hold nothing in their hands.

Their hands are pointed accusingly toward the ground in a soldier's stance. Their bodies are held rigid. They wear none of the brocade and silk you would expect from the daughter and the wife of a chieftain. Tashi looks fierce in the picture. Two ambers, the size of small tangerines, sit tightly on the two sides of her forehead. The dress stops at her ankle. My mother's look is one I have never seen in photos from her life in India and Nepal. She looks timidly into the camera as though she was hoping to define herself to the person who was taking the photo. She was aware that she would see herself for the first time imprinted on a piece of paper.

I tell Ashang she looks like an ordinary nomad in the photograph. The world of the Dhompas he is so proud of, the glory of over two hundred years of power, should have been evident.

Ashang laughs; they were nomads on a pilgrimage to Lhasa.

He lived many years of his life in the labor prisons because the Chinese believed, as he did, that blood set him apart. Being the son of the chief of Bachen in Nagchukha and the nephew of the chief of Dhompa, and a young lama, he had far too many privileges. Just one of these circumstances warranted a long imprisonment under the clause of counterrevolutionary crime.

Ashang remembers there were as many as five hundred people, a substantial number of them aristocrats from central Tibet, in the prison near Nagchukha. He worked outdoors all day, building roads and digging the intransigent ground in preparation for the great fields that were supposed to feed the huge nation of China. He said he worked for twelve hours and then attended the thought-reform study sessions in the evenings. The sessions were meant to obliterate his identity and gradually have him submit to the Communist party. He does not use the official Chinese term for the prison system—he does not know the word. He refers to it simply as prison and says that because he was a lama he was naturally suspected of being a dangerous enemy. Lamas and chiefs were seen to be more resistant to Communist ideology. It was true, he says, they could not easily be molded into Communists.

The object of the labor reform camp was to render the prisoner into an obedient, unthinking subject. The prisoner had to acknowledge his crimes, submit to superiors, and finally pledge his loyalty to the state and its laws. It took Tibetans some time to figure out the game: prisoners had to admit to crimes they had not committed. There was no place for truth in the system, just the act of allegiance to the new government.

I remind him there are many Tibetans imprisoned today for expressing their loyalty to the Dalai Lama or for simply voicing their dissatisfaction with the current policies. They probably undergo similar torture and have to do hard labor.

He remembers there were six prisoners to a small cell. The prisoners who were real criminals were treated better than the lamas and the chiefs brought in on counterrevolutionary charges. The criminals were put in charge and he had been wary of them, for they were quick to report on little acts: saying prayers, favorable mentions of the past, complaints against the Chinese. Ashang says monks and lamas often gravitated toward each other and tried to help each other. He remembers well a Lhasa nobleman he befriended—he no longer recalls his name—who had a prayer bead given to him by the Dalai Lama and this man got great comfort from the beads during his years in prison. The man would enlist Ashang's help in hiding the beads when the guards inspected his cell.

They worked long hours every day and thought they would spend their entire lives in prison. Each day Tibetans died of starvation, disease, execution, torture, and sheer misery. Many were beaten up and left to die. The cries of dying Tibetans rang through the halls. It was astonishing to Ashang to witness how little the dying men and women meant to the guards; they dragged the dead away like a log of wood down the hallway and disposed of them in ditches. The lamas would quietly pray for the dead without moving their lips. Ashang tries not to think of those days. His heart hurts when he does, he tells me.

One early September morning in 1976, he was on the roof of one of the prison wings rearranging tiles, his task for the day, when he saw a guard beckon to three others. When the guard finished speaking, the men fell to their knees. They sobbed and beat their fists against their foreheads. Ashang wondered if the guards had committed a crime and were reacting to their punishment, but then two other soldiers came along and threw themselves upon the ground. He went over to a fellow prisoner and relayed the scene he had just witnessed. The man said somebody high up had died.

Not long after, as though reminded of their responsibilities, the guards instructed all prisoners to return to their cells. As the prisoners waited in their cells a second instruction was made over the loudspeaker for them to gather outside in the courtyard. A senior guard announced in a breaking voice that something terrible had happened; their leader, beloved as a father, had died. The guard warned the prisoners they would have real reason to grieve now because great sorrow was coming to them. It was due to Chairman Mao's great vision that Tibetans had been kept alive. Now without him, their days were going to darken. He told the prisoners to prepare to lament for the suffering that would come to them. The Tibetans were confused. They waited in their cells. Much to their surprise, the guards did not put them to work for a few days. The prisoners grew uneasy, finding it strange to be ignored and left without work. They could not go out and they could not socialize with each other. Everyone sat in their cells and waited. Ashang said he and the other lamas enjoyed that brief interlude from work and took the chance to concentrate on their prayers.

Tibetans were happy that Chairman Mao was dead, but they could not share their happiness or reveal their thoughts to each other. Mao was a phantom formed from slogans and songs they had been forced to memorize. They reasoned that with him gone, his plans for them would end too. They feared too that something worse would emerge as the guards had indicated, but could not foresee what could be in store for them that was worse than what they were already undergoing.

A few days later, a Tibetan inmate, who was the leader of their cell and who assisted the guards, warned the prisoners that they would be expected to weep or give woeful speeches as part of the mourning ritual. Ashang was distressed, as nothing would bring tears to his eyes. Lamas and chiefs were the only ones, he recalls, who had trouble crying. Others found tears easily enough. He laughs recalling the tears people had to shed, not for the suffering they endured day after day but for the death of the man who had brought them to such desolation.

Mao's death was followed by rumors of impending attacks from unnamed enemies. The prisoners were made to dig trenches night and day in preparation for these attacks. Tibetan prisoners feared unnameable forms of death and torture at the hands of the Chinese guards, and now all of a sudden the guards too feared an assault upon them. Ashang could not imagine who was coming to fight the Chinese. He knew it would not be his own people, for every Tibetan was aware that there were no bombs or army to free them. During this period of restive paranoia the Tibetan prisoners briefly felt as though they were on the same side as the Chinese guards.

After not too long Ashang was told the prison was closing down and that most of them were being transferred to different locations. Ashang does not give me an exact date except to say it was a few years after Mao's death. Like many of my other relatives, Ashang was not sent home in 1978 but transferred to what he calls a semi-prison camp near Xining.

Another relative says Ashang was perhaps in the *laojia*, the camp that formed the second category of the forced labor system, which provided a little more freedom because it did not have armed guards. However, they lived in the same repressive and confined conditions. After a few more years, he was transferred again. He says he and his friends called this time at this third camp *ta tserpa,* "tethered like horses."

Ashang was released in 1982 after more than two decades in prison. He likened his first steps outside the gates of the camp to waking up from a dream and trying to separate the dream world from the day world. His parents, he was soon to learn, had died in prison. So had his aunts (my grandmother and grandaunt), and other relatives. He did not know where the rest of his family was and so he went to his monastery. He closed his eyes and tried to remember it as he had left it: the main prayer hall, the kitchen, and the stupa. If it had been the old days, there would have been monks saying their prayers, and the kitchen would have been warm and fragrant with butter and tea. He said he walked within the silence of ruins and found a dark room that was still standing. There he discovered two monks and a horse. The monks wept when they recognized him and they offered him scarves. It was a simple but warm welcome for the returning lama. The three shared the room, and gradually, on hearing that their lama had returned, many former monks found their way to the monastery. The monks had not said their prayers out loud for a long time as they too had been in prison or on communal farms. They had lived in darkness for twenty-four years following the Chinese regime's law forbidding all religious activities and all private practices that formed the basis of their culture and identity. Everyone was afraid to say their prayers out loud or talk about what they had been through. It was a strange time, Ashang said. He was free because he was no longer in a prison cell but his tongue remained chained. He was now in a borderless prison wherever he lived.

Ashang stops his story to point to a photograph of me on his altar. I am in my school uniform and I am twelve. In the photo I am wearing a green blazer, a green and gold striped tie, and my hair is oiled and tidy. I am smiling shyly into the camera.

"Poor thing," he says as though the girl in the picture is a stranger to both of us. He had heard from my mother I was a good child.

He prays for me every single day, he says.

My mother sent that photo to him a year after it was taken. Since I was thirteen, this uncle has learned to love me and the way he loves is to pray for my happiness and for my safety every day. Ashang asks me if I remember how my mother had reacted on hearing her brother and sisters were alive. Had she cried?

I do remember clearly because it was the first time I had seen my mother weep. She had sobbed quietly for a long time and I had not known how to comfort her. I had simply clung to her, unable to control my own tears.

In 1980 when I was twelve, I tell him, a man came to visit us in New Delhi with news that my mother's brother, her two sisters, and some cousins were alive. It was a cold December day and we were living in a room on the topmost floor of a house in New Delhi. I recall my mother listening closely as this man, among the first to visit Tibet since 1959, told her he had met her brother and her two sisters. She had turned to me with tears in her eyes. She had taught herself to accept that all the people she loved were dead. I know now that she had been alone in her happiness and her grief. She had not known whether to cry for the death of her mother or celebrate because half of her family was alive.

From having no family other than my mother, I was told at the age of twelve that I had over twelve cousins, two aunts, and an uncle. And perhaps, my mother said, a few granduncles and grandaunts. She wrote down a list of names on a piece of paper and instructed me to memorize them. And because her existence was the one happiness I had known with such unwavering assurance in my young life, I memorized the names and prepared myself to love the people who were my family.

Ashang's eyes fill up with tears. Poor thing, she lived all alone in India. She thought they were dead just as they believed she was dead. Even relatives inside Tibet lived unaware of each other. It was a form of death, he says.

"Poor thing," he says to me. "Like your late mother you live all alone so far away."

He was in a camp when my mother visited Tibet in 1982. He was permitted to see her for a few hours. He had believed that times were better because he had been allowed to meet family. He is quiet again. "What men will do to each other," he says.

Five years ago he had been preoccupied with the notion of freedom. Now again he asks me to define it for him.

I do what I want to a certain extent. Perhaps that is freedom, I say to him.

He asks if I am free to practice my religion. He asks if I am free to travel, to live where I want, to say what I want.

I say I am and I do, to a degree.

He asks if I know freedom.

In India and Nepal my experience of freedom was contingent on citizenship, and since my mother and I did not have citizenship, to an extent we were confined by fear. In the United States

I have spent more time as an "alien" than as a resident, and so again I have not been at liberty to move as freely as I desired. Yet I have never been denied the right to be who I am and to live as a Tibetan Buddhist.

Ashang asks if the United States is a good place. He points toward a poster of a room opening onto clear, clean, blue water. The walls are white. The sofas are of soft leather, also white. It bears no resemblance to any room I have lived in. It is spotless.

Such whiteness he has never seen in his own country and certainly not in Nangchen, where dust is a red and intrusive pestilence. And the ocean in its turquoise stillness is a befuddling idea, for he had never seen a body of water bigger than a lake. He explains that the Chinese authorities say the world outside China is a drawing on paper. Perfectly formed but in essence false because it is easily licked to ashes by fire or shredded. The world outside China, he has been told, is fickle and evanescent. With a grin, he says, nothing lasts in America.

Isn't that the whole premise of Buddhism, I ask him.

He asks me if I am really free if I am acting on my desires. The world is essentially like paper. It is impermanent and alterable. Real freedom exists in the mind, he tells me. He is stating what he has been taught and what he therefore believes. The look on his face says he'll believe and at the same time disbelieve anything I say.

Prison was a good teacher, he says. Can the world accommodate a wise and foolish old monk who has lived half of his life in prayers? He knows his place is in Tibet. He feels his age.

He cannot change with the times. He has no time for hope. He says he will die after he has received a blessing from Gyalwa Rinpoche. That, he adds, is his only wish.

In my solitary existence in San Francisco I think of his question and ask myself if I am free. What does freedom mean in a capitalist country? In the West my aspirations are toward building structures of permanence. I am surrounded by fear. Fear precedes the way I plan for the future, in the way I surround myself with commodities, in the way I speak of my body as though I will live until I am old. In this free country, to build a life on the premise of impermanence is to invite failure.

Ashang understands impermanence as a key to freedom and to a life light of fear and want. I have yet to learn to be free in a free country.

CHAPTER TWENTY-ONE

Lost

All day my companion and I rode our horses, sometimes at arm's length, sometimes close enough to talk. For a historian and a storyteller, Samdup was taciturn. Pointing to ranges in the distance he said that a year or two before 1959, the deities of those mountains had been called to war with the deities of the mountains in China. The deities of Tibet had lost the fight. That is how we came to lose our country, he explained.

We passed by yaks and sheep roaming the pastures. Ahead of us a white horse nibbled on grass. My companion said the horse was homeless. Nobody knew where he had come from. When we came across a nomad we asked about the horse. She said he had been there for a few months. She said the owner would come for him someday.

I learned that almost all the people here, even the young, had given up meat for a year following the death of the lama of a regional monastery.

Samdup led me farther up to the top of the hill from where overlapping folds of valleys and mountains created the effect of a maze. He pointed to a spot ahead of us. He was eight years old when he walked over the same mountains with his mother after Chinese soldiers took his father away. Samdup's mother carried a bag of a sweet tuberous root called *droma* for food, and with that they had made their way to a village deep in the mountains where she had relatives and where she thought they would be safe. A group of Tibetans had robbed them of their bag of *droma*.

"Right there, right there we lost our food to thieves," Samdup said; the sadness never left him. The men had apologized and explained they were many people and desperate for food. After they had lost their food, they had come to a river and he had taken off his shoes to make the crossing. His mother had carried his shoes for him but the river had been too strong and in reaching out to steady him, her fingers had given up the shoes. He remembers it was September; the sun did not assist them. It was too much to bear, he said.

After two days of walking, they had come upon a group of Tibetans hiding in a cave. The men had a bag of meat and seeing that the mother and son were in want of food, one of them had tossed the mother a piece of meat. The meat had struck Samdup's head instead and blood had oozed out. He said he had opened his mouth to cry only to feel hands clamp hard on his mouth. He was told to be quiet because Chinese soldiers were searching for Tibetans hiding in the mountains. At the age of eight, he suffered much. He thought he was going to die from such suffering. Misery alone does not kill a body, he said.

He has told his children about that particular day but they have not suffered as he has and do not understand.

Samdup spoke for that young boy that was his young self, as though he were someone he once knew. The memory of that day wounds him still. Suffering alone does not kill, he repeated.

CHAPTER TWENTY-TWO

How a Wolf Killed a Lion

The snow arrives like a thief at night in the last week of September. The yaks are speckled with snow in the morning. It takes the morning sun to melt the snow and restore the land to a deep moss green.

Every morning I watch the snow line fall lower and lower on the mountains, which no longer wear the nascent green of summer. I have not listened to the news or read a newspaper for months. My iPod is lifeless. I had used its energy sparingly knowing that once it was depleted, I would not be able to charge it. Every now and then the old radio belonging to Dorje crackles and a song, any song in any language, brings tears to my eyes. Distance from the familiar becomes a different form of solitude. The voices from the old radio, from so far away, make my existence in Dhompa seem peripheral to what goes on elsewhere in the world. And what goes on in the wider world feels incidental to my life in Dhompa. I view the closest town of Nangchen as though it is a rumor. It is as though we are far away, even from the Chinese who rule us without our consent.

"Soon you will leave," says Tenzin. He and I often linger in the kitchen after dinner.

I ask for stories he heard as a child. He tells me again the story of the wolf and the lion.

Changku, the wolf, was constantly bullied by Singhi, the lion. Changku was smaller and had fewer skills on the battlefield, so he meekly suffered Singhi's jests. One day Changku went to the edge of the lake to reflect on the paucity of his life. The deer had his devotees, the yak his strength, even the ant was known for his diligence, whereas he, Changku, had nothing. As he held that thought in his head and peered into the water, he saw someone exactly like him staring back at him. The other wolf would not drop his gaze. Changku snarled at him. The wolf snarled back. Changku was deeply offended. Who was this fellow? Changku lifted his shoulders as though to pounce and the wolf retaliated by making the same pose. Changku looked carefully and recognized something of a sorrowful look in the other wolf's eyes. Suddenly it dawned on him that he was looking at himself. He smiled and the reflection smiled back at him.

An idea erupted in his head. He shook his head to dislodge it but it returned. He wondered if he could get away with it. The more he thought on his plan, the more his smile lengthened. Without further deliberation, he ran to the lion who was sunning himself near the entrance to his cave. Ants were scuttling nearby, on tiptoes.

Singhi, Singhi, there is a lion as big as you in the water.

Are you crazy? Do you know what you are saying?

You know I would never dare to tell you this if it weren't true.

Singhi was doubtful of the existence of a lion who matched his size and strength—after all, he was known to be the biggest cat around. On the other hand he knew there was no reason for Changku to fabricate a story. He walked down to the lake. Singhi looked into the water and saw a lion with a head as big as a boulder. He was taken aback, then incensed at the thought of this other lion showing up in his domain. He bared his teeth. The lion did the same. His mouth was wide and cavernous. He had long, sharp teeth. Singhi roared as loudly as he could. The other lion thundered back at him.

This fellow needs to be taught a lesson, Singhi thought. He stepped backward and lunged at him. He disappeared into the water's blue depths. Changku had no reason to worry anymore. He had led Singhi to his death.

Tenzin smiles. A wolf led a lion to his death, he says.

Watching Tenzin in the dim glow of the kitchen fire, I can believe that the story originated in a nomad's warm tent. Looking at his kind face, it is possible to believe in big changes, and that smaller and less powerful beings can claim their independence from bullies.

Saffron insects fling themselves into the flames of the candle and leave the room in darkness. Almost every night the drama is enacted. What is it about fire that makes the moths so silly? I am content to be enveloped by the night. The sun has traveled to the other side of the world.

Amorphous large shadows appear in play when I light a candle in my room. The walls become a mobile theater. Tashi sleeps soundly, making a soft rustling sound in her throat. She must be riding a horse in her dream, I imagine. Perhaps she is racing my mother and they have stopped by the river.

In the room next to ours, Tenzin reads his prayers in the feeble light of a bulb lit by the solar panel. His voice is unable to keep to a particular note or volume.

The fields of turnips and wildflowers in our yard are needled with the sleep of all the little creatures taking shelter in their stalks. The river Kyichu greets rain with negligible fuss. I hadn't even noticed the rain. This is a place that makes me forgetful. I try not to think of anything. It is dark inside the house. I can see stars through the plastic sheet covering the window near my bed. I do not know their names in Tibetan to greet them one by one.

Tenzin quotes the words to a song he turns to every year at this time.

The loving parents have left and the enemy is arriving.

The cold is a callous foe and every winter he worries heavy snow will bury the short grass that nourishes the animals through winter.

Winter is a cruel enemy, Tenzin says. He makes garlands of the stems and leaves of the turnip plants and hangs them to dry on the eaves and the roof of the house. He cuts dry grass from the block of land he has held from the yaks all summer. The animals will feed on these. Even with his planning the animals will become weak over the long winter. He airs his warm clothes and gathers as much manure as he can from the mountains. He piles the dried manure in the kitchen and tells me the autumn manure will bring sweet thoughts during bleak winter days. He has butter stored in leather pouches, semi-dry yak meat, dried cheese, and bags of tsampa.

Day by day, the air cools and the grass turns brown. The heads of small round balls of turnips are visible and Tenzin will harvest them in late October or early November. He is eager to make *chole*, a turnip soup special to Nangchen. He says we have sour yogurt soup in the summer and sweet turnip soup in the winter. The turnip is diced into small cubes and cooked with meat and salt. Some prefer to cook the turnip until it is pulpy; some want to be able to taste a little of its flesh. Even without a pinch of sugar the soup is sweet.

September is also the month when water is said to have healing properties. It is believed the moon bores into every drop of moisture on earth and removes all impurities from the sky, the rivers, the lakes, and the springs. Everything water touches, water heals, in this period. I see monks bathing in the river. Elders plan trips to dip their feet in the river; they place their heads underwater if they are brave. If they are averse to any washing, they take a handful of water and anoint themselves.

I am unable to believe entirely in the moon's magic to turn all water into healing nectar and yet I do not disbelieve what I hear. I put my feet in the Kyichu and pray for good health to see me through the year.

On all of my four visits to Dhompa, I have left before the arrival of winter. I cannot endure the bitter cold: I will not be able to bathe anymore in the river, the outdoor bathroom will no longer seem a charming adventure, and there will be no milk and yogurt to bring rhapsody to my body. I know if I were to live through the winter in Dhompa, I would write a different book. One that says nobody should have to endure such poverty and such travails. Soon, the nomads will return to their winter bases and hide there. The animals will live indoors: they will eat the grass stored for them and the grasslands and flowers of summer will slip away from their memories. They will become lean and some of them will die. If the snow is heavy, there will be more deaths.

I walk around the mountains seeking to commit the landscape to memory. I do not want to leave this land. Like my mother, I too now carry images of Dhompa inside me. It is easy to love this land.

On the night before we are to leave, Dorje, my walking companion, sits at my bedside and tells me he does not wish for me to go away. I pat him on his shoulder and he bursts into tears. I would like to say something simple like "I will miss you" or "Thank you" to him. But it is not through words that we express our feelings. He weeps quietly and his shoulders heave.

My aunt, who has untangled her hair from its braid, slipped out of her heavy robe, and is now halfway into her bed, says, "Poor thing, don't cry," as though she's consoling herself at the same time.

Dorje continues to squat at my bedside, his head in his hands. I pat him once more and tell him to sleep. I have never had a grown man cry at the thought of my departure.

The road that brought me into Dhompa will take me back. I may not see Yungyang, Tenzin, and Dorje on my next visit. I am aware the nomadic life itself will undergo more changes. My attachment to the land makes me want for it to remain unchanged but I know this world is desirable because I can leave it anytime I want. It is a world I can escape to but not live in. Why should the nomads live without electricity, roads, bathrooms, shopping centers, and heating? Change is inevitable and it will come just as it always has in the past. Who am I to hope that nothing changes when I don't live here every day? I don't worry as they do when their loved ones fall ill and they have no roads that take them to a doctor or a hospital. Still, I feel a pang of loss when I think that there will come a time when the need for modern conveniences will transform the nomad way of life and these pristine mountains and rivers.

There are no words for the way my heart feels when Tashi and I take our leave in the morning. Tenzin's lips move in prayer; he tells me he will pray for me every single day. We allow our foreheads to meet and we say, *Ku tse ring*. May you live long.

Road trips in Tibet take longer than strictly required. First, there are intermittent toilet stops, then the necessary tea and snack breaks. A four-hour trip warrants at least two stops to eat what Tenzin has packed for us: a bag of bread, boiled meat, and *thi*, the protein snack of butter, small chunks of dried cheese, and sugar welded into a ball. It is creamy, crunchy, sweet, and addictive.

Our driver points out all the places where vehicles have fallen off the road in the past ten years. He announces the number of fatalities and tells us the stories of those who died. Tashi says her prayers and drops blessed rice grains whenever we go through accident zones.

I tease the driver, saying he has memorized Kham through its accidents and its sacred places.

He says he is a driver and must know his roads. He points out sacred hills, sacred trees, springs, and rivers. He recites his prayers out loud when he is not showing us prime spiritual grounds and accident spots. I ask him if the prayers keep him safe.

They make him feel safe. The problem with the new generation is that they think too much. They must have proof for everything. "There are many things you must accept on the basis of faith," he says.

I know what he means. I cannot ease myself into a sunny Californian disposition when I am in California. And within the Tibetan community I am not traditional enough as my appetite for independence and doubt is larger than my inclination to conformity.

We pass a man wearing an uncommon red hat with pink roses sewn onto a lace trim. He looks delectably masculine even with the accessory. Under him, his motorbike appears tiny. There are so few people visible that when we do see some they come as a surprise. A nomad rides by with a basketball bag. He has made a big hole on one side of the sphere and run a leather strap through it so that he can sling it over one shoulder.

Those of us in the vehicle with some sweetness of voice sing.

Because there is no consistency to what we drink
Sometimes hot, sometimes cold
We have thirty-two teeth

My hair is white because I am a wanderer
The snow falls on me and all night long
My head lies on a frosty saddle
Otherwise this is not my time for gray hair

The driver tells me there are bandits in parts of Kham who leap out from behind rocks and bushes and take away everything from travelers. There are none, however, on this road.

The hawk is the ornament of the sky and the earth
The rocks stand sad and alone when he does not sit on them
They are naked without him

Every now and then we see women or young girls minding sheep and yaks: shy women, laughing women, women who are on their feet and not stretched out on the grass like the men. They wear black chubas and blouses in brilliant shades of red or pink. Their clothes make them appear larger than they are and when we pass them on the road they look as broad as their yaks. They are easily amused and hide their faces and giggle when our driver pokes his head out of the jeep to flirt with them.

There are, I say, very few austere women here.

Rocks on either side of us are shaped like witches and wizards with tall hats. On and on we go, alone on the long road. A river hits our eyes like a silver chain. It is a serpentine creature glittering a few hundred feet below us.

Two figures appear in the distance; they grow tall and then disappear into the ground. As we get closer to them, I realize they are monks doing full body prostrations on the road. They wear woolen hats, more than one pair of gloves, and a full body apron of some thick padded fabric to keep them dry and protect them from cuts and abrasions. Ahead of them two men push a cart with their tent, and other belongings. We stop the jeep to offer money to the two monks. They will need help on this six-month journey to Lhasa. They will prostrate, an exertion not unlike push-ups, all the way to Lhasa, through snowstorms and rainstorms, and it will be the heart of winter when they traverse some of the highest passes of Zatou and Nagchukha. Maybe they will suffer from severe fatigue or illness, and if they should die along the way, they will be considered fortunate to have died while attempting a noble act. Every year more and more people go on these prostrations and when they return to their villages and monasteries, they are admired as heroes. Their future transgressions will be forgiven for people will remember their remarkable achievement.

Our jeep screeches to a stop behind a man who stands in the center of the road with a horse and a yak. He prods his yak to move to the side, but the animal is confused and runs toward and then away from the road. The wooden bucket the yak carries on its back is dislodged. Yogurt spills from its load. The man laughs and quickly retrieves what he can. He calms his yak down. He could have yelled at us for frightening his yak, but instead he is all apologies for stalling us. I wonder if we have just ruined a picnic. Maybe the yogurt was for a lama or for his family or maybe he was on his way to sell it. Tashi pokes her head out of the window, asks if he is all right and if he needs help. He says he is fine and waves to her. He says some greater loss has been averted and only a portion of his yogurt has been lost. He adjusts to his loss without rancor. The jeep starts and we throw dust and distance in his face as we drive toward Kyegu.

CHAPTER TWENTY-THREE

Month of Sin

In early September, a few hours into a much-anticipated Tibetan concert in Nangchen, a man unfurled a Tibetan flag in public and scattered leaflets calling for Tibetan self-governance. I had been in Nangchen the evening before the concert and had considered staying back to hear the concert, but good sense had made me return to Kyegu to renew my visa. It turned out to be a good decision: a day after I got my visa, the visa officer informed me that he had been instructed to deny all renewals. The incident in Nangchen had upset the Chinese, he explained.

The man who was said to have acted alone in Nangchen had disappeared into the crowd as soon as the police arrived at the hotel where the concert was being held. Some people told the police he had hopped on a motorbike, some people said he had slipped into a car waiting for him. Nobody in Nangchen offered a clear description of the man—they professed he was not one of them. This one incident was sufficient to bring the army to the streets from morning until night in Nangchen as well as Kyegu.

Eighteen soldiers with shield in one hand and a baton in the other march the streets in pairs. They are so serious and so young. Behind the foot soldiers an armored vehicle crawls like a sleepy bug. Soldiers stand in the tank with guns pointed at Tibetans ambling about their daily duties. I view the soldiers as though they are members of a street theater group. It is the only way I can look at them and not despair. The message is not lost to us: they are always watching us. My throbbing heart sits uneasily in my chest. All this because one man walked down a small dusty town waving a Tibetan flag and shouted for self-rule?

A woman standing beside me watches the soldiers, as I do. What does the great nation of China fear, she asks. "I have only a rusty knife that will not even go through their cotton shirt. What can we do to them? We are not treated like equals—not what the Chinese leaders say on television," she says. "Now they have an airport. It is not to make travel easier for us. How can we afford the fare? It is to bring these people here." She throws a contemptuous look at the soldiers and spits.

I walk around town seeking distractions, and meet throngs of people, wandering like me. Perhaps they too seek to be distracted in order to survive the oppression. From conversations on the street I learn there is a new healer visiting from Lhasa. They say she can banish diseases from your body. I wander to the courtyard of the hotel she is staying in. I wait for her to reveal herself to the crowd.

The crowd pulsates like tsampa grains roasting in fire. People jostle to the front of the queue, even though there is no real advantage in being in the front row. The handlers who manage the crowd only allow people they know or people of some prominence to enter the hotel to see her. The crowd continues to push regardless of these facts. They toss around jokes.

The next day the healer is gone. The authorities were nervous of the crowds gathering outside the hotel and asked her to leave, I am told.

All day long, young men who make up the Chinese army walk up and down the streets in a neat line.

Some Tibetan devotees follow the healer to the outskirts of town where she camps for a few days. The rest cast their lot with the local healer, who is known simply as the *khandro*, a term usually employed for a lama's wife. She is said to possess such power in her voice that people feel tears pricking their eyes when she prays out loud. She is mesmerizing, a nomad tells me, and it is mostly nomads who go to see her.

"Her prayers can heal you," a nomad visiting from Dhompa tells me. He had heard her sing her prayers while circumambulating the stupa in Shinze, a few miles outside Kyegu.

The khandro was married twice, both times to Chinese Muslim men. She had even converted to Islam. After her separation from her second husband she traveled to India and found her way back to Buddhism. On her visit to India she is said to have been blessed by the Dalai Lama, who singled her out from a crowd to tell her she had the ability to benefit people. Some say she cried so loudly when she stood before the Dalai Lama seeking his forgiveness for her conversion to Islam that he had no option but to give her his attention.

What really transpired during her India pilgrimage is a mystery, but the khandro underwent a change and returned to Kyegu full of spiritual fervor. She began full-body prostrations for hours every morning around the large stupa in Shinze. (Women remark she did it to lose weight.) Her prayers rang out in the air and caught the attention of regular worshippers who grew fond of her euphonious voice. Their initial skepticism turned into mild admiration. The khandro's transformation to healer happened quite suddenly and nobody can verify if it was a single incident or a series of them that resulted in the genesis of a kaftan-wearing goddess.

The walls to her waiting room are adorned, I hear, with gigantic posters of the Dalai Lama and Sakya Trizin. She is featured in many photos, standing beside lamas and other religious figures. Important people, nomads remark. They are stunned by her authoritative air and her full figure. They say she is grand. They go to her with their sicknesses, eschewing the doctors in town. And benefit she does, but not necessarily the patients who seek her help. She has increased the workload of the doctors in the local government hospital. A woman suffering from chest pain had been asked to lie down while the khandro, not yet reduced to an insignificant weight, stood on the patient's chest and thrice bore down her whole weight on the sick woman. When the patient coughed blood and felt a sharp pain along her sides, the khandro expressed delight and stated the illness was absconding from her body. The patient could barely move and when the pain persisted she went to the town's main hospital where doctors found three of her ribs broken by the khandro's exuberance. The doctors advised the patient to lodge a complaint at the police station but she refused. She had sought the khandro out and therefore it was her fate, she argued.

I would like to visit the khandro but none of my relatives offer to take me to see her.

"She will beat you up," they say. "She will sit on you and your bones will be crushed. She is twice your size," they add.

I seek people who have met her and I have to be content to hear their stories. A man and this one from Dhompa had hearing problems. He was determined to consult the khandro, despite his wife's suggestion he go to the doctor. The khandro poked a finger into his ear, and then followed it with a sharp object—he was not sure what, he could not see, he explained—and permanently damaged his eardrum. His right ear is now a tomb. His wife was determined to lodge a complaint with the local court but her husband forbade her from doing so. It was his fate, he stressed.

"The hope of Tibetans and the suspicion of Chinese," is a quote used frequently by Tibetans to refer to our boundless dependence on fate. Our capacity for hope makes us believe in everything but in the hopelessness of our situation. Charlatans are permitted to thrive among our people, as easily as lamas or righteous women.

My days turn into short paragraphs. Wind takes over the sky and it is impossible to stay warm without lighting stoves all day. The hills surrounding us have turned brown and hostile. The afternoons bring cold dust storms. My limbs are no longer mine and I fear my blood will freeze in my body. I resort to sleeping with hot water bottles to warm my icy feet. As much as I want to stay for another month or two, I cannot endure the cold.

Tashi says we are not experiencing real winter yet. We are in the month of sin, the period from the middle of October through November when nomads slaughter their cattle for the year's meat. A nomad with a good herd will kill as many as fifteen sheep and five yaks. The meat is preserved in a few different ways: either cut into strips and dried completely or allowed to hang by the leg to dry partially.

In the past this was the month my grandmother would make the herbal tablet believed to be a potent restorative medicine. The medicine required certain herbs and flowers to be cooked for a day in milk collected from a hundred female yaks. The mixture was cooked until it thickened to a paste. It was then cut into small squares and dried. Every morning, my grandmother made sure my mother ate a bit of the medicine. Tashi says nobody makes this herbal pill anymore.

During the month of sin the sun does not come out. It grieves for all the animals being killed, Tashi says. She keeps to her room to pray through the day. Indeed, the sun hides and we have a few gloomy days and then the sun strikes us silly with its warmth and brilliance for a succession of days.

I ask her how it has come to be that the sun is out in the month of sin.

I was teasing her but she is disturbed. Perhaps it does not matter anymore to kill. Perhaps death is no longer a big deal, she wonders.

CHAPTER TWENTY-FOUR

The Business of Dogs

In November, if the sun is out, it is warm enough to wear a single jacket and if the sun sulks behind clouds, my blood turns seditious and neglects my feet and fingers. I wear two layers of socks and gloves at night. The people around me look like they're wearing space suits. It is not just the elders who tread slowly. Birds and insects are silent. Only dogs bark incessantly and keep us awake late into the night.

I have heard many elders remark that dogs can see spirits. Too many ghosts in Kham, I grumble.

But it is not ghosts that are troubling dogs. They are in heat, I am told.

It is then I notice the surge of nomads in town. These are not the men who come in summer from their villages to sell their collection of caterpillar fungus or bags of wool and butter. These men descend to town with Tibetan mastiffs. They come from small villages with monosyllabic names, where the precursors to winter have already transformed their land into a hard brown coffin. They come bearing one or two dogs, brought along in the back seat of a car or riding pillion on a motorbike either ensconced in the lap of the back seat passenger or bundled in a sack and tied to the seat like a bag of dried cheese.

It is a wonder that the dogs can unfold their legs and walk after the long, bumpy ride. As soon as they recover, they are led into the streets or to the dog market to be presented to prospective buyers. If the dogs are female, they will have the additional task of mating with one of the studs in town, in hope they will engender a beast so beautiful, he or she will lift an entire family out of a life of poverty. The fate of Tibetan mastiffs has changed since my first visit to Kyegu when dogs were only good for guarding homes.

It is the photograph of mastiffs that men pull out from their wallets, not of their children or wives. They seek each other out to compare notes on the size, demeanor, and health of their puppies and exchange tips on raising them. They are keen to amend the slightest inconveniences or slur that might befall their four-legged babies.

Billboards in downtown Kyegu proclaim the beauty not of Tibetan ladies in traditional dresses, but of colossal canine creatures posing in front of snowy mountains or reposing in fields of vernal splendor. Poetry, seldom employed by businessmen to aid them in sales, is used elaborately, and in traditional verse form, to extol the girth of calves, the expansive nostrils, the purity of lineage, and other virtues of the dogs. It is possible to read the verses and believe you will be better off trading your only child for one such beast. So loyal, so lucrative are these dogs!

"We are fortunate people," Tashi says over and over. "We have our mountains, we have our animals, and if that is not enough we have dogs that make us rich. What do the Chinese have?"

Yes, dogs are making millions for a few people. Fields of barley have acceded to streets that obliterate the shape of the past. I cannot find my way to my old haunts because of the upsurge of private homes built within the last three years from the profits culled from the sale of a dog or caterpillar fungus. Dog riches, also referred to as new riches, announces itself without delicacy: the houses they inspire are monstrous concrete structures with incongruous traditional Tibetan touches. It is enough for most people in town to frame their windows with a few flowers or with the auspicious motifs of conch shells, the endless knot, or two rings of blue and red paint. Such decorations do not satisfy the new breed of mastiff businessmen. Their windows use the traditional as a base on which they showcase tinted glass and walls of green or blue tiles. On columns at the entrance to their homes snow lions stare from patterned tiles. Dogs can be heard barking indolently inside these houses while large vans and jeeps idle outside metal gates.

Tibetan mastiffs are promised all the comfort and care available; they are treated better than kin. They are given handfuls of nibbles brought all the way from the United States and purchased for exorbitant prices in faraway Chinese cities. Their diet is carefully discussed with doctors and friends and four or five times a day they are coaxed to eat stewed yak meat, milk, and yogurt fresh from animals grazing in distant fields. Often, the dogs are rocked in laps and fed with spoons like favored sons of emperors.

What if the men's own children clamor for the same administrations?

The answer I have heard is: "Not yet. Once the dogs are full, the family can relax and eat." And who can blame these men? It is inconceivable that someone of their own flesh and blood will ever fetch sixty thousand yuan a day in the cold winter months when nothing flourishes. Or command millions of yuan on sale.

Owang, King of Dogs, was sold for nearly 3.1 million yuan. He resides in a mansion in China and has more than one attendant, I am told. There are rumors the Chinese pay two hundred thousand yuan for one mating with Owang. In October 2008, Lhayou (meaning "favored by the gods" or "turquoise of the gods") was purchased by a Chinese businessman for four million yuan. The mastiff will have his own personal butler, perhaps even his own apartment, people speculate. A day before he left town, he was presented to the public. One of my cousins wore a stunned look after seeing him. That is no dog, he remarked. Lhayou is a lion.

And that is exactly what traders hope for their dogs: to be mistaken for any other animal but a dog. These are the names they give their dogs: Singda ("lion's own"), Lhayou ("favored by the gods"), Zurmang Nha Ki ("flat-nosed from Zurmang"), Bala ("the furry one"), and Yugu ("turquoise head"). None of them are named as we are or mistaken for what we are—ordinary and mortal.

A dog entrepreneur dreams of a perfect dog with a head the size of a large watermelon, a nose that spans the length of a face, a jowl that hangs like a giant bow, thick legs, thicker body, and long hair. A few years ago dreadlocks were fashionable; now traders say the preference is for lustrous hair and flaring nostrils.

What do the Chinese do with these dogs and why do they want them?

There are many opinions. The Chinese are superstitious and believe the purity of the dogs will bring them success and keep them safe, Tibetan traders say. Or the Chinese like something they can show off. Some say the Chinese are crazy and have a lot of money. Others surmise the Chinese are not stupid, so they must know something Tibetans do not. The dogs are often sold once they reach China or they become stud dogs.

It is difficult to trace the story of how the dogs have come to be so popular. Two traders, both nomads turned businessmen, tell me their version of it. A few years ago a Tibetan mastiff was taken to mainland China to be a mascot at dogfights. He was paraded before and after a fight to entertain patrons. Every day dogs fought for millions of yuan and every day the Tibetan mastiff performed his gig. One day it struck the owner that the mastiff might be good inside the ring. His customers argued that the dog was no fighter. He moved too sluggishly, he was too calm and friendly, they said. Despite his doubts, the owner put the mastiff up against a famous dog that had devoured every other dog. Within a few minutes the dog was a mangled heap. The Tibetan mastiff rose to instant fame in the dogfight world and was established as a fierce warrior, in addition to being in possession of the more endearing qualities of steadfastness and patience.

Tibetan mastiffs are the oldest and purest breed of dogs, the nomads say. Tibetan mastiffs are the most loyal dogs in the world.

How do they know this?

Why, the Chinese buyers have told them so.

The dog trade is a male world. I beg cousins of cousins to take me with them to see dogs. They cannot refuse the request of a guest, so I become the only Tibetan woman in this circle. The men assume I am Chinese, because in their minds only an outsider female would inspect dogs and argue about the unsavory business of stud dogs.

Men speak of stud dogs as though they are the famous courtesans of the day. Those in the business, and it appears to me that every man in town is dabbling in this trade or hopes to, know the names of all famous dogs and the men who own them. Karma Gelek is a name that is often chanted. His dog is Nyuthu's son. He charges twenty-five thousand yuan for one "encounter," as a mating session is called in the business. He offers a special price: forty-thousand yuan for two encounters! Amongst their own, the men are free with their assessment of the ability of the dogs to sire good pups. In my presence they alter their words and they speak a little less of the tactics to ensure an "encounter." They restrain their enthusiasm and information.

The first encounter is permitted as early as six or seven in the morning. Prospective clients form a line starting at dusk outside the house of the stud dog. The lines are very long outside Karma Gelek's house in the morning.

I am astounded: Must the stud encounter all the females waiting in line?

My cousin's husband blushes. He is young and educated, and he is not related to me by blood, so he is more relaxed about taking me to see the dogs. Still, he is uneasy when the word "encounter" comes between us. I am not his wife or girlfriend, and the word is sufficient to make him shuffle his feet and look away. I come away thinking the male dog must mate with each of the twenty or thirty female dogs waiting outside.

The next day he explains it to me. The dog has an encounter with one female dog in the morning and one in the evening. If the dog refuses the first one, the second one goes in, and then the third if the second is refused. Once the dog has chosen someone, the rest of the people in line take their dogs away and return in the evening. "You must have patience," he says. "Sometimes it takes a while for your turn." People wait in line at night so they can be in front of the line in the morning. Those who want to try their chance in the evening wait in line early in the morning.

I finally understand. What if the dog is not in the mood for anyone?

Then the owner loses out on many thousands of yuan that day, he says. Some days the dogs just do not cooperate.

If the stud dog ignores a female suitor one day, is it safe to suggest he will not be interested in her another day?

He blushes. I have arranged the question as delicately as possible and do not know any other way to pose it to him, not in this language at least.

It is possible he will like her another day, he says.

We drive in silence to see a red dog. I have never cared for a pet. I like to imagine I might have one someday, knowing full well that it is unlikely. When I am in San Francisco I abide by the etiquette that those of us without pets and children seem to adopt: I smile at dogs and children and occasionally say hello, in a soft, baby voice. It is not necessary to smile at the mastiffs or their owners in this town. The dogs do not need affirmation or recognition for their existence. They are taller than me if they stand on their hind legs. They have more hair on their head than I do. They are worth more in yuan.

The dogs get a brief reprieve after a successful morning encounter. Afternoons are spent with visiting dog traders. Tibetans have not adopted the habit of appointments, so there are no scheduled visiting hours; all afternoon long, groups of men walk in and out inspecting and deliberating on the stud dog they will choose. Sometimes they do not feel a gut response to any one dog and so they make many more visits. I don't know why the men bother on deliberating so much because eventually they seek a lama's divination.

The ten dogs I visit are monstrous. They will not be easily led for a walk or put in a handbag. The tall gates to the homes of these famous stud dogs are covered with their posters. A few owners put up placards signaling their membership to registered mastiff associations. The signs are meant for Chinese businessmen who may be comforted to see the name of a familiar business association. They do not matter to the Tibetan traders, most of whom cannot read Tibetan or Chinese.

The dogs are housed in large concrete cages fitted with metal doors. I expect them to be ferocious, but they are usually lying on their stomachs when I visit. They turn to me with insouciant gazes. They ignore the coaxing of their owners to stand up. They do not strut or lift their faces toward the groups of men who wait with quiet faces. The owners grab the hairs on the top of the dogs' head and pull the skin up, a mile high, to show how amply they are blessed, or they measure their ankles. All the while, the dogs move slowly, bored by the incessant attention from men in dark clothes and dark hats.

Who is the father? Who is the mother? How old is he? The questions are repeated at each house. Sometimes a famous dog's mother is owned by the same businessman and she is brought out so people can see mother and son side by side. If a female mastiff is known to have produced one good son, then all her puppies can fetch as much as one hundred thousand yuan as soon as they are born.

The most desired dogs of this season are referred to as *olas*— dogs who are between nine to eighteen months old. They are resplendent little bears.

How much do you spend feeding your dog, I ask one trader.

"Sixty thousand yuan a year," he says. "It is too much. I feed my entire family on less," he adds.

His dog has golden hair. He charges fifteen hundred yuan per encounter. He is hoping to sell his dog for a good price. He brings out two puppies. He says it is a strange business but the dogs eat well and even after they are sold, they live a king's life. Some days they are force-fed, he admits to me.

Why?

He wants them to grow big.

He brings a big bag of food. Was it made in America, he asks me. He says the food helps the dogs grow big and protects them against parasites.

I translate the words into Tibetan: *Professional food for giant baby dogs*. Nowhere do I see the place of manufacture. It is a company registered in the United States but the food could have been made in any of the distributing countries. There are directions in many languages.

I tell the trader the meat, the milk, and the yogurt he gives the dogs are probably better for them than the processed dog food.

The food is made in America, it must be good, he responds.

I know nothing about dogs and canine cuisine. I defer to his expertise and experience.

He asks me if I can look up the company when I return home and tell him if he is feeding the right kind of food. He says each year the dogs get better and bigger because they get such good care.

On days when I sit around the house feeling restless, I think of the dogs and tell myself it is impossible to feel bored in this town. I could always go to the dog market on the outskirts of town where men hang out with their dogs. Some of them keep their dogs in their vehicles. Sometimes I witness a sale. Sometimes ordinary dogs are purchased and everyone assumes the dogs will feature as a special on a menu in a faraway Chinese restaurant.

The women in my family are amused by my interest in the mastiffs. They giggle when I tell them I have learned to ask questions in a discreet manner. Tashi says there is no discreet way to speak about copulation. She has never seen any of these famous dogs in town. She looks eagerly at the photos I take on my visits.

"What about our dog?" she asks. "How does our dog compare to the famous ones?" The nameless dog who guards our house has loose limbs and hides his upper body inside his belly like an inverted comma. He cannot be ignored, for he does possess the demeanor of a bestial thing. He has a thunderous voice and he can be a threat to intruders. But he is no star. He is not walked, nor does anyone bestow pats, baths, and hugs on him. He remains tied all day and all night. I tell Tashi he makes a good guard dog, not because he recognizes potential threats to the household he guards, but because all movement makes him jealous. This is a theory that does not sit well with anyone in my family.

"His father and grandfather were tied to similar poles; bondage is his fate. Just look at the dog," Tashi says, "does he look like he needs our pity?"

Ordinary dogs are not kept as pets here: they are workers, and they guard the house in exchange for shelter and food. My cousins are shocked to hear that dogs are loved as much as family members in the United States. They themselves would be afraid to hug their dogs. Do the dogs in America make money for their owners for them to be so loved, they ask.

Our dog is big and toothy and if he were untied, I imagine he could disengage my head from my body with effortless speed. His fur hangs in formidable dreadlocks around his neck and he looks like the offspring of a lion and a donkey. I am scared of him, even terrified, if he comes close. He does not care to form attachments to any of us. He cannot be caught off guard. He cannot be cajoled into doing anything by anyone except by the one person who feeds him every day. Only at midday does he become lethargic and adopt a discriminating system that makes him bark only at visitors to the house. Only at midday does he ignore the gray birds that make merry over worms. When they are near the doghouse, there is a touch of defiance in their frog-like hop.

Our dog is too old to make anyone rich. "What a world we live in," Tashi says. All you need is an impressive dog to be able to make a living.

There are a few different routes to the dog trade. You may buy a young male pup—you would of course strive to buy one with a famous father and pay anywhere from fifty thousand to four hundred thousand yuan and hope the puppy resembles his father in a year; you may also buy a female pup and mate it with the famous dogs with each encounter costing thirty or forty thousand yuan for the best dogs and as low as fifteen hundred yuan for the rest. Once you acquire the dog, you embrace all kinds of anxieties: the dogs are easy prey to coughs, colds, and parasites, and many die in their first year. And there's the food to consider. All this with no assurance that the dog will grow to be spectacular.

Then again, but for hope, we would not be so interested or engaged in the world around us. Those who are lucky to see their puppies grow into big and beautiful mastiffs get to business as soon as the dog is ready to mate. From mid-October through mid-January or early February, all owners hope for their stud dog to mate two times a day. It is the easiest way to make money but of course the owners will tell you they have made many sacrifices to reach this level of ease. On a happy day, a dog makes ten to sixty thousand yuan for his owner.

Once in the morning and once in the evening is everyone's secret song.

⁂

The dogs in town are said to have descended from a mastiff brought from Lhasa to Parthang about eighty or ninety years ago by the previous incarnation of Sangye Nyenpa, a lama in Parthang valley. The native mastiffs guarding nomads and their cattle are overlooked in discussions of this pedigree. They are seen as being of unreliable heritage.

Most dogs I visit are sons, daughters, or grandsons of Nyuthu, who was sold for 3.8 million yuan. People say he was the one who taught them to dream big. He is now somewhere in China. Nyuthu is a descendent of Thikoo. I am pleased to state I know of Thikoo. In 2006, during the nascent stages of this business, he was the most coveted mastiff of the region. His name was whispered even in the neighboring counties of Chumaleb, Nangchen, and Dritou. In fact, his name is still uttered with awe.

Thikoo was given to Kesang Tashi, a nomad, in lieu of a loan and accepted not without some reservations. After all, in Kesang's mind, money was preferable to a dog whose only worth was in guarding the house and cattle. Kesang paid the dog no attention. On his visits to Kyegu he heard of the strange interest that wealthy Chinese families in Hong Kong, mainland China, and Taiwan had in Tibetan mastiffs. A few of his neighbors spoke of raising pups and said they'd been listening to traders comment on the potential of a good mastiff. Come to think of it, one man said, Thikoo was a fierce-looking dog and could probably fetch a thousand or so yuan. As the dog grew so did the compliments. One day, a Chinese man came inquiring about Thikoo and, on seeing him, offered to pay one hundred thousand yuan to have him. Kesang was shocked at the offer, but he had the audacity to calculate that if a man was willing to part with so much money so easily, the dog was probably worth a lot more. He kept the dog and the rest is history in the valley of Parthang and beyond.

Thikoo brought in more than one hundred thousand yuan a year for his owner. People from all over Yushu brought their female dogs to have an encounter with the famous dog of Parthang. Kesang purchased two apartments in Kyegu and a brand-new white Toyota jeep in the first two years of Thikoo's successful career as king stud. Kesang was bestowed the respectful title of Ahu, "Sir." His life became the theme of many discussions for years. People say he left his wife of many years and spent lavishly on a voluptuous younger woman in town.

The story goes that one day Kesang's son told his mother he wasn't well. His mother suggested he take a medicine and rest. A few hours later, Thikoo could not keep his food down. The mother roused the sick son and asked him to take the dog to the doctor. This provokes a laugh, even now after three years. Yes, a dog's life is more valuable than a son's life, perhaps even more valuable than a husband's life, traders joke. Kesang was not fed as well and as frequently as Thikoo was, state the rumors.

People are still inspired by Kesang's story. If it could happen to him, then it can happen to any of them. At age five, Thikoo's reign is over. His children are all over town and a handful carry the mark of his majesty. The rest are ordinary—a deal gone wrong. They have cost their owners a good sum and must remind them for the rest of their lives of their bad luck.

It is thus that the people of Kyegu engage in business. I do not ask what is produced in town or if there are factories, for there are none. I simply ask whose dog has a mean visage.

Thikoo lives in Parthang, where Kesang continues to maintain partial residence. A few miles down from his house is a river and a hot spring. The Parthang valley is famous for its summer flowers and the pilgrimage site Bu Namsto, where the Chinese princess Wen Cheng, the niece of Emperor Taizong of Tang China, stopped to rest on her one-year journey from Chang'an to Lhasa to wed Songtsen Gampo, Tibet's most renowned king in 640 CE. She carried with her many gifts, most precious of all, the statue of Jowo Shakyamuni, which sits in the Jokhang Temple in Lhasa and is the statue Tibetans long to see at least once in their lifetime. When people from Kyegu make a day trip to Bu Namtso or to the hot spring, they stop and visit Thikoo for a viewing.

Fourteen of us, all cousins and children of cousins, pile into four jeeps and head out of town and across the Zachu River. We have with us one of Thikoo's blood—a four-month-old pup named Gyachap—wrapped in a warm blanket and rendered helpless by the bumpy ride. My cousin's husband holds him in his lap while in the back seat his four-year-old son sits crushed against the door alongside five other children. This dog could be his lottery ticket, the cousin's husband tells me. A month ago, when the pup was quite ill, an elder placed the Dalai Lama's picture on his head and recited a prayer. The dog recovered and hence the name that means "saved by Gyalwa Rinpoche's blessing."

As we climb up the mountain, we see snow on the tips and in corners where sunlight does not reach. We then descend into a field of verdant grass and silver streams and rest for a while. Our bags of dry meat, noodles, and bread are taken out; the children frolic in the water and the rest of us lie on the grass and look out on beautiful country. From where we sit, we can see Kesang's house.

He is not home. His jeep is not outside. A woman answers our call and says the dog is resting but on hearing that I've traveled a great distance to see Thikoo, she relents. She drags Thikoo out from one of the cement kennels built outside the house. At first sight I am unimpressed; he looks smaller than the pups he has engendered. A cousin tells me to peer closely and see what he sees: Thikoo is onyx in complexion; he stands like a lion; his neck hangs in many layers like a sweater that's folded over; his ears are massive. He walks with great indolence and accepts the obeisance of our cameras without interest. He sits down and gazes in the opposite direction. The woman says he is tired. To his right sits his mother. She too is famous, not just for giving birth to a wondrous being like her son but because she herself is quite grand. Her face is meaner than her son's. She barks at us. Thikoo does not look up.

Gyachap does not stir in the arms of the cousin who carries him. Father and son face each other but do not recognize each other.

CHAPTER TWENTY-FIVE

How to Say Goodbye

Tashi counts the days to my departure and pictures the life to which I will return. "Alone and on her own in America," she says often to herself. "What if you get sick? What if you are sad? Who will take care of you?" She wishes a child for me, and a good husband. Sometimes she wishes a house for me. She grasps for something, anything that will add to this image she has built of a lonely life lived by a solitary self in exile.

She believes that having somebody, to be something to somebody, will balance or make the contrarieties of life easier. It has been so in her life and so she believes it must be in mine. I tell her she is right, and it makes her happy and hopeful.

Otherwise my remaining weeks with my family allow for little sentimentality. Instead of slow days with elders and walks with cousin sisters, I find myself hiding in my room to stay warm or engulfed with tasks from strangers. I get inundated with requests to help people write business signs or notes in English, such as the monk who knocks peremptorily at our gate to ask if I can translate the name of his monastery into English. He comes from a monastery in Chamdo, a day's journey by jeep, and he is in Kyegu to print stationery for his monastery. He had heard from someone in town that I speak and read English. I invite him into the house and write the name of his monastery in English on the piece of paper he provides me. He brings out a laptop from his bag and asks if I can help him set up his computer. I offer him tea. He is more adept at using the computer than I am and I cannot do what he seeks. He puts away the paper with the name of his monastery in his shirt pocket and thanks me as he leaves, banging the door behind him. Another person asks if I can give a few English lessons to his employees. Even seven days of lessons is better than nothing, he says.

Friends of friends stop me on the streets to ask if they have the correct pronunciation of a word. They state their preference for the American accent over the British. I have an Indian accent with British inflections—it is not the desired accent, but I am the only one in the neighborhood for now who can speak the dialects as well as English so I am tolerated. Such requests are usually saved for the few foreigners who happen to pass by and there are more now—Christian missionaries, international aid agency employees who run humanitarian projects in and around Yushu, and the occasional backpacker—but not frequent enough for the people of the town to avoid gawking in wonder when they see a Westerner.

Because I am leaving soon for the land where Tibetans are a minority, my family members speak more and more of the foreigners they have met over the years as though somehow that will offer me protection when I am alone and out of their view. The elders speak of their first sighting of a Caucasian by resorting to terms they reserve for their introduction to such inventions as the car, the airplane, and the solar panel. An uncle remembers Pascal from Canada, from sixteen years ago. Pascal had sported a beard, he was tall, and he did not utter a word of Tibetan even after living in my uncle's house as a guest for more than a week. When a friend visits me in Kyegu, my uncle calls him Pascal, in spite of my repeated reminders that he has his own name. My uncle says he can only keep long-gone Pascal's name in his memory.

My aunt saw her first white man fifteen years ago. She says

he looked like a little bird with his ginger-colored hair. His arms were covered with similar hair. Like a yak, she says, and then—thinking perhaps she has been a little untoward—a monkey, she offers. How does hair grow like grass on the body, she wonders.

Even the tough young khampa men are a little in awe of Caucasian travelers. So hardy they are, they remark. They are surprised people take the trouble to travel so far from their comfortable homes to see a small town like Kyegu.

A young lama in his early twenties is on his way to Nepal. He has visited big cities in mainland China, Hong Kong, Taiwan, and Singapore to teach Tibetan Buddhism to Chinese practitioners. He tells me he took English lessons from a teacher in Xining. He proceeds to practice what he knows: "How are you? I am from Kham." The words are thrown out breathlessly as though he is reciting his prayers. He speaks an English that has so heavy a Nangchen accent that it sounds like some other language. It is such effort for his tongue and his jaw to accommodate the vowels, he says. His mouth hurts. Speaking in English is a physical exertion.

I ask him to repeat the words slowly.

Where are you from?

I am a Tibetan monk.

Yes, I eat meat.

I tell him he is ready for the world of English.

He plans to take the Lhasa Express from Xining to Lhasa. I tell him the names for the train allude to celestial force: the Sky Train, Rocket to the Rooftop of the World. I had taken the train in 2006, a month after it was inaugurated. It had been amusing to watch Chinese passengers grow excited every time they spotted an animal in the distance. The first yak had incited a fight for the window. As the day sped by and yaks had come and gone, the travelers had retreated to their berths. A few, anticipating headaches and nausea, had kept their hands trained to grasp the oxygen tube by the headrest.

The train had cut through fields that for centuries had played host only to animals. Now everyday at the scheduled hour a train snakes its way across the landscape disturbing the monotony and long habit of the land. An announcement had informed us that the train brought joy and prosperity to Tibetans. It reminded us of the wonders of the train itself: the world's highest passenger railroad travels for most of this route at altitudes above 13,000 feet and through the world's highest railroad tunnel; much of the tracks are laid above permafrost. I had thought then there was no reason for fellow travelers, almost all of them Chinese, to disbelieve those words. It was enough for them to gaze out of the large windows of the train to see that indeed something marvelous had been achieved.

I tell the young lama the Chinese on the train were not disturbed that there were only a handful of Tibetans inside and outside the train. How ironic it is the Chinese government should blame the nomads for the degradation of the Tibetan grasslands when they bring a train across miles of grassland all the way from Xining to Lhasa. More trains are to follow, including a luxury sightseeing train, I hear.

The lama says the train is just one more step the Chinese have taken to secure their position in Tibet and to assert their dominance over Tibetans. Some Tibetans say the Chinese don't need a train to bring them to Tibet; they come anyway through the many highways and airports that link China to Tibet. Nomads I spoke to in Dhompa hoped the train would be a vehicle that fulfilled their long-held Buddhist dream to see the Jokhang and the Potala, and perhaps even take them to Samye and beyond.

The lama is curious to see the train. He says he misses the mountains when he is away.

I prepare myself to leave by imagining the city I will return to: the block I live on in San Francisco that is home to two or three hundred people of whom I recognize four or five; Golden Gate Park where I run or walk a few times a week; the coffee shop at the end of the street where bikers recuperate in their tight clothing, coffee in hand.

I am full of sadness at the thought of leaving my family. I cannot choose to live freely in my own country and yet if I were given a choice, I would not leave the life and places I have come to know to live under Chinese rule. I have come to rely on Dhompa with the foolish comfort that comes in knowing there is a place in the world where generations of my family have lived and died. That thought serves to ground me when I feel unmoored by my transnational nomadic existence.

For now I enjoy the luxury of fourteen brothers and sisters: we have no word for cousin in our dialect so we are brothers and sisters. I call on all the thirteen nieces and nephews to kiss me repeatedly. And every night after dinner my cousin brother looks at me with something of an eagerness, asking if he can peel an apple for me. Ready for apple, he asks. If the old days had continued he would have been the chieftain of Dhompa. He smiles with his whole body when I say yes. Thin circles of apple rind curl around his fingers. He takes his time to peel the apple. This is his love. He says soon I will be alone and nobody will be there to peel an apple for me.

His wife admits he will not willingly peel an apple for her.

And so it is with my aunt's husband. When I visit him for the last time, he packs a small bag of dried meat. I know he has selected the softest bits for me. He begins to cut them into bite-sized pieces so that I can eat them more easily.

I beg him not to take the trouble.

How will you find a knife in Beijing before you fly home to cut the meat into small pieces, he asks.

Here in Tibet live the people my mother taught me to love before I met them. We are family, and love has undetermined aptitude and great hunger. I wander around town with a heavy heart. You can love a place as you love a person and it is especially easy to feel that way here, where man and nature are intertwined deeply. I commit to memory little things: the thin film of dust incited by the ends of chubas dragging on the earth; the gentle contours of the mountains; the steady gaze of a yak; the alacrity with which children submit to authority; the patience of women who sit in the main square with bottles of milk and yogurt for sale; the songs on the streets.

My cousin tells me I am behaving like a matriarch of a village after he hears me berating schoolboys playing outside our gate to speak in Tibetan.

Speak in Tibetan. You are Tibetan, I said to them.

The young boys had looked at me in surprise and then nodded in assent. Just like that. As I walked through the gate, I had heard them command each other to speak in Tibetan because "that foreign woman" had said so.

I make offerings at the Kyegu monastery before I leave. There are prayers to amend, to prevent, to protect, and there is one for those making a journey. I ask for obstacles to be removed. It would be unacceptable for any Tibetan to set off on a journey without making at least a small gesture toward the divine beings. I am not a knowledgeable Buddhist. I recognize just a few deities and can say a handful of prayers but I have been brought up to acknowledge the unknown. Besides, it seems an apposite ritual considering the long journey ahead of me.

Inside the monastery's shrine, the presence of faith and devotion is palpable, akin to the kind of collective immersion rock stars command while performing to hundreds of devoted fans. It is not difficult in the midst of such faith to feel the vulnerability of Tibet—that Tibetan Buddhism is our sole defense against the Chinese. Our faith in these gilded images, and the prayers we carry on our lips, bind us from the east and the west, and to the center.

A woman prays quietly for all sentient beings in the world. Her eyes are shut, her hands folded in front of her breasts. She offers her merits in exchange for the happiness of countless beings unknown to her. When she opens her eyes, I see they are full of tears. I sense the futility of such effort. What are prayers when held against the progress promised by China? But I say this with profound admiration, for there is great strength in believing that things will eventually right themselves. Because they must.

CHAPTER TWENTY-SIX

Love

Every winter of my childhood my mother took three months leave from her job to coincide with my school holidays. We traveled to Bodh Gaya where the Buddha attained enlightenment, then Sarnath where he gave his first sermon, and the last month we spent in Kathmandu. This annual pilgrimage allowed me to develop relationships with monks, elders, and distant relatives from Nangchen who cared deeply for my mother. She wanted me to have people who loved me so that if something happened to her, I would have familiar faces to turn to. In this way my mother took care of my future.

We would take the train from Delhi to Bodh Gaya and then slowly make our way toward Nepal by train and by bus. The long days on the road gave us the chance to be with each other as traveling companions.

I was always anxious when my mother stepped out of the train to get food or water for us. It was my great fear that she would be left behind on the platform of some unknown town and that I would be taken far away and we would never be reunited. I would keep my eyes trained on her, my face squished against the bars of the train compartment, and if she slipped from my view for even a moment, my heart would ache as though I had already lost her. She would return to the train compartment to find me near the door with tears in my eyes. Sometimes she took me with her, leaving our luggage unattended in the train, a risk she was willing to take if I looked particularly stricken. I knew I came first with her.

My mother would use each setback in my life or each little loss as a way to teach me to be less wary. I was not careful with my belongings and would lose one earring of a pair or leave my jacket in my neighbor's home. She never scolded me for being careless and if I showed signs of distress she would tell me the loss of something precious was a good thing because it removed a larger obstacle from taking place. I never quite understood the logic or the lesson. She never wavered in this belief, whether I lost my collection of earrings and silver rings at fifteen or when at twenty, I returned home after a round of kora at the stupa and found a thief had taken three pairs of shoes and two pairs of jeans I had bought and left to dry in the garden. Nor did she alter her words after my purse was stolen with seventeen thousand rupees and a hundred dollars in it the day after I returned to Delhi to rejoin college. I wept and asked her to forgive me for losing the money. It always pained me to be careless with money because she worked so hard. She did not ask me why I had carried all my money in a plastic bag in a crowded bus. She simply hugged me and said, "It is only money. Do not worry. It has removed a bigger obstacle from your path."

CHAPTER TWENTY-SEVEN

May the Gods Be Victorious

We are traveling through a cotton shroud. The blinding white of the road can only be viewed through dark glasses. The driver feels he will be led off the road and into some secret land and never find his way out. The snowbound ground melts into the mountains and the sky in a hazy absence of color.

My cousin says winter brings all sadness to the surface.

A remorseless beautiful white surrounds us. It is an entirely new world and unrecognizable from the land's summer garb. I observe tiny footprints. They cannot be of deer because the imprints are singular and in a neat row. I see birds and realize it is they who walk as though they have one foot. Darker dots speckle the distant white of the land; these are yak and human footprints. It does not matter if we mistake one of them for the other; they are too blinded and cold to care, I imagine.

A small section of the road is under repair and workers are breaking stone at the side of the road. The Chinese government has spent a lot of money building this highway; they began working on it in 1949. The workers are all Chinese and they have come from places that are warmer, where they do not eat yak or wear sheep wool all year round. They have light and unblemished skin. Even after a full day in the snow's glare, they look fresh and youthful. They cannot look like they belong to this land even if they wanted to.

I think of the Tibetan overseer of the road in Dhompa who had said the Chinese were good workers. They could stay away from their homes and do a good job. They had the gift of endurance. Tibetans on the other hand, he said, were utterly lazy. Tibetans liked picnics, they ate several times a day, and they needed to rest several times a day. He had complained that for Tibetans every working day was a picnic.

This is not the road my mother took when she left Tibet at the age of eighteen. Perhaps she had walked not too far from where I travel now by jeep. She had wandered for three years seeking a way out of her country. She had traveled with her husband and her husband's people, her own had been left behind. In her notes my mother wrote that she and her group fled without any awareness of night and day.

> Sometimes we had to move for days and nights without any food. When we started we were a large camp with lots of wealth, cattle, servants, and retainers but gradually with the long journey and many skirmishes with the Chinese soldiers, we were left with only the clothes and shoes we wore when we reached Mustang in Nepal. We had to beg for our food but we were relieved and happy that we were in a free land away from the Chinese. For many days I used to wonder whether it was all a dream or if we had really escaped from the Chinese. We were always scared that the Chinese would kill us.

> When I thought of the sufferings of our people left behind in Tibet, I felt great sadness.

> My mother mentioned to me that she considered stopping her horse and surrendering to the Chinese on many occasions during the long escape. She had turned back every so often wishing she had the strength to stop her horse. She said those days kept

returning in her dreams and even in her dreams she could not surrender to the Chinese.

The land is big and startling in its starkness. It commandeers my eyes wherever I look. I wonder if for the rest of my life I will have to enter and exit my country like an uninvited guest, totally dependent on the whims of the Chinese to see my family.

The past still has a place in the future for me. That is perhaps why I am nostalgic about Dhompa and also why I return again and again to the elders. When I consider the lives they have lived, I am able to garner a little more strength than I am actually capable of.

As we come to the top of another pass we fling our paper prayers and shout, *La so, La so.* May the Gods be victorious. I thank the deities for having watched over me. I entreat them to bring me back again. I allow myself to believe it will take a long time for the land to change and for Tibetans to forget this land. The tall posts with prayer flags and the large rocks with the carvings of prayers and deities will be here for a while yet. It will take time for Tibetans to be forgotten and to forget.

We travel with ease as fresh snow crackles under the vehicle. The mountains surround us so that I feel I am carried within them. I am watched over by the deities of the land. I tell myself a story so I remember. A long time ago, the mountain deities of Tibet and the mountain deities of China went to war . . .

And because beautiful daydreams are made of mountains, home, and freedom, I dream a different ending.

Epilogue

On 14 April 2010, my aunt was wrapping up her prayers and enjoying her morning tea when she felt the windows in her room rattle and the bed beneath her shift. She ran out of her room to join the rest of the family in the yard.

"Tsering Wangmo, Kyegu is gone. Everything is gone and I am still here," she said when I managed to get through to her by phone, hours after an earthquake hit the town of Kyegu.

Tashi could not describe what had happened to the houses on her street. She could not see very far; dust hung in myriad shapes in the air. She had lived on this street for two decades and it was now unrecognizable.

Every family in Kyegu lost a loved one or knew someone who was killed. The neighbor across the street dug into the debris of his house with his hands, hoping his wife, daughter-in-law, and his young grandchildren would still be alive.

The living moved into canvas tents. Many of my relatives lived in tents for as long as three years.

I have not been able to visit my family since 2009. An employee at the Chinese consulate in San Francisco reminded me in 2010 that she was not obliged to give me a reason, when I asked why I was denied a visa two years in a row.

When I do visit Kyegu, I will have to acquaint myself to its new shape. My aunt's neighbor's family will not be there. The streets of "the town of nine lives" will not be the same as I have recorded in the pages of this book.

The memory of the town is not erased but has merely been rearranged, I tell myself. The new has traces of the old. New injuries build on the old. When I return to the towns and villages of Amdo, Golog, and Yushu, I will hear the stories and the names of Tibetans—over a hundred in number—who have sacrificed their lives by immolating themselves. Their names are part of the narratives of these villages and towns. And, of Tibet.

It is not possible to speak of death, someone else's death, in the ways I have already attempted in this book. The wide, deceptively empty spaces of the high grasslands can no longer be categorized as just beautiful stretches of land. They are also spaces of continuing protest or contestation. It does not suffice to speak of someone else's death, to inscribe meaning, to speak of the past and future solely through the custom of the old language and religion. We must find a language that responds to the present reality where it is possible to speak of the present only if we give it up. A language that seeks to understand what it means when an individual takes death to be hope for the future. What does it say about the possibilities of the future? How do we read the silence framing the self-immolations and in what language and register must we learn to respond? Are we listening to the aspirations of Tibetans inside Tibet to guide policies toward a future for all Tibetans?

San Francisco

Acknowledgments

I thank my aunts, Tashi, Dontso, and Parchen; my uncle, Phuntsok Wangdak Dhompa and Ashang; my ten to thirty cousins, and my mother's childhood companions.

I am grateful to Mr. Howard Junker of ZYZZYVA, for allowing excerpts of an earlier incarnation of this book to be seen in the pages of ZYZZYVA many years ago.

To Anne Edelstein and Krista Ingebretson of the Ann Edelstein Literary Agency for their months of guidance and work on the book. To Sivapriya at Penguin Books, India, for saying Yes.

My gratitude to the Galen Rowell Fund, MacDowell Colony in New Hampshire, Hedgebrook at Whidby Island, Michael Monhart and Dana in New York, and Jamyang Khyentse Rinpoche and Metok Lhatso in Bir, India, for giving me places where I could write.

I thank my editor, Beth Frankl.

Thank you Bhuchung D. Sonam, Dechen Tsering, Elaine Seiler, Eva Herzer, Jasjit Mangat, Karma Gyaltsen Neyratsang, Kesang Tseten, Lhanze Sakya, Melvin Shaffer, Myung Mi Kim, Norbu Tenzing Norgay, Orgyen Topgyal Rinpoche, Parnaz Farouton, Rom Srinivasan, Sashikala Imchen, Sherub Wangmo, Tashi Tsering (Dharamsala), Tsedo, Tsering Dolma (TD), Prof. Tsering Shakya, and Tshering Yangzom. My deep gratitude to Dhondup Tashi Rekjong, James Andrews, Kabir Mansingh Heimsath, Marie-Helene Bertino, Marilyn Seaton, Samantha Skinazi and Prof. Wlad Godzich for protecting me from the errors I write.

There are those who have always been there, and to whom I continue to turn to: Dickey Wongmo, Marilyn Kennell, and Maush and Valerie Melvin.

Kading-che.